FREE Test Taking Tips Video/DVD Offer

To better serve you, we created videos covering test taking tips that we want to give you for FREE. **These videos cover world-class tips that will help you succeed on your test.**

We just ask that you send us feedback about this product. Please let us know what you thought about it—whether good, bad, or indifferent.

To get your **FREE videos**, you can use the QR code below or email freevideos@studyguideteam.com with "Free Videos" in the subject line and the following information in the body of the email:

a. The title of your product

b. Your product rating on a scale of 1-5, with 5 being the highest

c. Your feedback about the product

If you have any questions or concerns, please don't hesitate to contact us at info@studyguideteam.com.

Thank you!

NMLS Study Guide 2023 and 2024

3 Practice Tests and MLO SAFE Exam Prep Book for Mortgage Loan Originators [Includes Detailed Answer Explanations]

Joshua Rueda

Written and edited by TPB Publishing.

ISBN 13: 9781637755228
ISBN 10: 1637755228

Table of Contents

Welcome

Dear Reader,

Welcome to your new Test Prep Books study guide! We are pleased that you chose us to help you prepare for your exam. There are many study options to choose from, and we appreciate you choosing us. Studying can be a daunting task, but we have designed a smart, effective study guide to help prepare you for what lies ahead.

Whether you're a parent helping your child learn and grow, a high school student working hard to get into your dream college, or a nursing student studying for a complex exam, we want to help give you the tools you need to succeed. We hope this study guide gives you the skills and the confidence to thrive, and we can't thank you enough for allowing us to be part of your journey.

In an effort to continue to improve our products, we welcome feedback from our customers. We look forward to hearing from you. Suggestions, success stories, and criticisms can all be communicated by emailing us at info@studyguideteam.com.

Sincerely,
Test Prep Books Team

FREE Videos/DVD OFFER

Doing well on your exam requires both knowing the test content and understanding how to use that knowledge to do well on the test. We offer completely FREE test taking tip videos. **These videos cover world-class tips that you can use to succeed on your test.**

To get your **FREE videos**, you can use the QR code below or email freevideos@studyguideteam.com with "Free Videos" in the subject line and the following information in the body of the email:

a. The title of your product
b. Your product rating on a scale of 1-5, with 5 being the highest
c. Your feedback about the product

If you have any questions or concerns, please don't hesitate to contact us at info@studyguideteam.com.

Quick Overview

As you draw closer to taking your exam, effective preparation becomes more and more important. Thankfully, you have this study guide to help you get ready. Use this guide to help keep your studying on track and refer to it often.

This study guide contains several key sections that will help you be successful on your exam. The guide contains tips for what you should do the night before and the day of the test. Also included are test-taking tips. Knowing the right information is not always enough. Many well-prepared test takers struggle with exams. These tips will help equip you to accurately read, assess, and answer test questions.

A large part of the guide is devoted to showing you what content to expect on the exam and to helping you better understand that content. In this guide are practice test questions so that you can see how well you have grasped the content. Then, answer explanations are provided so that you can understand why you missed certain questions.

Don't try to cram the night before you take your exam. This is not a wise strategy for a few reasons. First, your retention of the information will be low. Your time would be better used by reviewing information you already know rather than trying to learn a lot of new information. Second, you will likely become stressed as you try to gain a large amount of knowledge in a short amount of time. Third, you will be depriving yourself of sleep. So be sure to go to bed at a reasonable time the night before. Being well-rested helps you focus and remain calm.

Be sure to eat a substantial breakfast the morning of the exam. If you are taking the exam in the afternoon, be sure to have a good lunch as well. Being hungry is distracting and can make it difficult to focus. You have hopefully spent lots of time preparing for the exam. Don't let an empty stomach get in the way of success!

When travelling to the testing center, leave earlier than needed. That way, you have a buffer in case you experience any delays. This will help you remain calm and will keep you from missing your appointment time at the testing center.

Be sure to pace yourself during the exam. Don't try to rush through the exam. There is no need to risk performing poorly on the exam just so you can leave the testing center early. Allow yourself to use all of the allotted time if needed.

Remain positive while taking the exam even if you feel like you are performing poorly. Thinking about the content you should have mastered will not help you perform better on the exam.

Once the exam is complete, take some time to relax. Even if you feel that you need to take the exam again, you will be well served by some down time before you begin studying again. It's often easier to convince yourself to study if you know that it will come with a reward!

Test-Taking Strategies

1. Predicting the Answer

When you feel confident in your preparation for a multiple-choice test, try predicting the answer before reading the answer choices. This is especially useful on questions that test objective factual knowledge. By predicting the answer before reading the available choices, you eliminate the possibility that you will be distracted or led astray by an incorrect answer choice. You will feel more confident in your selection if you read the question, predict the answer, and then find your prediction among the answer choices. After using this strategy, be sure to still read all of the answer choices carefully and completely. If you feel unprepared, you should not attempt to predict the answers. This would be a waste of time and an opportunity for your mind to wander in the wrong direction.

2. Reading the Whole Question

Too often, test takers scan a multiple-choice question, recognize a few familiar words, and immediately jump to the answer choices. Test authors are aware of this common impatience, and they will sometimes prey upon it. For instance, a test author might subtly turn the question into a negative, or he or she might redirect the focus of the question right at the end. The only way to avoid falling into these traps is to read the entirety of the question carefully before reading the answer choices.

3. Looking for Wrong Answers

Long and complicated multiple-choice questions can be intimidating. One way to simplify a difficult multiple-choice question is to eliminate all of the answer choices that are clearly wrong. In most sets of answers, there will be at least one selection that can be dismissed right away. If the test is administered on paper, the test taker could draw a line through it to indicate that it may be ignored; otherwise, the test taker will have to perform this operation mentally or on scratch paper. In either case, once the obviously incorrect answers have been eliminated, the remaining choices may be considered. Sometimes identifying the clearly wrong answers will give the test taker some information about the correct answer. For instance, if one of the remaining answer choices is a direct opposite of one of the eliminated answer choices, it may well be the correct answer. The opposite of obviously wrong is obviously right! Of course, this is not always the case. Some answers are obviously incorrect simply because they are irrelevant to the question being asked. Still, identifying and eliminating some incorrect answer choices is a good way to simplify a multiple-choice question.

4. Don't Overanalyze

Anxious test takers often overanalyze questions. When you are nervous, your brain will often run wild, causing you to make associations and discover clues that don't actually exist. If you feel that this may be a problem for you, do whatever you can to slow down during the test. Try taking a deep breath or counting to ten. As you read and consider the question, restrict yourself to the particular words used by the author. Avoid thought tangents about what the author *really* meant, or what he or she was *trying* to say. The only things that matter on a multiple-choice test are the words that are actually in the question. You must avoid reading too much into a multiple-choice question, or supposing that the writer meant something other than what he or she wrote.

5. No Need for Panic

It is wise to learn as many strategies as possible before taking a multiple-choice test, but it is likely that you will come across a few questions for which you simply don't know the answer. In this situation, avoid panicking. Because most multiple-choice tests include dozens of questions, the relative value of a single wrong answer is small. As much as possible, you should compartmentalize each question on a multiple-choice test. In other words, you should not allow your feelings about one question to affect your success on the others. When you find a question that you either don't understand or don't know how to answer, just take a deep breath and do your best. Read the entire question slowly and carefully. Try rephrasing the question a couple of different ways. Then, read all of the answer choices carefully. After eliminating obviously wrong answers, make a selection and move on to the next question.

6. Confusing Answer Choices

When working on a difficult multiple-choice question, there may be a tendency to focus on the answer choices that are the easiest to understand. Many people, whether consciously or not, gravitate to the answer choices that require the least concentration, knowledge, and memory. This is a mistake. When you come across an answer choice that is confusing, you should give it extra attention. A question might be confusing because you do not know the subject matter to which it refers. If this is the case, don't eliminate the answer before you have affirmatively settled on another. When you come across an answer choice of this type, set it aside as you look at the remaining choices. If you can confidently assert that one of the other choices is correct, you can leave the confusing answer aside. Otherwise, you will need to take a moment to try to better understand the confusing answer choice. Rephrasing is one way to tease out the sense of a confusing answer choice.

7. Your First Instinct

Many people struggle with multiple-choice tests because they overthink the questions. If you have studied sufficiently for the test, you should be prepared to trust your first instinct once you have carefully and completely read the question and all of the answer choices. There is a great deal of research suggesting that the mind can come to the correct conclusion very quickly once it has obtained all of the relevant information. At times, it may seem to you as if your intuition is working faster even than your reasoning mind. This may in fact be true. The knowledge you obtain while studying may be retrieved from your subconscious before you have a chance to work out the associations that support it. Verify your instinct by working out the reasons that it should be trusted.

8. Key Words

Many test takers struggle with multiple-choice questions because they have poor reading comprehension skills. Quickly reading and understanding a multiple-choice question requires a mixture of skill and experience. To help with this, try jotting down a few key words and phrases on a piece of scrap paper. Doing this concentrates the process of reading and forces the mind to weigh the relative importance of the question's parts. In selecting words and phrases to write down, the test taker thinks

about the question more deeply and carefully. This is especially true for multiple-choice questions that are preceded by a long prompt.

9. Subtle Negatives

One of the oldest tricks in the multiple-choice test writer's book is to subtly reverse the meaning of a question with a word like *not* or *except*. If you are not paying attention to each word in the question, you can easily be led astray by this trick. For instance, a common question format is, "Which of the following is...?" Obviously, if the question instead is, "Which of the following is not...?," then the answer will be quite different. Even worse, the test makers are aware of the potential for this mistake and will include one answer choice that would be correct if the question were not negated or reversed. A test taker who misses the reversal will find what he or she believes to be a correct answer and will be so confident that he or she will fail to reread the question and discover the original error. The only way to avoid this is to practice a wide variety of multiple-choice questions and to pay close attention to each and every word.

10. Reading Every Answer Choice

It may seem obvious, but you should always read every one of the answer choices! Too many test takers fall into the habit of scanning the question and assuming that they understand the question because they recognize a few key words. From there, they pick the first answer choice that answers the question they believe they have read. Test takers who read all of the answer choices might discover that one of the latter answer choices is actually *more* correct. Moreover, reading all of the answer choices can remind you of facts related to the question that can help you arrive at the correct answer. Sometimes, a misstatement or incorrect detail in one of the latter answer choices will trigger your memory of the subject and will enable you to find the right answer. Failing to read all of the answer choices is like not reading all of the items on a restaurant menu: you might miss out on the perfect choice.

11. Spot the Hedges

One of the keys to success on multiple-choice tests is paying close attention to every word. This is never truer than with words like *almost*, *most*, *some*, and *sometimes*. These words are called "hedges" because they indicate that a statement is not totally true or not true in every place and time. An absolute statement will contain no hedges, but in many subjects, the answers are not always straightforward or absolute. There are always exceptions to the rules in these subjects. For this reason, you should favor those multiple-choice questions that contain hedging language. The presence of qualifying words indicates that the author is taking special care with his or her words, which is certainly important when composing the right answer. After all, there are many ways to be wrong, but there is only one way to be right! For this reason, it is wise to avoid answers that are absolute when taking a multiple-choice test. An absolute answer is one that says things are either all one way or all another. They often include words like *every*, *always*, *best*, and *never*. If you are taking a multiple-choice test in a subject that doesn't lend itself to absolute answers, be on your guard if you see any of these words.

12. Long Answers

In many subject areas, the answers are not simple. As already mentioned, the right answer often requires hedges. Another common feature of the answers to a complex or subjective question are qualifying clauses, which are groups of words that subtly modify the meaning of the sentence. If the question or answer choice describes a rule to which there are exceptions or the subject matter is complicated, ambiguous, or confusing, the correct answer will require many words in order to be expressed clearly and accurately. In essence, you should not be deterred by answer choices that seem excessively long. Oftentimes, the author of the text will not be able to write the correct answer without offering some qualifications and modifications. Your job is to read the answer choices thoroughly and completely and to select the one that most accurately and precisely answers the question.

13. Restating to Understand

Sometimes, a question on a multiple-choice test is difficult not because of what it asks but because of how it is written. If this is the case, restate the question or answer choice in different words. This process serves a couple of important purposes. First, it forces you to concentrate on the core of the question. In order to rephrase the question accurately, you have to understand it well. Rephrasing the question will concentrate your mind on the key words and ideas. Second, it will present the information to your mind in a fresh way. This process may trigger your memory and render some useful scrap of information picked up while studying.

14. True Statements

Sometimes an answer choice will be true in itself, but it does not answer the question. This is one of the main reasons why it is essential to read the question carefully and completely before proceeding to the answer choices. Too often, test takers skip ahead to the answer choices and look for true statements. Having found one of these, they are content to select it without reference to the question above. The savvy test taker will always read the entire question before turning to the answer choices. Then, having settled on a correct answer choice, he or she will refer to the original question and ensure that the selected answer is relevant. The mistake of choosing a correct-but-irrelevant answer choice is especially common on questions related to specific pieces of objective knowledge.

15. No Patterns

One of the more dangerous ideas that circulates about multiple-choice tests is that the correct answers tend to fall into patterns. These erroneous ideas range from a belief that B and C are the most common right answers, to the idea that an unprepared test-taker should answer "A-B-A-C-A-D-A-B-A." It cannot be emphasized enough that pattern-seeking of this type is exactly the WRONG way to approach a multiple-choice test. To begin with, it is highly unlikely that the test maker will plot the correct answers according to some predetermined pattern. The questions are scrambled and delivered in a random order. Furthermore, even if the test maker was following a pattern in the assignation of correct answers, there is no reason why the test taker would know which pattern he or she was using. Any attempt to discern a pattern in the answer choices is a waste of time and a distraction from the real work of taking the test. A test taker would be much better served by extra preparation before the test than by reliance on a pattern in the answers.

Introduction to the NMLS SAFE MLO Exam

Function of the Test

In order to protect consumers and reduce fraud in connection with mortgage loans, Title V of the Housing and Economic Recovery Act of 2008, also known as The Secure and Fair Enforcement for Mortgage Licensing Act (SAFE Act), mandated that all mortgage loan originators (MLOs) must either be licensed by their states or registered federally. The SAFE Act requires every state to have a process for MLO licensing that meets standards laid out by the Nationwide Mortgage Licensing System & Registry (NMLS).

To successfully achieve state licensure, a prospective MLO must score at least a 75 percent on the SAFE Mortgage Loan Originator Test, developed by the NMLS.

Test Administration

Each MLO candidate must create an account with NMLS in order to enroll to take the SAFE MLO Test.

Once the candidate has enrolled, they can pay for a test enrollment window as an individual or through a company. As of 2023 the fee for test enrollment is $110 and the test enrollment window is 180 days. During this time, the candidate must accept the Candidate Agreement, schedule the test, and take the test. The Candidate Agreement must be accepted before scheduling the SAFE MLO Test. Test enrollment windows cannot be refunded or transferred. If the test enrollment window closes before the candidate is able to take the test, the candidate must create and pay for a new test enrollment window.

The SAFE MLO Test is offered both at Prometric testing centers and via online proctoring, during which the test will be monitored and recorded. Test appointments can be scheduled either through the NMLS Manage Test Appointments page or through the Prometric website. Group appointments for five or more candidates can be scheduled by a company through the Prometric website. Online proctoring is not available for group appointments.

Scheduled appointments may be cancelled or rescheduled no later than two business days before the scheduled appointment. There are limited exceptions for emergencies.

If a candidate fails the SAFE MLO Test they must wait thirty days to schedule a new test date. If a candidate fails the test three times, the waiting period is extended to 180 days before a new test date can be scheduled. Candidates must pay for each new test enrollment window.

Test Format

The SAFE MLO Test consists of 120 multiple-choice questions, each with four answer options. Out of the 120 questions, only 115 are scored. The five unscored questions are being tested for future use and are scattered throughout the test. The unscored questions are not marked in any way and cannot be differentiated from the scored questions.

The SAFE MLO Test itself lasts for 190 minutes. The overall test appointment will last for an additional thirty to thirty-five minutes due to a mandatory test tutorial and an optional survey.

The SAFE MLO Test has five major content areas. The table below shows each content area as well as the percentage of the test and approximate number of questions for each content area:

Content Area	Percentage of Test
Federal Mortgage Related Laws	24% (approx. 29 questions)
Uniform State Content	11% (approx. 13 questions)
General Mortgage Knowledge	20% (approx. 24 questions)
Mortgage Loan Origination Activities	27% (approx. 32 questions)
Ethics	18% (approx. 22 questions)
Total	**100% (total 120 questions)**

Scoring

Each candidate will take a unique form of the SAFE MLO Test. This is achieved through the use of Linear on the Fly Testing (LOFT), which ensures that candidate scores are comparable despite some candidates receiving slightly harder or slightly easier versions of the test.

Candidates who take their test at a testing center will receive an unofficial printed score report at the end of the test that includes their overall percentage score as well as details regarding their performance on the various sections of the test. The score report becomes official once it is posted in NMLS, which will occur within 72 hours. Candidates will also receive an email with access to their NMLS record. Candidates who take an online test will receive an official score report via email within three business days.

The minimum passing score for the SAFE MLO Test is 75 percent.

Expiration

The test results for an MLO who successfully passes the SAFE MLO Test will expire after five years or longer if the MLO fails to get or maintain a valid license. If test scores expire, the MLO must retake the SAFE MLO Test.

Updates and Changes to the Test Information

Occasionally legislation relating to MLOs may be revised or updated during a test administration cycle. Candidates are required to educate themselves about these changes and answer questions according to the most recent statutes, rules, and regulations.

Study Prep Plan for the NMLS Test

1. **Schedule -** Use one of our study schedules below or come up with one of your own.

2. **Relax -** Test anxiety can hurt even the best students. There are many ways to reduce stress. Find the one that works best for you.

3. **Execute -** Once you have a good plan in place, be sure to stick to it.

One Week Study Schedule

Day 1	Federal Mortgage Related Laws
Day 2	Uniform State Content
Day 3	Mortgage Loan Origination Activities
Day 4	Ethics
Day 5	Practice Tests #1 & #2
Day 6	Practice Test #3
Day 7	Take Your Exam!

Two Week Study Schedule

Day 1	Federal Mortgage Related Laws	Day 8	B. Ethical Behavior Related to Loan...
Day 2	E. Other Federal Laws and Guidelines	Day 9	Practice Test #1
Day 3	Uniform State Content	Day 10	Answer Explanations #1
Day 4	B. Mortgage Loan Products	Day 11	Practice Test #2
Day 5	Mortgage Loan Origination Activities	Day 12	Answer Explanations #2
Day 6	C. Closing	Day 13	Practice Test #3
Day 7	Ethics	Day 14	Take Your Exam!

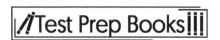

One Month Study Schedule

Day 1	Federal Mortgage Related Laws	Day 11	Answer Explanations	Day 21	Ethics
Day 2	B. Equal Credit Opportunity Act...	Day 12	General Mortgage Knowledge	Day 22	B. Ethical Behavior Related to Loan...
Day 3	C. Truth in Lending Act (TILA), 12 CFR Part...	Day 13	B. Mortgage Loan Products	Day 23	Take a Break!
Day 4	D. TILA-RESPA Integrated Disclosure...	Day 14	C. Terms Used in the Mortgage Industry	Day 24	Practice Test #1
Day 5	E. Other Federal Laws and Guidelines	Day 15	Practice Questions	Day 25	Answer Explanations #1
Day 6	F. Regulatory Authority	Day 16	Mortgage Loan Origination Activities	Day 26	Practice Test #2
Day 7	Practice Questions	Day 17	B. Qualification: Processing &...	Day 27	Answer Explanations #2
Day 8	Answer Explanations	Day 18	C. Closing	Day 28	Practice Test #3
Day 9	Uniform State Content	Day 19	D. Financial Calculations	Day 29	Answer Explanations #3
Day 10	Practice Questions	Day 20	Practice Questions	Day 30	Take Your Exam!

Build your own prep plan by visiting:
testprepbooks.com/prep

As you study for your test, we'd like to take the opportunity to remind you that you are capable of great things! With the right tools and dedication, you truly can do anything you set your mind to. The fact that you are holding this book right now shows how committed you are. In case no one has told you lately, you've got this! Our intention behind including this coloring page is to give you the chance to take some time to engage your creative side when you need a little brain-break from studying. As a company, we want to encourage people like you to achieve their dreams by providing good quality study materials for the tests and certifications that improve careers and change lives. As individuals, many of us have taken such tests in our careers, and we know how challenging this process can be. While we can't come alongside you and cheer you on personally, we can offer you the space to recall your purpose, reconnect with your passion, and refresh your brain through an artistic practice. We wish you every success, and happy studying!

Federal Mortgage Related Laws

A. Real Estate Settlement Procedures Act (RESPA), 12 CFR Part 1024 (Regulation X)

RESPA Origins and Purpose

The **Real Estate Settlement Procedures Act (RESPA)** is legislation that was passed by Congress to protect and educate homebuyers and sellers by creating transparency in mortgage financing transactions. The statute, enacted in 1975, contains four primary provisions: 1) disclose financing and settlement costs to borrowers and sellers; 2) eliminate referral fees and kickbacks; 3) regulate and limit the amount of monies required to establish escrow accounts; and 4) update recordkeeping requirements for land title information. RESPA applies to loans for purchases, home improvements, assumable mortgage loans, refinances, and home equity lines of credit (HELOCs) involving one- to four-family residential dwellings. It was enforced originally by the Department of Housing and Urban Development (HUD); however, the Consumer Financial Protection Bureau (CFPB) took over those responsibilities when it was created in 2011. RESPA is also referred to as **Regulation X**, or Reg X, because it is part of Chapter X of the Bureau of Consumer Financial Protection guidelines. RESPA is found under Title 12, Chapter X, Part 1024 of the **Code of Federal Regulations**, which lists all the rules and regulations of the U.S. Federal Government.

Required Disclosures Under RESPA

Note that this section describes the original provisions of RESPA; please see page twenty-one for changes made in 2015 as a result of the TILA-RESPA Integrated Disclosure Rule.

RESPA requires the disclosure of all transaction-related information to the borrower, including information about settlement services, consumer protection laws, business relationships between any of the parties involved in the transaction, and all information related to the cost of the financing. Specific forms and information must be provided to the borrower at different stages of the transaction process. At the time of the loan application, borrowers must be given a Good-Faith Estimate (GFE) detailing the anticipated amounts of the closing costs and the charges associated with the loan, a mortgage servicing disclosure explaining whether the loan is expected to be sold or transferred after the closing, and a **Special Information Booklet**. The **Special Information Booklet** must include an explanation all of the costs in the settlement; explanations and samples of standard settlement forms; an explanation of escrow accounts; information about the borrower's choices in selecting service providers; and an explanation of unfair practices, costs, and requirements.

The **Good-Faith Estimate (GFE)** is a particularly important disclosure. It details all of the relevant information and expected costs associated with the requested loan. The first page of the GFE includes information about the loan originator; important dates (such as the expiration date for the quoted interest rate); and a summary of the loan, which includes the loan amount, the expected interest rate, the loan term, the monthly payment amount, and details about any changes to the information, as in the case of adjustable-rate mortgages (ARMs).

The second page of the GFE includes an itemization of all expected settlement charges, including origination fees, costs for title insurance and services, appraisal fees, and initial escrow deposit

requirements. The third page includes information on possible variations or changes to the expected charges and a **shopping chart** that borrowers can use to compare the estimates from multiple mortgage brokers or lenders. Loans made after 2015 use a new form called the Loan Estimate, but much of the required information is the same.

At least three days prior to closing, RESPA requires that borrowers be given an Affiliated Business Arrangements (AfBA) Disclosure and also a Closing Disclosure (formerly known as the HUD-1 Settlement Statement). The **Closing Disclosure** is a five-page form that details information about the loan terms, including the loan amount, interest rate, repayment terms, and all costs and fees associated with the loan and the closing. The Closing Disclosure itemizes which fees and costs are being paid by which party (borrower-paid, seller-paid, or paid by others) and includes contact information for the real estate agents, the mortgage broker, the lender, and the settlement agent.

Initial Escrow Statements

The borrower must be given an **initial escrow statement** at closing or within forty-five days of closing. The initial escrow statement includes the monthly mortgage payment, what portion of that payment goes towards the escrow account for taxes and insurance, an itemization of the estimated taxes and insurance that will be paid from the escrow account, estimated disbursement dates for those payments, the amount of the **cushion** (any monies that will remain in the account after payments are made), and a trial running balance of the account. After the closing, the borrower must be provided with an annual escrow statement that details all monies paid into the escrow account and all payments that were made from the account. This statement must be given to the borrower once for every twelve-month period after the closing of the loan.

Mortgage Broker Definition

The burden of providing the financial information and disclosures about the mortgage loan transaction to the parties involved falls on the mortgage and loan professionals, including those working as mortgage brokers. RESPA defines a **mortgage broker** as any person who originates loans and/or serves as an intermediary between a borrower and a mortgage lender or finance company. The mortgage broker is typically the person who collects the documentation from the borrower, puts together the loan package for submission to the lender, and works with the borrower and the lender to get the mortgage transaction approved and funded.

RESPA Prohibitions and Limitations

RESPA prohibits certain practices, including payments for referrals, charging unearned fees, and kickbacks. A **kickback** is a payment or financial compensation given for preferential treatment. For example, if a title company gives a mortgage broker financial compensation or gifts in exchange for the broker using them in all of their mortgage transactions, that would be an illegal kickback. The payment of referral fees is also considered a form of kickback and is prohibited. The mortgage broker can suggest service providers to the borrower, but they cannot require that any particular provider be used. The borrower must be given the choice of whom to use, and the broker cannot receive any type of compensation from the service provider.

RESPA also governs how escrow accounts can be used and prohibits excessively large deposit requirements. An **escrow account** is used to hold monies that will pay annual property taxes and homeowners insurance when the borrower pays those together with their mortgage payment (a **PITI mortgage** payment refers to principal, interest, taxes, and insurance). Typically, a borrower will be required to pay two months' worth of taxes and insurance payments at closing to establish the escrow account, though this amount may be adjusted depending on when the tax and insurance payments are due. Then the tax and insurance money that is collected as part of the mortgage payment each month is put into the escrow account so that when it is time for taxes and insurance to be paid, the account is fully funded.

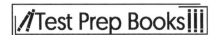

Business relationships and affiliations between service providers, mortgage brokers, and lenders in a transaction are not prohibited, but such relationships must be disclosed to the borrower. The borrower must also be informed of the charges for services and the nature of the relationship, such as a broker's financial interest in a particular title company. Finally, the borrower is not required to use any affiliated company and must be given a choice of service providers.

Settlement Services

RESPA covers a number of settlement services in conjunction with mortgage loan financing. The term **settlement services** refers to any provider involved in the loan transaction, including loan origination and processing services, title services, attorney services, document preparation, credit reporting, appraisals, inspections, insurance services (including homeowners insurance, hazard insurance, flood insurance, and mortgage insurance), and settlement agents. All of these providers and services are governed and bound by RESPA.

RESPA Exemptions

There are some exemptions to the RESPA requirements. RESPA does not apply to commercial, business, or agricultural transactions nor to temporary loans, such as construction loans or bridge loans. RESPA also does not apply to any loans for unimproved properties, such as vacant lots or raw land, so long as the loan proceeds will not be used to build a residential dwelling on the property.

Borrower's Loan Application Information

Part of RESPA specifically addresses what information is required from the borrower on the loan application. RESPA requires that the borrower's **loan application** includes 1) the names of all borrowers, 2) the gross monthly income for all borrowers, 3) the social security numbers for all borrowers, 4) the address of the property being used to secure the loan, 5) the estimated value of the property, and 6) the amount of the loan being requested. The loan originator, broker, or lender may also require additional information, such as current and previous employment and any outstanding debts or credit obligations of the borrower(s).

Loss Mitigation and Foreclosure Process

RESPA also includes certain **loss mitigation** procedures, the remedies available to borrowers and lenders should a borrower fall behind on repayment of the mortgage loan. Loss mitigation is intended to help borrowers keep their homes and to help lenders avoid having to foreclose on the property. These procedures require that the lender contact the borrower at regular intervals in an attempt to resolve the delinquency.

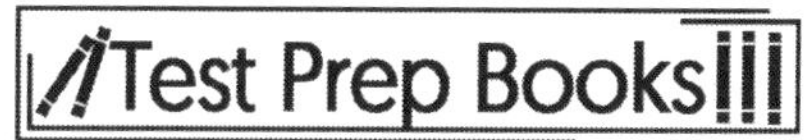

Within forty-five days of the first delinquency, the lender must contact the borrower by phone, in writing, or in person to discuss the borrower's options for avoiding foreclosure. The lender must appoint a contact person or team who are assigned to work with the borrower and who are available for the borrower to contact with questions about the loss mitigation process. The contact person must be able to discuss available loss mitigation programs with the borrower; assist the borrower with completing the loss mitigation application; inform the borrower as to the status of any submitted mitigation applications; and explain the appeals process to the borrower, should that become necessary.

There are often several loss mitigation options that help borrowers remain in their homes. A forbearance allows the borrower to temporarily stop making payments, or to make smaller payments, for a certain amount of time. A repayment plan allows borrowers to resume making payments while paying an extra amount each month that will be applied towards the past due amounts. Loan modification plans restructure the terms of the loan, such as the interest rate or the length of the loan, to reduce the monthly payments. If the borrower can come up with the money to bring the loan current, a reinstatement plan may also be an option.

If staying in the home is not an option, the borrower can still avoid foreclosure by requesting a **short sale**. A short sale is when the lender agrees to allow the home to be sold for less than the amount owed on the mortgage. The borrower can also relinquish ownership by surrendering the deed in lieu of foreclosure, in which case the lender accepts the deed to the home rather than foreclosing on the mortgage.

The borrower must request a **loss mitigation application** from the lender in order to take advantage of any of these options. The application package typically includes an application form; income documentation, including paystubs, tax returns, and bank statements; and a signed hardship statement. The lender must review the application and notify the borrower within five days if the application package is complete. If the package is missing information, the lender must provide the borrower with information as to what is needed and must provide a reasonable time frame for the borrower to submit the information. The lender then has thirty days to evaluate the application package and notify the borrower in writing of the loss mitigation options. The borrower can then accept or reject the offer(s) and also has the option to appeal the modification decisions of the lender. During the loss mitigation application process, the lender is prohibited from continuing with foreclosure proceedings, depending on the timing of the foreclosure process and the lender's receipt of the borrower's loss mitigation application.

B. Equal Credit Opportunity Act (ECOA), 12 CFR Part 1002 (Regulation B)

The Equal Credit Opportunity Act Purpose

The **Equal Credit Opportunity Act (ECOA)** is legislation that prevents lenders from discriminating against borrowers based on factors having nothing to do with their ability to repay a loan. **Regulation B** is the rule that implements the Equal Credit Opportunity Act. It specifically defines unlawful behavior with regards to ECOA and details lending practices that are required, permitted, and prohibited with regards to borrower credit applications. Regulation B was enforced by the Federal Reserve until the Consumer Financial Protection Bureau (CFPB) was created in 2011 and assumed regulation of the industry. Violations of Regulation B are handled by the CFPB in conjunction with the **Federal Trade Commission**

(FTC) and the **Department of Justice**. Regulation B is found under Title 12, Code of Federal Regulations Part 1002, or 12 CFR Part 1002.

The purpose of ECOA and Regulation B is to ensure that credit is available for all "creditworthy applicants" without discrimination. The law also includes requirements regarding notifications to the borrower of all decisions and actions taken on credit applications, as well as disclosure, credit reporting, and recordkeeping requirements.

Factors That Cannot Be Used to Discriminate

ECOA lists specific **identifiers** that cannot be used in the determination of creditworthiness. These factors include race, color, religion, national origin, sex, marital status, and age, as well as whether the borrower participates in any public assistance program or has exercised any consumer rights protections under the Consumer Credit Protection Act. This means that lenders cannot deny a credit application solely based on any of these factors. For example, a person cannot be denied credit because they are not married or because they are too young (so long as they are at least of the legal age of maturity). Prior to the enactment of ECOA and Regulation B, lending discrimination was common. Women, for example, were prohibited from obtaining a credit card without their husband's express permission. ECOA was established to prevent these types of discriminatory and prohibitive lending practices.

Prohibitions on discriminatory behavior are not limited solely to credit decisions. Lenders also cannot use discriminatory language in their marketing materials or in any oral or written statements, and they cannot discourage people from applying for credit based on these identifiers.

ECOA Permissible Information Collection

ECOA does allow for the collection of some information solely for regulatory and reporting purposes. For example, a lender may ask a borrower's sex or race for federal reporting purposes, but the information cannot be required. That is, borrowers may opt out of providing the information if they wish. If the borrower does opt to provide the information, the information cannot be used in the evaluation of the loan application.

Avoiding discriminatory behavior does not mean that lenders cannot require reasonable information from potential borrowers in order to determine their creditworthiness, meaning their ability to repay the loan and evidence of their past handling of credit accounts. ECOA allows lenders to collect information such as a borrower's credit report and income documentation, including paystubs, tax returns, and bank statements.

Loan Application Information

Loan applications, especially for mortgage loans, typically include a great deal of information about the borrower; the property; and the borrower's employment, income, and debts. While ECOA prohibits the use of specific information in determining creditworthiness, some information can be requested on the loan application so long as it is optional. For example, the borrower may choose whether or not to include a courtesy title, such as Mr. or Mrs., and the borrower can choose whether or not to disclose information concerning income from child support or alimony.

In addition, the borrower's birthday is required, but this may only be used for identification purposes and for ensuring that the borrower is of legal age to enter into a contract. In some cases, lenders may

take the age of an **elderly borrower**, anyone age 62 or older, into account if the use of such information provides the borrower with a favorable distinction. The age of an elderly borrower may not be used as a negative factor.

When an application is submitted for the purpose of purchasing or refinancing a residential dwelling, federal regulations require the collection of information regarding a borrower's sex, race, ethnicity, marital status, and age for monitoring purposes. However, the borrower is not required to provide that information. If the borrower opts not to provide the information, the mortgage broker is permitted to note the pertinent information based on visual observations and the borrower's surname. The information may only be used for federal reporting purposes and may not be used in determining whether to extend credit to the borrower.

Income Evaluation

Evaluating a borrower's income is a key aspect in determining the creditworthiness of the borrower. The lender may require documentation for income derived from employment, such as pay stubs, tax forms such as W-2 or 1099 forms, or tax returns. Lenders may require profit and loss statements for self-employed borrowers; statements for investment, annuity, or pension accounts; and other documentation that demonstrates the borrower's ability to repay the loan. The lender may request information about child support, alimony, or other support payments the borrower receives if the borrower wishes for that income to be considered in the loan application. The lender is permitted to evaluate the reliability of the income and the probability of its continuance, but the lender may not deny the loan application because the borrower receives this type of income. Similarly, the borrower may wish to include Social Security income or Social Security Disability income in the evaluation of the loan application. The lender may consider this income, but may not deny the loan based on the borrower's receipt of it. Other creditworthiness factors include the amount of existing debt as compared to the borrower's income (referred to as the debt-to-income ratio or DTI) and the borrower's history of timely repayment.

Co-Signer Requirements

There are specific requirements with regards to co-signers under ECOA as well. First, if a borrower meets all of the necessary credit requirements, then a co-signer cannot be required. Additionally, if a borrower does not meet the creditworthiness guidelines, then the lender may require a co-signer for the loan; however, the lender may not require that the co-signer be a spouse. This would be considered discrimination based on marital status.

Notification of Actions Taken

Once the full loan package and all documentation has been submitted to the lender, the lender has thirty days to notify the borrower of the credit decision. Actions taken include approval; **counteroffer**, such as a change in loan terms; or adverse action, such as on an incomplete application or denial of the loan.

Loan Denials

Lenders can deny loans for a variety of reasons, including insufficient income, inadequate debt-to-income ratio (DTI), and unacceptable property condition or valuation. Loan applications can also be denied if they are incomplete or if the borrower fails to provide supporting documentation as required by the lender. For example, a lender may deny a loan application if the borrower does not have sufficient income to be able to repay the loan based on the lender's debt-to-income (DTI) guidelines. Similarly, lenders can require minimum credit scores and/or demonstration of a sufficient credit history showing the borrower's ability to handle debt responsibly, and if a borrower does not meet those requirements, the lender may deny the loan. However, a lender would be in violation of ECOA if they were to deny a loan based on any of the protected distinctions such as race or marital status.

Adverse Actions and Required Disclosures

Adverse action occurs when a lender has refused to grant a loan or credit based on the contents of the borrower's application, income documentation, or credit history. For example, if a lender determines that a borrower does not have sufficient income to pay the mortgage payment in addition to the borrower's other existing debts, the lender will take the adverse action of denying the loan application. The lender has thirty days to notify the borrower of the adverse action. Notification must be made in writing and must contain the name and address of the lender, identification of the federal agency that has oversight of the lender, a statement of the action taken, and either the specific reason for the adverse action or information on the applicant's right to request such disclosure of reason within sixty days of the notice of adverse action. The notification must also include an ECOA notice, such as the suggested statement provided in section 1002.9, paragraph b(1): "The Federal Equal Credit Opportunity Act prohibits creditors from discriminating against credit applicants on the basis of race, color, religion, national origin, sex, marital status, age (provided the applicant has the capacity to enter into a binding contract); because all or part of the applicant's income derives from any public assistance program; or because the applicant has in good faith exercised any right under the Consumer Credit Protection Act. The Federal agency that administers compliance with this law concerning this creditor is…."

Credit Reporting and Record-Keeping Requirements

ECOA also includes sections regarding credit reporting. Lenders are not required to report accounts to the credit bureaus. However, if they do, they must do so in compliance with ECOA guidelines. This includes reporting information equally for all parties to the account, such as including specific information for each spouse such that the credit reporting agency can include information for both parties on their respective credit reports.

Finally, ECOA includes provisions regarding record-keeping requirements. Lenders must keep applications on file for twenty-five months after the last date of action taken, including applications on which adverse action was taken. Lenders must also retain records for existing accounts for at least twenty-five months after the date of an adverse action, such as a denial of credit line increase.

C. Truth in Lending Act (TILA), 12 CFR Part 1026 (Regulation Z)

Purpose and Definitions

The **Truth in Lending Act (TILA)** was enacted by Congress in 1968. It is designed to inform and protect consumers when they deal with lenders. TILA applies to most types of consumer credit, including closed-end loans such as mortgages and auto loans as well as open-end accounts like credit cards. TILA protects consumers against unfair and inaccurate credit billing practices and requires the full disclosure of loan

terms, including the interest rate, the annual percentage rate (APR), and all costs associated with the loan. TILA also gives borrowers the right to cancel some types of transactions that involve their primary residential property. TILA regulations are enforced by the Federal Reserve and the CFPB. Similar to Regulation X and Regulation B, **Regulation Z**, found in Chapter 12, Part 1026 of the Code of Federal Regulations, is the rule that implements TILA.

The Truth in Lending Act (TILA) applies to mortgage loans in some very important ways, and it is important to understand some key terms. The **interest rate** is the amount that the lender will charge for the loan. It is usually expressed as a percentage and is calculated based on the current loan balance, known as the principal. **Finance charges** are the monies that lenders make as profit on the loan. Finance charges include the charged interest on the loan as well as origination fees and other charges associated with obtaining and maintaining the loan. The **annual percentage rate (APR)** is the total cost of the loan. It includes the interest as well as any additional finance charges. The APR is meant to reflect the true cost of the loan. It is important to note that **seller contributions**, costs and fees that are paid by the seller in a purchase transaction, are not included in the APR calculation.

A **residential mortgage loan** is any loan used to obtain financing for the purchase or refinance of a borrower's primary residential dwelling. Borrowers must disclose whether the property being used to secure the loan is their primary residence versus a second home or an investment property, as the rules governing mortgage finance vary depending on the property's intended use.

Truth in Lending (TIL) Disclosure Form

Note that this section describes the original provisions of TILA; please see page twenty-one for changes made in 2015 as a result of the TILA-RESPA Integrated Disclosure Rule.

When a borrower obtains a mortgage loan, whether it is for a purchase or a refinance, they must be provided with a **Truth in Lending (TIL) Disclosure** form. The mortgage broker must provide the borrower with a TIL within three days of receipt of the borrower's loan application. This initial TIL should be based on the requested loan and anticipated interest rate and costs as provided on the initial Good Faith Estimate (GFE). If the terms of the loan change, a new TIL must be provided to the borrower, and a final TIL must be provided to the borrower at least seven days prior to the closing of the loan transaction.

The TIL includes a chart at the top of the page that clearly shows the APR for the loan, the finance charge, the amount financed, and the total payments. Also included are simple explanations of each of these amounts. The APR is "the cost of your credit as a yearly rate." The finance charge is "the dollar amount the credit will cost you." The amount financed is "the total credit provided to you." This is the amount of the loan being given. Finally, the total of payments is "the amount you will have paid after you have made all payments as scheduled." The purpose of this section of the TIL is to be as transparent as possible with the amount of money the loan is going to cost the borrower.

The next section of the TIL shows the breakdown of the borrower's monthly payments. For a fixed-rate mortgage loan, one that does not change over time, there are usually two lines. The first line shows the monthly payment for each month of the loan. The second line shows the last month's payment, which can sometimes be slightly different due to the interest rate calculation. Some types of loans may have increasing or decreasing monthly payments, and these will be specified in this section. Also, balloon mortgage payments will be shown here. A balloon mortgage is one in which the borrower pays a monthly payment for a set period of time with the full balance due on the loan at the end of that time.

This section will also indicate if the borrower's loan is an adjustable-rate mortgage (ARM), meaning that the interest rate on the loan varies over time. The remaining sections of the TIL include information about any late charges that may be assessed, if there is a prepayment penalty if the loan is paid off in advance of the final due date, and whether or not the loan is assumable. An **assumable mortgage** is one that can be assumed by a new borrower with qualification and approval from the lender.

Mortgage Refinance Loans

A mortgage **refinance** loan is one that is obtained when a borrower is seeking to get a new loan against a property they already own. This can be a property they own outright or a property that already has a mortgage. One of the key provisions of TILA applies to mortgage refinance loans that involve the borrower's primary residence. This provision is the borrower's **right to rescind**, also known as the **right of rescission**. TILA gives borrowers three days after the closing of a refinance transaction to review and consider the loan and change their mind, or rescind their agreement to the loan terms. Borrowers may opt to rescind their refinance loan for several reasons. They may have found a better deal, such as a loan offer with a lower interest rate, or they may have read something in the loan documents that they do not agree with. Borrowers can also simply change their minds and decide they do not want to accept the new loan after all. Borrowers are not required to disclose their reasons to the lender.

The lender must provide the borrower with a notice of right to rescind, which explains this right to the borrower. The notice must disclose the security interest in the borrower's principal dwelling, the borrower's right to rescind the transaction, how to take action to rescind the transaction, and the effects of a rescission. The notice must also include the deadline for the rescission period, typically three days after the close of the transaction. The refinance loan typically will not be funded until after the three-day right of rescission period has ended.

The right of rescission applies to refinances, home equity loans, and home equity lines of credit (HELOCs). It does not apply to mortgages used to purchase residential properties. Rescission also does not apply to refinances that are for less than the current mortgage balance or for consolidation of loans with the same lender.

Home Ownership and Equity Protection Act and High-Cost Mortgages

The **Home Ownership and Equity Protection Act (HOEPA)** is an amendment to the Truth in Lending Act (TILA). It was enacted to protect consumers from high interest rates and fees imposed on home equity and mortgage refinance loans. HOEPA requires special disclosures for any loan that meets specific high-cost mortgage guidelines, particularly with regards to the fees charged for the loan and the APR of the loan as compared to the average prime offer rate. The **average prime offer rate** is an interest rate calculation based on the current rates, points, and loan pricing being offered on mortgage loans to low-risk borrowers. The average prime offer rate is updated weekly by the Consumer Financial Protection Bureau (CFPB). Additionally, distinctions are made for first-lien mortgages and second-lien or subordinate mortgages. A **first-lien mortgage**, often just called a first mortgage, is one that will be paid off first should the property go into foreclosure. A **second-lien mortgage** or **subordinate mortgage** is one that will be paid secondary to the first mortgage in the event of a foreclosure.

High-cost mortgages are defined as loans that meet one or more of the following criteria:

- The APR of the loan will exceed the average prime offer rate by more than 6.5 percent for a first-lien mortgage.
- The APR of the loan will exceed the average prime offer rate by more than 8.5 percent for a subordinate mortgage or for mortgages under $50,000.
- The total fees for the transaction will exceed 5 percent of the total loan amount for mortgages over $20,000.
- The total fees for the transaction will exceed the lesser of 8 percent of the total loan amount or $1,000 for mortgages under $20,000.
- The prepayment penalty is more than 2 percent of the total amount prepaid.

These guidelines do not, however, apply to reverse mortgages, home construction loans, or USDA rural property loans.

In addition to the standard disclosures required for mortgage loan transactions, high-cost mortgages must also include the following statement, pursuant to section 1026.32 of TILA: "You are not required to complete this agreement merely because you have received these disclosures or have signed a loan application. If you obtain this loan, the lender will have a mortgage on your home. You could lose your home, and any money you have put into it, if you do not meet your obligations under the loan."

High-cost mortgage loans have specific limitations under HOEPA, as well. These loans may not include a final balloon payment of more than twice the regular monthly payment, advance payment requirements, raises to the interest rate in the event of a default, or prepayment penalties.

Higher-Priced Mortgage Loans

TILA makes a distinction between high-cost mortgage loans and higher-priced mortgage loans. A **higher-priced mortgage loan** is one in which the interest rate is 1.5 percent more than the average prime rate offer for a first mortgage, 2.5 percent higher for a **jumbo first mortgage** (a mortgage that exceeds the maximum amounts set by the Federal Housing Finance Agency), and 3.5 percent higher for a subordinate mortgage.

Higher-priced mortgage loans have additional requirements under TILA. The lender must maintain an escrow account for the payment of taxes and insurance, and the borrower does not have the option to waive this requirement and pay the taxes and insurance premiums directly. Additionally, the escrow account cannot be canceled for at least five years or until such time as the loan is paid in full, whichever comes first.

Lenders making higher-priced mortgages must also obtain a written appraisal of the property by a certified or licensed appraiser. The appraisal must also include an inspection of the interior of the property. If the property is being sold as a flipped property, then a second appraisal must also be obtained at no additional cost to the borrower. A **flipped property** is a property that the seller has owned for less than ninety days but is selling for more than 10 percent above the seller's original purchase price, or a property that the seller has owned for less than 180 days but with a selling price of more than 20 percent above the seller's original purchase price.

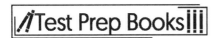

Mortgage Loan Originator Compensation

Lastly, TILA regulates the compensation that can be paid to **mortgage loan originators (MLOs)**. Loan originators are defined as anyone who takes a loan application or otherwise assists in obtaining or negotiating a mortgage loan in exchange for financial compensation. Mortgage brokers are typically considered loan originators unless they are directly employed by a lender.

Under TILA, mortgage loan originators may not be paid based on the terms of the loan with the exception of the loan amount. Loan origination fees are typically calculated based on the loan amount, and these are permitted. However, a loan originator may not be paid a higher fee based on a higher loan amount, such as a commission of 1 percent for loans up to a certain amount and 2 percent for loans above that amount. Additionally, a loan originator cannot, for example, be paid extra if a loan closes at a higher interest rate or for a specific term. Finally, loan originators cannot receive compensation from persons other than the lender or the borrower. This is to prevent **steering**, a term referring to an originator directing the borrower to use a particular lender or loan provider with less favorable terms or to use specific settlement service providers in exchange for compensation from those providers. Steering can also refer to originators or lenders pushing borrowers towards or away from particular communities and is typically a result of bias for or against the borrower based on the prohibited categories in the Fair Housing Act such as religion, race, gender, marital status, or disability.

It is important to note that the mortgage loan originator compensation rules only apply to closed-end mortgage loans. They do not apply to HELOCs or open-end lines of credit.

D. TILA-RESPA Integrated Disclosure Rule (TRID) ("Know Before You Owe")

Purpose of TRID

In October 2015, the CFPB instituted a series of guidelines designed to close some of the loopholes in the mortgage finance laws. Some unscrupulous lenders were finding ways to circumvent consumer protection laws, and the **TILA-RESPA Integrated Disclosure Rule (TRID)** is designed to fix those issues. The TRID rule is also referred to as the **Know Before You Owe** rule. The TRID rule applies to most closed-end mortgage loans. It does not apply to reverse mortgages or open-end lines of credit such as HELOCs.

TRID consolidates several of the disclosures into two forms. The new Loan Estimate form replaces the Good Faith Estimate (GFE) and the preliminary Truth in Lending (TIL) disclosures, and the Closing Disclosure replaces the old HUD-1 Settlement Statement and the final Truth in Lending (TIL) Disclosure.

Loan Estimate Form

The **Loan Estimate** form, federal form H-24, is a three-page document that includes the details about the proposed mortgage loan. At the top of the first page is an italicized note that says, "Save this Loan Estimate to compare with your Closing Disclosure." This is a reminder to the borrower to check that their final loan is the same as the loan that they were quoted up front and that they are aware of and understand any changes to the loan terms.

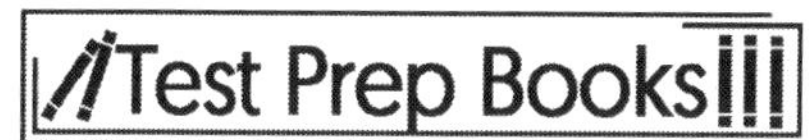

The top of page one also includes that date of the estimate, the name and address of the borrower, the property address, and the purchase price of the property. Also listed are the loan term (the length of the loan), the purpose of the loan (purchase or refinance), the loan product (a fixed-rate mortgage loan versus an adjustable-rate mortgage (ARM), for example), and the loan type (conventional, FHA, or VA). There is also a check box that indicates whether the interest rate is locked and the lock expiration date.

Beneath this information is a box that details the loan terms. It includes the loan amount, the interest rate, and the monthly principal and interest payment. There is also information regarding any prepayment penalties and whether the loan includes a balloon payment.

The next section of the form is the Projected Payments section. This includes the estimated monthly payment, including the principal and interest as well as any mortgage insurance and escrow amounts. There is also information about the property taxes and the homeowner's insurance premiums that will be collected and held in escrow. If the payment will change over the term of the loan, this information is explained here as well.

Finally, the bottom of page one includes the estimated closing costs for the loan and the estimated **cash to close**, which refers to the amount of money the borrower will be expected to bring to the closing. The breakdown of the closing costs and the cash to close can be found on page two of the Loan Estimate.

Page two of the Loan Estimate form is divided into two columns and includes a detailed breakdown of all of the costs associated with the loan. The first column includes all of the loan costs. Section A specifies the loan costs, including the origination charges as well as application and underwriting fees. Section B includes charges for settlement services that the borrower has no control over, such as the credit report fee and the appraisal fee. Section C lists the settlement services that the borrower can shop for, including pest inspection, surveys, and title fees.

The second column details all other costs associated with the loan, such as transfer taxes and deed recording fees. This column includes sections for **prepaids**, or **prepaid costs**, which are the insurance and taxes that have been paid in advance. For example, the homeowner's insurance is often paid in advance for the full year as part of the loan closing. There may also be prepaid interest if the loan closes in the middle of the month rather than at the end of the month. Finally, this column shows the amount of money being collected to establish the escrow account and any other fees. The bottom of page two shows the calculations that resulted in the closing costs and cash to close figures that are shown on page one.

The third page of the Loan Estimate form offers some comparisons that the borrower can use should they choose to shop for other loan offers. There are also notes about the appraisal, whether or not the loan is assumable, and late payment information.

Loan Consummation

One of the terms that is often referred to on the loan paperwork is **loan consummation**. This is a legal term that refers to the date when the borrower becomes legally obligated to the lender to repay the loan. This sounds somewhat complicated, but it usually just refers to the date that the loan paperwork is signed by the borrower, usually the closing date, though this can vary in some states. Settlement agents will verify the loan consummation requirements and date with the local state laws in order to provide the necessary disclosures within the allowed time frames.

Special Information Booklet

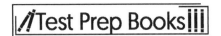

Under TRID, a borrower must still be provided with a **Special Information Booklet**, published by the Consumer Financial Protection Bureau (CFPB), as required by RESPA. The booklet is entitled "Your Home Loan Toolkit: A Step-By-Step Guide." If the loan is a HELOC, then the CFPB booklet entitled "When Your Home is On the Line: What You Should Know About Home Equity Lines of Credit" instead. The Special Information Booklet must be provided to the borrower within three business days of the lender's receipt of the loan application.

Closing Disclosure Form

The Closing Disclosure form is a five-page document that details all of the final loan transaction information. The borrower must receive the Closing Disclosure form a minimum of three business days before the loan closing date. In addition, the costs shown on the Closing Disclosure form should be very similar, or even identical, to the figures provided on the Loan Estimate form.

The Closing Disclosure form looks very similar to the Loan Estimate form and includes much of the same information. At the top of the first page is a statement reading, "This form is a statement of final loan terms and closing costs. Compare this document with your Loan Estimate." This is a reminder to the borrower to make sure that what is being charged in the final loan agreement is the same, or very nearly so, as what was disclosed to them on their estimate. The rest of the first page of the Closing Disclosure is nearly identical to the Loan Estimate form, making it relatively easy for the borrower to compare the two and make sure that all of the information is as expected.

The second page of the Closing Disclosure is different from the Loan Estimate in that all of the costs are broken down into three columns, "Borrower-Paid," "Seller-Paid," and "Paid by Others." The borrower should be able to compare the costs on this page with the costs listed on the Loan Estimate. At the bottom of the second page is the Total Closing Costs that the borrower is expected to pay. This figure should match the closing costs listed at the bottom of page one.

The third page of the disclosure shows the calculations involved in the total cash to close required by the borrower at closing. This includes the closing costs, the down payment, any deposits that have been paid, and any credits from the seller. The bottom of the page is the summary of the transaction for both the borrower and the seller.

The fourth page includes additional disclosures about the loan, including whether the loan is assumable or not, late payment and partial payment information, and information about the escrow account.

The fifth page shows the total loan calculation and the contact information for the lender, the mortgage broker, the real estate agents, and the settlement agent, including mailing addresses and phone numbers.

Disclosures Timing

The Loan Estimate form must be provided to borrowers within three business days of loan application. Additionally, if there are any changes to the loan terms, such as raising or lowering the loan amount or changing the interest rate, a new Loan Estimate form must be provided to the borrower within three business days of the change. Lastly, there must be at least seven business days between the borrower's

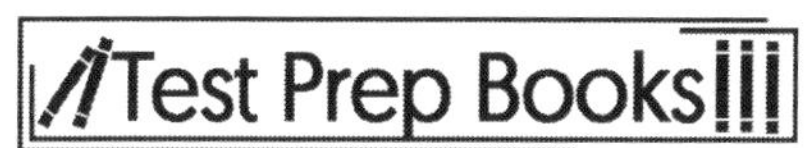

receipt of the Loan Estimate form and the closing of the loan. The borrower must be given the final Closing Disclosure form at least three business days before the closing date of the transaction.

Tolerance Limits and Good Faith

Lenders and mortgage loan brokers should make every effort to provide the borrower with a complete, correct Loan Estimate disclosure right from the start. Lenders and brokers are expected to act with **good faith**, meaning that they are acting with sincerity and integrity. There must be no hint of deception or deliberate misleading of the borrower.

Good faith is determined through the comparison of the final loan figures and the initial loan estimate figures. If the loan closing figures are less than or equal to those initially disclosed, the lender is considered to have acted in good faith. Costs that are higher than the original estimate must fall within the acceptable tolerance limits: zero tolerance, 10 percent tolerance, and unlimited tolerance. The **tolerance limits** dictate how much a fee can change from the initial Loan Estimate to the final Closing Disclosure.

Fees that are categorized as zero tolerance cannot increase from the initial Loan Estimate form. These include any fees that are under the lender's control, such as the loan origination fee. Zero tolerance fees also include fees that the borrower cannot shop for, such as the appraisal fee and transfer taxes. It is presumed that the lender has reasonable knowledge of these fees and should be able to accurately convey them to the borrower.

The 10 percent tolerance fees include third-party services, provided that the borrower is able to shop for and choose them. These fees are considered cumulatively when considering whether the lender has acted in good faith. The total of all of these fees on the Closing Disclosure must be within 10 percent of the total on the Loan Estimate.

Finally, some fees fall under the no tolerance, or unlimited tolerance, category. The fees in this category are not controlled by the lender and include fees like the prepaid interest (which is dependent on the loan closing date), property taxes, and homeowner's insurance.

There are very specific circumstances under which a lender or mortgage broker can revise the Loan Estimate disclosure, and simply making a mistake on the form is not one of them. If there is information missing from the initial Loan Estimate form, the lender or broker must make every effort to provide the borrower with the information as quickly as possible. If the lender does not have some of the information that is required for the estimate, they must use due diligence in obtaining the information and providing the borrower with the closest estimate possible. They must also note that the information is an estimate.

Change of Circumstances

It is important that lenders and mortgage brokers have their fees correct on the initial Loan Estimate form that is sent to the borrower, because the form generally cannot be modified except in certain circumstances, known as **changed circumstances**. When a changed circumstance occurs, it is known as a **triggering event** and allows for revisions to the Loan Estimate form. The most common changed circumstance involves the borrower's eligibility to qualify for the quoted loan and the value of the property being used to secure the loan. For example, if a borrower claims a certain income on their loan application, but the mortgage underwriter is unable to verify that income level, the borrower may no longer qualify for the original loan amount. In this case, the loan may be restructured to require a larger down payment, which would be a change of circumstances and would require a revised Loan Estimate form. Similarly, if the property being financed is appraised at a lower-than-expected value, that could significantly affect the amount of financing the lender is willing to offer on the property. In these circumstances, the lender is permitted to revise and reissue the Loan Estimate.

Another permissible changed circumstance is if the borrower requests a change to the loan terms. For example, if the borrower asks to change the loan from a 30-year fixed loan to a 15-year fixed loan, then a new Loan Estimate would be generated and provided to the borrower showing the new loan terms. Other changed circumstances involve changes to the interest stemming from locking a previously unlocked rate and borrower-initiated delays in the closing of more than ten days.

Borrower's Right To Rescission

The borrower's right of rescission does not change under TRID. On a mortgage refinance, the borrower has three business days to cancel, or rescind, the mortgage loan. The clock begins when the borrower signs the loan contract, called the Promissory Note, and receives the Truth in Lending (TIL) disclosure. In addition, the lender must provide the borrower with two copies of a notice that explains the borrower's right to rescind the loan. Generally, all of these documents are signed and provided at the closing of the loan transaction. The day after the closing is counted as day one, and Saturdays are considered business days, but Sundays and legal holidays are not.

The right of rescission does not apply to refinance loans that are the same or lower than the current mortgage and that are being refinanced with the same lender. In addition, there is no right of rescission on purchase loans or on properties that are not the borrower's primary residence.

If the borrower decides to rescind the loan, they should contact the lender immediately. There is not a standardized means of notification, but the lender should have provided information on how to rescind the loan. The form can be mailed to the address provided by the lender or, if an address was not provided, to the address listed for making monthly payments. The date and time of the rescission is considered to be the time the form was mailed. In the event of a rescission, the lender has twenty days to refund any monies that the borrower paid in conjunction with the loan.

Annual Escrow Statement

In addition to the Initial Escrow Statement that is provided to the borrower at closing, an **annual escrow statement** must be provided each year. The statement must show any activity in the escrow account during the course of the year, including all payments made by the borrower and any payment made out of the account, such as tax payments or homeowner's insurance premiums. The statement must also show the anticipated activity for the coming year.

There are seven specific items that must be included on the annual escrow statement. These include 1) the borrower's current mortgage payment, including the escrow amounts; 2) the monthly mortgage payment and escrow portions from the past year; 3) the total amount paid into the escrow account during the previous year; 4) the amounts paid for taxes, insurance, and other costs for the previous year; and 5) the balance in the account at the end of the period. In addition, the statement must include explanations for any surplus and how the lender is handling the extra amount, and an explanation of any shortages that the borrower is expected to pay. The statement must be provided to the borrower within thirty days of the end of the fiscal year.

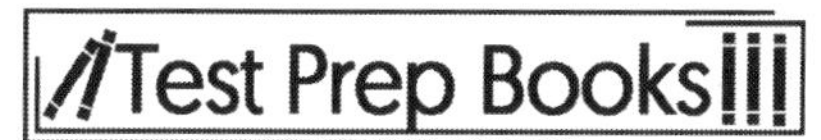

E. Other Federal Laws and Guidelines

Home Mortgage Disclosure Act (HMDA), 12 CFR Part 1003 (Regulation C)

Enacted in 1975, the **Home Mortgage Disclosure Act (HMDA)** requires certain financial institutions in the U.S. to report specific information for public disclosure. By providing the public with this loan information, the HMDA intends to make sure that financial institutions are adequately serving their communities' housing needs as well as identifying and preventing lending discrimination. The collected information can also help public officials determine the most effective distribution of public sector investments to indirectly support and encourage private sector investment in the most needed areas. It defines the necessary information to be reported as well as situations for exemptions. **Regulation C**, found in Chapter 12, Part 1003 of the Code of Federal Regulations, implements HMDA.

Data Reporting

All reported loans must have a unique **universal loan identifier (ULI)** to identify that specific loan. Within that identifier are special character requirements that allow identification of the institution involved with the loan at a glance. All reported loans must also specify a variety of information relating to each loan. The following is a list of all the information that must be reported. Most of it could be considered common-sense identifying information, but some aspects are defined separately in Regulation Z, 12 CFR 1026. That criteria is included at the end of this list.

- Whether or not a loan is guaranteed by the Rural Housing Service, the Farm Service Agency, the Federal Housing Administration (FHA), or the Department of Veterans Affairs (VA)
- The purpose of the loan (e.g., home improvement, refinancing, home purchase, cash-out refinancing, or another purpose)
- Whether or not a loan or application involved a request for preapproval
- Whether the residence on the property is being constructed on site or whether is it a manufactured home
- Whether the property will be a primary residence, secondary residence, or investment property
- The amount of the loan
- Whether the loan was originated or purchased, if the applicant did not accept the loan for any reason (including preapproval requests), and the date the institution took action
- The location of the property securing the loan, including address, state, country, and census tract
- Information about the borrower, such as ethnicity, race, sex, age, and gross annual income (if the credit decision considered it), as well as whether the information was collected on the basis of surname or observation
- What type of entity is purchasing the loan

- In situations where the loan falls under the Home Ownership and Equity Protection Act of 1994 (HOEPA), whether or not the loan meets the criteria for a high-cost mortgage
- The status of any lien on the property
- The credit score(s) used to make the credit decision and the scoring model used
- Any reasons that the financial institution denied the loan, if applicable
- The loan's interest rate
- Additional information regarding the credit decision, such as the ratio of total monthly debt to total monthly income and the ratio of total debt secured by the property to the property's value
- The number of months until the legal obligation matures or terminates
- The number of months until the interest rate may change
- The value of the property securing the loan
- If the dwelling on the property is a manufactured home, then whether the loan is secured by a manufactured home, as well as whether the borrower owns the land directly or indirectly, or leases it
- The number of dwellings related to the property
- If the property includes multifamily dwellings, then the number of dwelling units that are income-restricted according to affordable housing programs
- Whether or not the borrower submitted the application directly to the financial institution, as well as whether or not the obligation was initially payable to the same institution
- If necessary, the unique identifier assigned by the Nationwide Mortgage Licensing System and Registry (NMLS)
- The name of the automated underwriting system used to evaluate the application and the result generated
- Whether the loan is a reverse mortgage, open-end line of credit, or primarily for business or commercial purposes
- If the loan is subject to Regulation Z, 12 CFR part 1026 and is not an assumption, purchased loan, or reverse mortgage, then the difference between the loan's APR and the average prime offer rate (The average prime offer rate is an APR derived from average interest rates and loan pricing terms; it is published by the Consumer Financial Protection Bureau (CFPB) weekly.)
- If the loan is subject to Regulation Z, 12 CFR 1026.43(c) and a disclosure is provided according to 1026.19(f), then the amount of total loan costs as explained 1026.38(f)

- In situations where the loan falls under Regulation Z, 12 CFR 1026.43(c), but is not subject to 1026.19(f) and is also not a purchased loan, the total dollar amount of all points and fees charged for the loan
- In situations that require disclosures under Regulation Z, 12 CFR 1026.19(f), totals for every itemized amount the borrower has paid at or before closing and totals for lender credits
- In situations where the loan falls under Regulation Z, 12 CFR part 1026, but is not a purchased covered loan or a reverse mortgage, the number of months for the loan term and any prepayment penalties
- If the loan includes a balloon payment, interest-only payment, and any terms that would cause the loan to be a negative amortization loan or allow for payments other than fully amortizing payments, then all of these terms as defined in Regulation Z, 12 CFR part 1026

Exemptions

While federal law requires all financial institutions to comply, select institutions and transactions are exempt from being reported. A state-chartered or state-licensed financial institution is exempt from the HMDA if the Consumer Financial Protection Bureau (CFPB) determines that there is a similar and comparable state disclosure law that the institution is subject to. In this case, the institution may apply for exemption, and if accepted, will report and use forms required by its state law instead. If the institution loses that exemption, it will comply with the HMDA starting from the calendar year after the last year it reported under state law. There are also a number of loan transactions that are exempt or partially exempt from reporting. These are listed below.

- If the financial institution is acting in a fiduciary capacity, then a closed-end mortgage loan or open-end line of credit is exempt.
- If a closed-end mortgage loan or open-end line of credit is secured by a lien on unimproved land, it is exempt.
- Temporary financing is exempt.
- Buying an interest in a collection of open-end lines of credit or closed-end mortgage loans is exempt.
- Buying the sole right to manage open-end lines of credit or closed-end mortgage loans is exempt.
- When done as part of an acquisition or merger, buying loans or credit is exempt.
- Open-end lines of credit and closed-end mortgage loans for less than $500 are exempt.
- The purchase of partial interest in open-end lines of credit or closed-end mortgage loans is exempt.
- When used principally for agriculture, open-end lines of credit and closed-end mortgage loans are exempt.

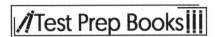

- When used principally for business or commercial enterprises, open-end lines of credit and closed-end mortgage loans are exempt. This does not apply if the line of credit or mortgage is used for a home purchase loan, home improvement loan, or refinancing.
- Closed-end mortgage loans are exempt for financial institutions that have generated fewer than one hundred of these loans in one of the two preceding calendar years.
- Open-end lines of credit are exempt for financial institutions that have generated fewer than two hundred of these lines of credit in one of the two preceding calendar years.
- If a borrower receives new funds that will be combined into a supplemental mortgage as a result of New York Tax Law section 255, the transaction is only exempt if the consolidation is completed in the same calendar year in which the transaction providing new funds to the borrower was also completed.

Fair Credit Reporting Act (FCRA)/Fair and Accurate Credit Transactions Act (FACTA) 15 USC § 1681 et seq.

The **Fair Credit Reporting Act (FCRA)** was enacted in 1970 and sets several rules for the collection and use of information in consumer reports, more commonly called **credit reports**. Credit reports contain a variety of credit and bill repayment information, such as how often someone makes their payments on time, but it can also contain rental repayment information, liens, and bankruptcies. The **Fair and Accurate Credit Transactions Act (FACTA)** was enacted years later in 2003 and acts as an amendment to the FCRA, allowing consumers to request a free credit report every year and adding provisions that allow individuals to place alerts on their credit. Together, both acts help shield consumers from erroneous or fraudulent situations regarding their credit history.

Credit in Mortgage Banking

A **credit score** is a general measure of how likely a person is to make timely and full repayments on their obligations. Higher credit scores indicate better repayment behavior. When a person applies for a mortgage, lenders will check their credit score in addition to other factors. If they find a high credit score (typically around or over 700), then they may be more willing to offer lower interest rates and better deals. Therefore, the steps that the FCRA and FACTA take affect mortgage lending by allowing consumers to keep better track of issues with their credit reports and dispute them as necessary. This means borrowers can get better interest rates on the mortgages they take, and lenders will see more accurate credit reports to make informed lending decisions.

Federal Trade Commission Red Flags Rule, 16 CFR Part 681

The Federal Trade Commission (FTC) created the **Red Flags Rule** to set up a system for how businesses and institutions must organize an **Identity Theft Prevention Program**. The rule was passed in January 2008, but enforcement did not begin until the end of 2010. It sets a clear definition as to which organizations must have these programs, including financial institutions, car dealerships, utility companies, and mortgage brokers.

Identity Theft Prevention Programs

A mortgage broker meets all of the definitions of a creditor under the Red Flags Rule. Brokers obtain consumer credit reports, provide information to consumer reporting agencies, and advance funds that

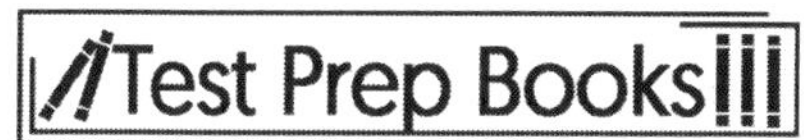

are repaid in the future. While the Red Flags Rule allows any organization the opportunity to create a program that is appropriate for itself, it does require four basic elements for addressing identity theft:

- Identify relevant red flags.
- Detect red flags.
- Prevent and mitigate identity theft.
- Update program.

The organization must be able to identify any business-relevant red flags for identity theft, and to have procedures in place that will detect those red flags during regular operations. It must then be able to act on preventing and mitigating damage once red flags are identified, and the program as a whole must have a method for maintenance, such as by educating staff and improving procedures.

There are five categories of red flags:

- Alerts or warnings from a consumer reporting agency
- Suspicious documents
- Suspicious identifying information like a suddenly new or incorrect address
- Unusual activity from a customer's account, like a sequence of abnormal transfers
- Warnings from customers, victims, or law enforcement about identity theft connected to a customer's account

Bank Secrecy Act/Anti-Money Laundering (BSA/AML)

The **Bank Secrecy Act of 1970 (BSA)** sets several regulations that all financial institutions must follow and establishes reporting requirements to combat the criminal activity of money laundering. Because of this, the law is also sometimes called an anti-money laundering law (AML). The act has been amended several times to require institutions to establish internal policies, procedures, and training to strengthen the anti-money laundering programs they have implemented. As mortgage brokers are a type of financial institution, it's important to be aware of the different types of reports they must file according to the BSA. Failure to comply with BSA reports carries a heavy fine and a potential prison sentence.

BSA Reports

There are five major types of reports that all financial institutions must regularly submit, sometimes even daily. A **currency transaction report (CTR)** reports any cash transactions that exceed $10,000 in a single business day. They include the individual's bank account number, name, address, and Social Security number. The occasional CTR filed for one client is usually not a concern to the Financial Crimes Enforcement Network (FinCEN), but many forms across different banks or in combination with other reports will draw attention.

The second type of report is a **suspicious activity report (SAR)**. An SAR must be filed any time a cash transaction is conducted where the customer seems to be avoiding BSA requirements, such as not filing a CTR, or when the customer's actions lead to suspicion of fraud. As these reports are meant to alert authorities to potential criminal activity, customers or businesses must not be informed that an SAR has been filed against them.

A **Foreign Bank Account Report (FBAR)** is only applicable to U.S. citizens and residents with some direct connection to a foreign bank account. Anyone with a foreign bank account with an aggregate value of

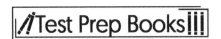

$10,000 or more must file one of these reports annually by October 15, as well as report the account on a Form 1040 tax form.

A **monetary instrument log (MIL)** has to be filed if any cash purchases of monetary instruments valued between $3,000 and $10,000 are made. The log must be kept on hand for at least five years so it is available to any examiners or auditors. These monetary instruments include items like money orders, traveler's checks, or cashier's checks. Additionally, a **Currency and Monetary Instrument Report (CMIR)** must be filed by every institution that is physically involved with the transportation or shipping of currency and other monetary instruments into or out of the U.S. if the aggregate amount exceeds $10,000.

Gramm-Leach-Bliley Act (GLBA) – Privacy, Federal Trade Commission Safeguard Rules and Do Not Call Registry

The **Gramm-Leach-Bliley Act (GLBA)** was passed in 1999 and is also known as the **Financial Services Modernization Act**. The initial function was to repeal a portion of the Glass-Steagall Act of 1933 and allow consolidation among financial institutions such as commercial banks, investment banks, insurance companies, and securities firms. However, it also placed several restrictions on mergers and created three important sets of rules for maintaining the security of private consumer information. Regardless of whether or not a financial institution discloses that private information, compliance with the GLBA is mandatory and each institution is required to maintain policies to prevent foreseeable data security threats.

Financial Privacy Rule

The **Financial Privacy Rule** sets the basis for how financial institutions handle private information. They must have a privacy policy in place to explain to consumers what information they collect, how they use and share it, and how it is protected. Each institution must also allow consumers to opt out of any of that information being shared with unaffiliated parties. This policy must be shown to the consumer at the time the business-consumer relationship is established, every year thereafter, and any time the policy changes to maintain consumer acceptance.

Safeguards Rule

The GLBA also requires all financial institutions to develop a written security plan to explain how they are prepared to protect their clients' private information. This is called the **Safeguards Rule** and forces institutions to closely examine their data management and risk levels. An institution must include the following in their plan:

- Specifying at least one employee to manage the institution's safeguards
- Thorough risk analysis on every department handling private information
- Developing and monitoring a system or program to keep the information secure
- Maintaining the flexibility to alter and upgrade safeguards to reflect changes in information storage, collection, and use

Pretexting — Do Not Call Registry

Finally, the GLBA requires all financial institutions to be prepared to deal with pretexting. Generally, **pretexting** refers to trying to access private information without permission or authority. Phishing is a common form of pretexting; it uses a fake website, email, or phone call to try to gain private information. Institutions typically plan for this by training employees to recognize these attempts and

deflect any pretexting inquiries, or by performing random checks with employees to test their attention and recognition. For consumers, the Federal Trade Commission (FTC) manages a National Do Not Call Registry to allow consumers to deny sales calls. Several types of calls are still allowed, such as charity, political, informational, and debt-related calls, but any telemarketing company is required to opt in to the registry and remove any numbers on the Registry from their call lists. Failure to comply with the Registry can result in a fine of over $40,000.

Mortgage Acts and Practices — Advertising, 12 CFR Part 1014 (Regulation N)

In 2009, the Omnibus Appropriations Act was passed. The act is primarily a spending bill to fund a variety of Cabinet departments and earmarks, but it featured a notable new policy for mortgage acts and practices related to advertising. The rules of the policy were originally written by the Federal Trade Commission (FTC), and while the FTC still retains enforcement authority, it is now the Consumer Financial Protection Bureau (CFPB) that has rulemaking authority. 12 CFR Part 1014 **Regulation N** sets out a number of rules regarding the advertising of mortgage credit to prevent misleading or false advertising.

Prohibited Representations

12 CFR Part 1014.3 sets the specific rules for what types of false advertising of mortgage credit is punishable by law, and also lays out that it is also a violation to request a waiver from the consumer to bypass these protections. It also states that every **commercial communication** (defined by Part 1014 as any written or oral statement, illustration, or depiction designed to effect a sale of a good or service) conducted by any person or organization subject to the law must maintain copies of said communication for at least twenty-four months from the last date it was disseminated in the event of an investigation. It is a violation to misrepresent any of the following about a mortgage product:

- The interest on the mortgage, including details such as the monthly interest payment and whether or not interest owed vs. interest paid affects the total payment due
- Any mortgage rate (e.g., simple annual rate, annual percentage rate, or periodic rate)
- Mortgage costs or fees, including the type and amount, and statements that there are no mortgage fees
- Whether or not there are any additional products sold along with the mortgage, including the cost and terms of any such product (e.g., credit insurance)
- Information regarding taxes and insurance for the mortgage, including but not limited to terms, payments, amounts, or other requirements (e.g., are taxes or insurance paid separately from the mortgage and how much, if any, of the payment for taxes or insurance is included in the loan amount, loan payments, or total due)
- Any information regarding a prepayment penalty (e.g., whether or not there is a prepayment penalty and the amount and terms of the penalty)
- Whether or not the payments, interest, or any other mortgage terms are variable or fixed
- Comparisons between rates or payments (e.g., any rates/payments that last for only part of the mortgage term, actual rates/payments, and hypothetical rates/payments)

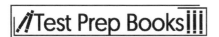

- The kind of mortgage (e.g., fully or partially amortizing)
- The total amount of the mortgage and any cash or credit given to the consumer as part of the mortgage
- Any information about required payments (e.g., amount, number, timing, or no payments due to reverse mortgage)
- Default information, including any circumstances under which a mortgage would be considered in default and any obligations necessary to prevent defaulting on the mortgage
- How helpful a mortgage may be with debt repayment, including any reduction, elimination, or restructuring of debt
- Any connection between the mortgage or mortgage provider and another entity (e.g., any organization or program, or any government entity or program), including the use of logos, symbols, or formats similar to those used by the connected entity
- The origin for commercial communications, including whether or not any such communications are made by or made for a consumer's present mortgage lender
- What rights the consumer has occupy their property under the terms of the mortgage (e.g., the duration of the right to occupancy and occupancy conditions under a reverse mortgage)
- The ability or potential for a consumer to get a mortgage (e.g., preapproval or guarantee)
- The ability or potential for a consumer to get a refinance or alteration to their mortgage (e.g., preapproval or guarantee)
- Any counsel or expert advice available in reference to the mortgage, as well as the credentials of the counselor or expert

Electronic Signatures in Global and National Commerce Act (E-Sign Act)

The **Electronic Signatures in Global and National Commerce Act (E-Sign Act)** was enacted in 2000 with the goal of making electronic signatures as authentic as pen and paper signatures for contracts. It mandates that no one can deny the legal validity of electronic signatures or of contracts where electronic signatures are used simply because they are in electronic form rather than paper form. An **electronic signature**, as defined in the E-Sign Act, is a symbol, sound, or process that is linked to the contract or other document being signed. It must be implemented by the signer with the intent to use it as a signature on that document.

Disclosure and Consent

Financial institutions are required to make several things clear to consumers before obtaining their consent to use electronic signatures:

- Whether or not there is a right or option to sign non-electronically, the right to retract consent for electronic signatures, and any consequences or conditions for retracting consent

- Whether this consent is effective for this transaction alone or whether it is effective for specific types of records that may be produced between the consumer and the financial institution
- What procedures are necessary to retract consent and update electronic contact information for the consumer
- How to get a paper copy of a signed record, including records that are signed electronically, and any fees for the paper copies

Electronic consent must be conducted in a manner that can reasonably demonstrate that the consumer has understood the information in the form or contract that is the subject of consent. Oral communication or recordings are not accepted as electronic signatures for consent. Electronic consent must also be **affirmative consent**, meaning it must be deliberately stated that the consumer consents to the electronic signature. Assuming consent because the consumer does not deny consent or has not responded does not qualify. Any electronic agreements that were made before October 1, 2000, are considered grandfathered under the E-Sign Act and are the only electronic agreements exempt from the act.

USA PATRIOT Act

In response to several terrorist attacks on the U.S. in 2001, the **USA PATRIOT Act (Patriot Act)** was passed. Most of the provisions and goals of the Patriot Act relate to matters of national security, but there is one section that affects financial institutions significantly. Title III of the Patriot Act sets a variety of new rules and restrictions requiring financial institutions to cooperate with law enforcement, improve recordkeeping, and increase responsiveness to money laundering crimes that connect to possible terrorism.

Patriot Act, Title III

Title III of the Patriot Act is divided into three subtitles with the purposes of detecting, preventing and combating the financing of terrorism. It amends portions of the Money Laundering Control Act of 1986 and the Bank Secrecy Act of 1970 (BSA). Many of the rules that were changed or added will be covered here, but for a full description, see the following sections of the USA PATRIOT Act: 311, 312, 313, 314, 319(b), 325, 326, 351, 352, 356, 359, and 362.

The first subtitle created a number of new changes and restrictions. Financial institutions were required to record aggregate transaction amounts that were processed in any area of the world where the U.S. government was concerned about money laundering taking place. Assets could be seized if money laundering was uncovered, and institutions with a bad track record of dealing with money laundering could have mergers blocked by the Department of the Treasury. Shell banks were prohibited, and institutions had to identify the interests and identities of any privately owned bank from outside the U.S. that had an account with them. Deposits from a U.S. bank to a foreign bank account became subject to restraining orders and warrants. The definition of money laundering was also expanded, incorporating new descriptions such as making a financial transaction in the U.S. with the intent to commit a violent crime, bribery of public officials, and smuggling of controlled or unauthorized munitions. Finally, the Secretary of the Treasury is required to encourage foreign governments to include the name of the originator in wire transfers sent to the U.S. or other countries with the information to remain with the transfer the entire time.

The second subtitle modified the Bank Secrecy Act of 1970 (BSA) to shift the balance toward law enforcement, making it easier for them to police money laundering and harder for criminals to perform it. Designated agencies that receive suspicious activity reports (SARs) were allowed to contact U.S. intelligence agencies. Existing BSA reporting requirements were strengthened. Reporting suspicious transactions became mandatory, and it became illegal to structure any transactions to try to evade BSA reporting. The **Financial Crimes Enforcement Network (FinCEN)** became a bureau of the Department of the Treasury to create a more secure network for reporting transactions. The BSA's definitions of money laundering were refined and the civil and criminal penalties for money laundering were increased. U.S. Executive Directors at any international financial institution were told to openly support countries that support the U.S.'s War on Terrorism, and had to provide constant audits of disbursements to make sure no money was paid out to anyone who supported or committed acts of terrorism.

The third and final subtitle focused on currency crimes that avoided using banks when laundering money to circumvent the BSA. The BSA was amended to include concealing over $10,000 on a person or luggage as a crime penalized by up to five years in prison and forfeiture of property up to the smuggled amount. Violations of currency reporting cases had their penalties drastically increased to include all property involved in the offense, plus any property traceable to the defendant. Unlicensed money transmitting businesses became prohibited, and money laundering was expanded to include provision of material support to designated foreign terrorist organizations. Lastly, it specified that anyone conspiring to commit a fraudulent activity outside the U.S. that would be an offense inside the U.S. could be prosecuted under 18 USC Section 1029.

Homeowners' Protection Act (Private Mortgage Insurance (PMI) Cancellation Act)

The **Homeowners' Protection Act** was passed in July 1998 and went into effect one year later in July 1999. It is often also called the **PMI Cancellation Act** because its primary focus was to set clear rules and requirements regarding homeowners canceling their **private mortgage insurance (PMI)**. Most loans require the borrower to obtain private mortgage insurance if the down payment of the loan is less than 20 percent of the property value. However, many lenders had different rules or requirements for allowing borrowers to cancel PMI, leading to confusion and frustration since this didn't benefit the borrowers in any way and only added slight protection for the lenders.

PMI Cancellation

The PMI Cancellation Act lays out rules for both borrower requests and automatic termination of mortgage insurance. Borrowers can request cancellation if they are the current borrower on the loan, submit a written request, and have a good payment history. They must also satisfy any requirements from the lender to prove that the property remains at or above its original value and that there are no subordinate liens on the borrower's equity. If these requirements are all met, then the loan servicer is required to take action to cancel the PMI when the principal of the loan is reduced to eighty percent of the original loan value, regardless of any amortization schedules.

PMI must also be automatically canceled by the loan servicer on the date that the principal of the loan is reduced to seventy-eight percent of the original property value. In the event it is not automatically canceled in this way, it must undergo **final termination**, meaning it must be canceled on the first day of the month following the midpoint of the loan's repayment period. The borrower must be current on their payments for either automatic cancellation to occur. In any instance of PMI being canceled, loan servicers generally cannot request further PMI payments after another thirty days.

All of this information about the right to request PMI cancellation and automatic cancellation must be disclosed to borrowers at the time of transaction, as well as every year. Loans defined by the lender as high risk, however, are only subject to final termination at the midpoint of the loan's repayment period.

Dodd-Frank Act

In the wake of the Great Recession of 2007–2008, the **Dodd-Frank Wall Street Reform and Consumer Protection Act** was passed in July 2010. More commonly known as the **Dodd-Frank Act**, its focus was to improve accountability and transparency among financial institutions and encourage financial stability. It created and changed several regulatory agencies, and was behind the formation of the Consumer Financial Protection Bureau (CFPB). As far as mortgages are concerned, the primary focus is Title XIV of the act.

Title XIV: Mortgage Reform and Anti-Predatory Lending Act

Prior to the Great Recession in 2007–2009, mortgages were granted extremely easily, as there were ways for banks to package mortgages into a bond that was worth more to them than an individual mortgage. When the housing market crashed in 2008, many borrowers discovered that these mortgages had been given out with provisions that made the mortgage difficult to pay off in the event the value of their property had decreased. The eight subtitles of Title XIV of the Dodd-Frank Act sought to crack down on this predatory behavior and set new standards and disclosure requirements.

The first three subtitles focused on setting standards for mortgage loan originators (MLOs) and the mortgages themselves. All mortgage loan originators (MLOs) must be properly qualified, registered, and licensed. The Federal Reserve Board is allowed to create any regulations to monitor MLOs, and the originators must comply. Compensation related to the face amount of a loan became prohibited to discourage MLOs from pushing borrowers into mortgages they had no hope of repaying. MLOs must be able to determine that the borrower can reasonably repay the loan using factors such as credit history and expected income, or else they may not create the mortgage. Borrowers can seek legal damages against MLOs who violate these minimum standards, giving them more legal accountability. **Balloon payments** (where the scheduled payments become rapidly more expensive) were prohibited, and MLOs may not encourage actions such as defaulting on prior loans, prepayment fees, or structuring a loan to avoid any requirements of law.

Title XIV also created the **Office of Housing Counseling** in its fourth subtitle. The purpose of this office is to coordinate and administer any regulations related to housing or mortgage counseling. The OHC is also responsible for assisting borrowers as they apply for mortgages by providing information about their rights and details about the process. The fourth subtitle also requires the Department of Housing and Urban Development (HUD) to conduct studies of foreclosures and defaults, and to maintain a database of information on all foreclosures and defaults.

The fifth and sixth subtitles set even more specific requirements for MLOs to follow. They must create five-year escrow accounts for taxes and any necessary insurances. Any consumers who waive these services must be clearly informed of the consumer's responsibilities. Force-placed insurance can only be required by MLOs when they have good reason to believe that a borrower has allowed their property insurance to lapse or is non-compliant with other obligations laid out as part of the loan. Higher-risk mortgages must have a written property appraisal before MLOs can offer them to borrowers. These appraisals must be at the creditor's expense and may not be influenced or falsified between the creditor and appraiser. Several new regulations were implemented to guarantee the quality of appraisals and the qualifications of appraisal companies, such as State certified appraisers being required for certain transactions.

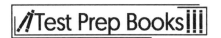

The seventh and eighth subtitles set out a few miscellaneous provisions. The Protecting Tenants at Foreclosure Act was extended through 2014, and a Government Accountability Office study was requested on efforts to catch foreclosure rescue scams and loan modification fraud. Finally, the Emergency Homeowners' Relief Fund was made available at the beginning of October 2010, and a program was created to provide legal assistance to low and moderate income homeowners undergoing foreclosure.

F. Regulatory Authority

Consumer Financial Protection Bureau (CFPB)

The **Consumer Financial Protection Bureau (CFPB)** was established with the Dodd-Frank Act in 2010. As the name suggests, it is responsible for consumer protections in financial situations. Any financial institution operating in the U.S. with at least $10 billion in assets is under the CFPB's jurisdiction and subject to its rules and scrutiny. It monitors and receives consumer complaints about financial institutions while focusing its regulations on three major areas: mortgages, credit cards, and student loans. For the purposes of this study guide, we will focus only on mortgages.

Mortgages

The CFPB is the organization that financial institutions must report to about mortgage disclosures and information required by the Home Mortgage Disclosure Act (HMDA). All of the information required to comply with the CFPB can be found online on its website at www.consumerfinance.gov/compliance/compliance-resources/mortgage-resources. This includes resources like HMDA reporting requirements, rules for mortgage appraisals or escrows, and rules on mortgage servicing. Additionally, the CFPB occasionally issues warning letters to institutions if their actions come close to violating federal law. Three mortgage-related warning letters have been issued in the past, two of which were variants of the same warning. The two similar warnings were issued on November 19, 2012, to companies that may have been using misleading mortgage advertisements targeting older Americans or service members. The third warning was issued on October 27, 2016, to companies that were not correctly complying with disclosures from the HMDA.

There is also consumer information about mortgages available online. The CFPB defines many mortgage terms and explains the entire mortgage application process in detail online at www.consumerfinance.gov/consumer-tools/mortgages. The bureau's stance on mortgages is to provide a wealth of information to consumers to help them understand it while monitoring financial institutions for suspicious or abusive behavior against consumers.

Department of Housing and Urban Development (HUD)

The **U.S. Department of Housing and Urban Development (HUD)** was created in 1965 in order to create and execute policies on housing and city development. Its origins trace back to the Housing and Home Financing Agency, which was responsible for U.S. housing programs from 1947–1965. In more recent times, HUD's focus is on helping consumers find the right housing solution for them, whether that's home ownership, rental assistance, or disaster recovery help.

Housing Assistance and Mortgage Insurance

The Department of Housing and Urban Development (HUD) is host to the **Federal Housing Administration (FHA)**, which was created in 1934 and absorbed into HUD in 1965. It is one of the largest mortgage insurers in the world and provides mortgage insurance and assistance for people seeking to own a home, rent an apartment, or rent a home. The FHA maintains a list of approved lenders that their mortgage insurance and assistance covers, as well as information about loan limits, homes for sale, and disaster relief options. For businesses, it has several detailed FAQ lists about how to interact with their coverage in various situations to keep things smooth when dealing with FHA-insured mortgages, Treasury Homeowner Assistance Funds, and partial claims. It even has information on how COVID-19 has affected their coverage, all of which can be found at www.hud.gov/federal_housing_administration.

For those looking to buy a home, HUD also has a step-by-step list for approaching the process of becoming a homeowner, covering topics such as knowing your rights and planning your budget to shopping for loans, homes, and homeowners insurance. Every step is supplemented with links to articles to read or tools to use to help with the planning process. Aspiring homeowners can find this information at www.hud.gov/topics/buying_a_home.

Practice Quiz

1. TILA is enforced by which government agencies?
   a. The Department of Housing and Urban Development and the Department of Justice
   b. The Department of Justice and the Consumer Financial Protection Bureau
   c. The Federal Reserve and the Consumer Financial Protection Bureau
   d. The Federal Reserve and the Department of Housing and Urban Development

2. Which of the following would be considered a violation of Regulation B?
   a. Thomas submitted his income documents to the lender as requested. In reviewing Thomas's pay stubs, the lender determined that his income is less than Thomas originally stated. Determining that Thomas no longer qualifies for the loan, the lender denied his loan application.
   b. Jordan opted not to complete the sex, race, and ethnicity section of the loan application. The mortgage loan originator (MLO) made a determination of this information based on Jordan's physical appearance.
   c. Susan has applied for a mortgage loan, and in casual conversation, she told her loan originator that she would like to have children in the future. The loan originator revealed this information to the lender, who denied her loan because they determined that Susan would likely quit her job and be unable to afford to repay the loan.
   d. William did not qualify for a mortgage loan based on his own credit and income. The mortgage broker suggested that William ask his wife to agree to co-sign the loan.

3. If a borrower closes on their refinance mortgage on a Friday afternoon, when is the deadline for them to rescind the loan?
   a. Saturday night
   b. Monday night
   c. There is no right of rescission on refinance loans.
   d. Tuesday night

4. Which of the following would NOT be a red flag for identity theft?
   a. A warning from the Consumer Financial Protection Bureau
   b. A request to close an account
   c. A change in address to one across the country without warning
   d. Repeated attempts to transfer large amounts of money out of an account

5. You need a customer to sign an updated terms of service document. Which of the following is the most convenient method to use?
   a. Email the file to them to print, sign, scan, and send back to you.
   b. Email them the updated terms of service and tell them to email back if they want to opt out of any changes.
   c. Have them select an accepted e-signature for the document.
   d. Assume they agree once they've read the document completely.

See answers on the next page.

Answer Explanations

1. C: TILA regulations are enforced by the Federal Reserve and the Consumer Financial Protection Bureau (CFPB). The Department of Housing and Urban Development (HUD) originally enforced RESPA before it was handed over to the CFPB in 2011, but it never enforced TILA regulations, making Choices *A* and *D* incorrect. The Department of Justice does not enforce TILA regulations, making Choice *B* incorrect.

2. C: Denying a loan to a woman because she may decide to leave her job and have a child in the future would be discrimination based on sex. In Choice *A*, lenders are permitted to review a borrower's income and take that into consideration in deciding whether to approve the loan or not. In Choice *B*, the loan originator is permitted to make visual assessments as to a borrower's sex, ethnicity, and race in the event that the borrower declines to self-disclose that information. The mortgage broker, originator, or lender is permitted to suggest a co-signer for a borrower who does not otherwise qualify, as in Choice *D*. They may not, however, require that a spouse be included on a loan.

3. D: The borrower has a three-day right of rescission. The clock starts on the day after closing and includes Saturdays, but not Sundays or legal holidays. Thus, a Friday closing has a three-day right of rescission that ends at midnight on the following Tuesday night. Choice *A*, Saturday, would be the first of the three days. Since Sundays do not count as business days, Monday, Choice *B*, would be counted as day two. Choice *C* is incorrect in that there *is* a right of rescission on refinance loans; there is no right of rescission on purchase loans.

4. B: A request to close the account is not enough of an indicator of identity theft, since the consumer may genuinely want to close out their account. A direct warning from the Consumer Financial Protection Bureau (CFPB) is certainly a red flag, so Choice *A* is incorrect. Sudden address changes and repeated money transfer attempts are also red flags, so Choices *C* and *D* are also incorrect.

5. C: In order for an electronic signature to be legally valid, it must demonstrate affirmative consent. The most correct and convenient way to do that would be Choice *C*, having the customer choose from a selection of signatures or symbols that you and the customer agree upon. Choice *A* does involve a traditional signature so it would be legal, but the process of printing and scanning could be inconvenient for the customer, so it's not the best answer here. Choices *B* and *D* assume consent rather than asking for affirmative consent, so they are both incorrect.

Uniform State Content

A. SAFE Act and CSBS/AARMR Model State Law

SAFE Act

In response to the impending financial crisis in 2008, the U.S. Congress passed the **Secure and Fair Enforcement for Mortgage Licensing Act (SAFE Act)** as a component of the Housing and Economic Recovery Act. More commonly abbreviated as the SAFE Act, the focus of the Act was to standardize licensing and registration procedures for mortgage loan originators (MLOs) who lend mortgages to borrowers. In addition to creating a foundation for MLOs to become appropriately licensed, it also laid groundwork to allow different regulatory agencies to share information more easily as well as to improve consumer protections by allowing them to freely access a registered database of all MLOs and their work history.

MLOs are responsible for providing a lot of detailed information about themselves for their initial registration. This includes personal identifying information, employment history, criminal and civil lawsuit history, and fingerprints for a background check conducted by the Federal Bureau of Investigation. Once verified and submitted, new MLOs get a unique identifier number with the **Nationwide Mortgage Licensing System and Registry (NMLS)** and must maintain their registration status by confirming or updating any information annually. If there are significant changes, such as employment termination, name changes, or legal action taken, this information must be updated within thirty days of the event. Financial institutions that are federally chartered or insured must also submit contact and tax information to obtain an NMLS identification number and must follow the same annual or thirty-day timeline to update or maintain their registration.

State Mortgage Regulatory Agencies

Although many MLOs work for private financial institutions such as banks, they can also work for state mortgage lenders and regulators in a similar capacity. A state-level mortgage agency may be responsible for monitoring and collecting information about the mortgages that are loaned in their state, or they may offer government-sponsored mortgages for special situations such as loans backed by the Federal Housing Administration (FHA) for borrowers who don't meet the minimum requirements for traditional loans or the loans backed by the U.S. Department of Veterans Affairs (VA) for citizens who have served in the armed forces. However, no matter what agency an MLO works for, they must still maintain registration with the NMLS.

In order to become an MLO, a person will need to take an MLO license exam. These exams can be proctored in person at specific testing facilities or conducted through the NMLS online systems and can be scheduled anytime. Once a new MLO is fully licensed and registered with the NMLS, they receive a unique MLO identifier number. These identifiers can never be changed and are assigned exclusively to one MLO, allowing the NMLS to more easily track and keep a record of all licensed MLOs and what mortgage business they are licensed to perform. In addition, the SAFE Act mandates that MLO identifiers be publicly and easily available. The MLO must provide the number upon request and on any initial communication with a consumer, such as in a Loan Estimate form. In addition, any institutions that employ an MLO are required to make the identifier numbers of all their MLOs easily available to the public. It can be a list on their website with directions to find it or a physical post in an accessible place,

such as the building's lobby. The method does not necessarily matter as long as the public is able to easily access the identifier numbers.

The Consumer Financial Protection Bureau (CFPB) is responsible for enforcing various rules regarding mortgages and MLOs, but there is one specific rule that is noteworthy to mention. In Regulation Z (12 Code of Federal Regulations [CFR] Part 226), there is a specific rule regarding MLOs and paid compensation for their work. It essentially prohibits an MLO from receiving extra compensation from a creditor for a mortgage the MLO originates based on the mortgage terms and conditions. Instead, only the amount of credit offered as part of the loan can affect their compensation. This prevents a conflict of **dual compensation** in which the MLO would be incentivized to base the mortgage terms on how they will be paid, not what is best for the borrower, and also prevents the MLO from being paid by both the creditor and a borrower.

License Law and Regulation

Mortgages cannot be given out except by a licensed MLO, whose job is to take mortgage applications and negotiate terms between creditors and borrowers. These licensing requirements are taken very seriously to ensure that borrowers receive protection through fair terms and conditions and that lenders receive protection due to a thorough analysis of the risk of lending to a given borrower. The primary service that MLOs offer is to translate a borrower's application for a mortgage into a negotiation with a financial institution, leading to an offer of mortgage credit for the borrower.

Although this process of negotiating the mortgage must be conducted by a licensed MLO, other people with different roles may provide assistance. **Underwriters** examine the risk of providing a service to a consumer; this most commonly happens with insurance, but MLOs also use underwriters to get an analysis of the risk in lending to a particular borrower. Clerical staff such as mortgage clerks may simply handle the more mundane tasks such as typing up forms and documents, recording and updating information, and answering basic consumer questions. **Loan processors** will verify all information the borrower submits and perform the physical task of collecting, assembling, and processing loan application paperwork. So, although a licensed MLO is the only person able to actually negotiate mortgage terms and originate the mortgage, they may receive assistance from other staff with many of the other formalities and paperwork preparation to keep things moving.

Qualifications and Licensing Process

Some specific qualifications for an MLO license may vary depending on the specific license someone is applying for as well as the state they will be working in, but many of the basic requirements are the same. Applicants must undergo background checks by the Federal Bureau of Investigation and demonstrate financial responsibility in their credit report. They must also have already spent significant time learning about mortgage laws and procedures prior to applying for a license. All education hours must be received from NMLS-approved courses. Applicants often also require a sponsorship from a financial institution that is already registered with the NMLS. Finally, applicants must pass written tests at the state level, federal level, or both depending on the license. If they pass, they earn their license as an MLO. If they fail, they may retake the test with some caveats. Test retakes must have a thirty-day waiting period between each attempt, and after the third consecutive failure this waiting period is extended to 180 days before a new retest is allowed.

MLO license applications may be denied for several reasons. If the applicant was convicted of a felony within seven years prior to applying, their application will be denied. Applicants may also be denied if they have had a previous loan originator license revoked in any jurisdiction or demonstrated a lack of financial responsibility or character.

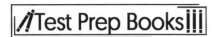

MLO licenses can also be revoked. If an MLO is convicted of a felony involving fraud, dishonesty, breach of trust, or money laundering, their license will be permanently revoked and they will be barred from ever obtaining an MLO license again.

Licenses must be renewed annually with the NMLS directly. This renewal period is between November 1 and December 31 every year. An MLO who doesn't renew their license within this window does not lose their license, but their license is considered inactive and they may not resume acting as an MLO in any capacity until it is renewed and active again. In this case, the renewal period time window is unnecessary; an inactive MLO may immediately update their registration for renewal. However, if an MLO's license has been inactive for five years, they will also have to retake the SAFE MLO test and score at least 75 percent. There is only one exception to this annual renewal requirement. If a new MLO obtains their registration less than six months before the end of the annual renewal period—in this case, the calendar year—they are not required to renew that year. Their first renewal will be in the next year's renewal period. In addition, MLOs need to maintain current education to stay qualified and licensed. Every year as part of renewing the license, MLOs need to take a seven- to eight-hour course of continuing education, keeping them up to date on legal changes and challenges.

MLOs need to report some information as it changes to keep the NMLS database accurate. If they have a change of employment, MLOs must log in to their account and update their employment information within five days of the change. When working as an MLO, they need to disclose their identifier number at the beginning of all transactions as well as upon consumer request.

There is also a special situation called **temporary authority**. If an MLO is otherwise nationally qualified but still needs to complete or update state-specific requirements, they are granted temporary authority to continue working on applications for originating loans for no more than fourteen calendar days. This is to prevent any significant delays in business operations while processing license or qualification renewals.

Compliance

The CFPB and various state-level regulatory agencies have the authority to examine the records and books of any MLO to check for compliance with all rules and regulations. If necessary, they may even require a direct summons of the MLO to present the information themselves as well as give testimony while under oath about the accuracy and details of the records. Any wrongdoing determined as a result of these investigations will be penalized depending on the offense. This study guide will discuss several different actions an MLO can perform that are required, permissible, or prohibited by the CFPB.

MLOs may not purchase real estate agent ads, as it could create a conflict of interest between the real estate agent and the MLO both wanting to collude to get a successful sale without considering the financial safety of the borrower. It is also illegal for an MLO to use the NMLS identifier of a supervisor as their own, as this creates false information within the NMLS database. All MLOs must use their own unique identifier to keep the information tracking accurate, including a requirement that they must display their NMLS identifier on any advertisements for themselves that solicit borrowers. Any debts, such as mortgages, must also be correctly reported in future credit reports—a requirement of the 1970 Fair Credit Reporting Act (FCRA)—and may not be omitted. MLOs also may not engage in **bait-and-**

switch tactics in which they advertise mortgage products in an appealing way only to switch them with mortgages that have worse terms and conditions after the consumer accepts the mortgage terms.

If an MLO is subject to a complaint investigation, they are required to comply and submit all relevant documents to investigating authorities. This is required by law whether the investigation is by federal or state regulators. All documents related to complying with mortgage regulations on a specific mortgage must be retained by MLOs for at least three to five years depending on the nature of the document. If the mortgage is sold off to another broker and the original MLO no longer services it, all those documents must also be transferred to the new servicer, and they must also follow compliance with record retention.

Several actions are defined specifically as MLO activities. When an MLO takes a loan application, the specific action being referred to is receiving information from a consumer that is used by the MLO to determine if they qualify for a loan. Verifying information, forwarding an application without reviewing it, and assisting a consumer by explaining the information needed or steps required are not part of this specific definition, so these are actions that someone does not need an MLO license to perform. Offering or negotiating loan terms also has a specific definition for MLOs, referring to the act of directly presenting the offer of a loan to a consumer, whether verbally or in writing. Generally presenting the loans that a consumer may qualify for without offering a specific one is not part of this definition, so someone does not need an MLO license to be able to explain or define various loan terms so long as it is not a direct offer to the consumer.

MLOs may add clauses to mortgage terms to make them assumable. Assumable mortgages are mortgages that a house's new buyer assumes in place of the house's seller, who is the original borrower. This generally requires permission from the mortgage lender to decrease the likelihood that a qualified borrower sells off homes with assumable mortgages to less qualified borrowers.

The exact penalties against an MLO for violating compliance will vary depending on the severity of the offense and damage done. At a minimum, an MLO will be required to pay a civil fine of up to $10,000 per violation in addition to any other remedial actions required. If it is a willful or otherwise intentional violation, this will also include up to a year in prison. In addition, all penalties carry the risk of revoking an MLO's license and barring them from ever obtaining a new license.

Practice Quiz

1. When a mortgage loan originator (MLO) completes their registration with the Nationwide Mortgage Licensing System and Registry (NMLS), what do they receive as proof of registration?
    a. Certificate of authorization
    b. Lapel pin with a unique serial number
    c. Unique identifier number
    d. Commemorative coin

2. In what circumstances can an MLO's unique identifier be changed?
    a. If the MLO quits working as an MLO, it can be reassigned to a new MLO.
    b. If the MLO is convicted of a felony and has their license revoked, it can be reassigned to a new MLO.
    c. If the MLO submits a written request to the NMLS, it can be changed.
    d. It can never be changed.

3. What is an MLO's primary service?
    a. To translate an application for a mortgage into a negotiation with a financial institution
    b. To be the point of contact for mortgage payments between a borrower and a financial institution
    c. To be the source of lending funds for a mortgage
    d. To offer extensive counseling and advice about which mortgage type best suits a borrower

4. A licensed MLO needs to take continuing education to fulfill the requirements for keeping their license. How many hours does the MLO need to sign up for?
    a. Two hours
    b. Four hours
    c. Six hours
    d. Eight hours

5. Today marks the receipt of the final payment of a borrower's mortgage, and it is officially amortized. At a minimum, how long does the MLO who originated the mortgage need to keep a record of the mortgage?
    a. One year
    b. Three years
    c. Six years
    d. Forever

See answers on the next page.

Answer Explanations

1. C: Once their registration is verified, a new MLO receives a unique identifier number with the NMLS, which is used to prove registration of that specific MLO. A certificate sounds likely, but they can be easily faked, so Choice *A* is incorrect. Physical items such as lapel pins and commemorative coins are not used as proof of registration, so Choices *B* and *D* are also incorrect.

2. D: MLOs can never get their unique identifier changed for any reason. This is to keep the identifiers unique and allow the system to track the business of every licensed MLO. Whether an MLO quits permanently, has their license revoked, or simply wants a different one, there is no circumstance that allows an MLO's identifier to be changed, making Choices *A*, *B*, and *C* all incorrect.

3. A: The primary service offered by an MLO is to negotiate a mortgage loan with a financial institution based on the application provided by a prospective borrower. They are not the point of contact when making payments on a mortgage, so Choice *B* is incorrect. They are not the direct source of the money loaned out on a mortgage, so Choice *C* is incorrect. Although an MLO may offer counseling and advice about mortgages to help a prospective borrower narrow down what they need, that is not the primary role they provide and must obtain their license for, so Choice *D* is also incorrect.

4. D: MLOs need seven to eight hours of continuing education every year from approved courses as a requirement of getting their license renewed. Two, four, and six hours are all not enough to satisfy this requirement, so Choices *A*, *B*, and *C* are all incorrect.

5. B: MLOs need to keep records of all their mortgages for at least three years. One year is too short, so Choice *A* is incorrect. Six years is above the legal minimum, so Choice *C* is incorrect. Keeping the records forever is not expected, so Choice *D* is incorrect.

General Mortgage Knowledge

A. Qualified and Non-Qualified Mortgage Programs

Mortgage loans are classified as either qualified mortgage loans or non-qualified mortgage loans depending on whether or not they meet strict guidelines designed to protect both borrowers and lenders from making risky loans. Qualified mortgage loans prohibit certain features that may make repaying the loans more difficult for borrowers. Some of these features include interest-only periods, balloon payments, and negative amortization. Qualified mortgages also place limits on the cost of the loan, as determined by the annual percentage rate (APR), and limits on prepayment penalties and upfront fees and costs.

Qualified Mortgages

Qualified mortgage loans must meet the requirements set forth under the **ability to repay** rule, which is part of the Dodd-Frank Wall Street Reform and Consumer Protection Act (Dodd-Frank Act). The ability to repay rule was implemented by the Consumer Financial Protection Bureau (CFPB) and became effective in January 2014. This rule states that lenders must make a reasonable determination as to a borrower's ability to repay a loan before making a loan.

A primary cause of the mortgage loan crisis of 2008 was the number of loans that were made to borrowers who were financially unable to repay their loans. Lenders made loans without properly verifying borrowers' income or debts, and some borrowers were qualified based on low initial interest rates that eventually rose dramatically, increasing the borrower's monthly mortgage payment. The borrowers were able to afford the initial mortgage payment, but when the interest rate, and thus the mortgage payment, increased, the borrowers were no longer able to make the loan payments. The ability to repay rule is aimed at preventing another mortgage and foreclosure crisis like the one in 2008.

Qualified mortgages are mortgage loans that have met compliance requirements for a lender's good faith efforts to verify that a borrower is indeed able to afford to repay the loan. Lenders are expected to use third-party records (such as credit reports, bank records, and pay stubs) to underwrite certain minimum factors when determining if a borrower is able to repay the loan. These factors include: 1) verifying the borrower's income and assets; 2) confirming the borrower's employment status; 3) calculating an accurate monthly payment on the mortgage loan; 4) determining the monthly payment on any concurrent loans, such as a second mortgage or home equity line of credit (HELOC); 5) calculating the monthly payments for other mortgage-related obligations such as homeowner's insurance and property taxes; 6) verifying all current borrower debts, including alimony and child support payments; and 7) reviewing the borrower's credit history.

Initially, lenders were also required to verify the borrower's **debt-to-income ratio (DTI)**, which could not exceed a strict 43 percent cap. However, in December 2020, that part of the rule was amended, removing the debt-to-income calculation and replacing it with a price-based maximum annual percentage rate (APR) calculation. The amended rule states that the loan's APR cannot exceed the average prime offer rate by more than 2.5 to 6.5 percent, depending on the amount of the loan and whether the property is a manufactured home. First-lien mortgage loans of more than $110,260 cannot have an APR of more than 2.5 percent above the average prime offer rate. First-lien mortgage loans of $66,156 to $110,260 are limited to 3.5 percent above the average prime offer rate. First-lien mortgage

loans under $66,156, as well as first-lien mortgage loans for manufactured homes, are capped at 6.5 percent above the average prime offer rate. Subordinate mortgage loans under $66,156 are capped at 6.5 percent, and subordinate mortgage loans over $66,156 are capped at 3.5 percent. All of these loan limits are subject to annual inflation adjustments.

Even with this new calculation, lenders are still expected to consider the borrower's debt-to-income ratio (DTI) and **residual income** (which refers to money left over after all the borrower's monthly payments have been made). However, there are no specific guidelines or requirements about what **consideration** entails.

Lenders must keep written records of their policies and procedures for underwriting and determining a borrower's ability to repay. Lenders must also keep documentation showing what information was used in considering a borrower's ability to repay, including underwriting worksheets or automated underwriting reports and underwriting standards, policies, and/or guidelines. Failure to perform due diligence or to maintain adequate records could result in the loan being reclassified as a non-qualified mortgage. This can negatively affect the lender's ability to sell the loan on the secondary market because non-qualified mortgage loans are generally considered riskier than qualified mortgage loans.

Some types of loans are exempt from the ability to repay rule. These include timeshares, construction loans, bridge loans, HELOCs, and reverse mortgages.

The ability-to-repay rule is designed to protect both borrowers and lenders and help avoid foreclosures. If lenders exercise their due diligence in analyzing a borrower's ability to repay and making loans based on those findings, there is a greater chance that the borrower will be able to repay the loan in full and the loan will not go into foreclosure for non-payment. Similarly, if the lender suitably underwrites the loan before approval, the lender is protected in the event the borrower defaults on the loan. Qualified mortgage loans are federally guaranteed by the Federal National Mortgage Association (Fannie Mae), Federal Home Loan Mortgage Corporation (Freddie Mac), the Federal Housing Administration (FHA), or the Department of Veterans Affairs (VA).

Conventional/Conforming Mortgages

Conventional mortgage loans—otherwise known as **conforming mortgage loans**—meet the standards and requirements set forth by the **Federal National Mortgage Association (Fannie Mae)** and **Federal Home Loan Mortgage Corporation (Freddie Mac)**. Fannie Mae and Freddie Mac are called **government-sponsored enterprises**, or **GSEs**. When a lender makes a mortgage loan to a borrower, the lender rarely holds and services the loan for the entire length of the term. Instead, the lender will often sell the loan on what is known as the secondary market. By selling the loan to another servicer, the lender frees up its capital in order to make more loans to other borrowers.

Fannie Mae and Freddie Mac were created by the federal government to fill this need on the secondary market. Fannie Mae and Freddie Mac buy qualified mortgage loans and then either hold the loans for the duration of the terms or sell packages of loans, known as **mortgage-backed securities (MBS)**, to other mortgage investors. Loans that qualify for purchase by Fannie Mae or Freddie Mac are called conventional mortgage loans because they conform to the requirements of these enterprises. By buying loans, Fannie Mae and Freddie Mac allow lenders to keep their funds fluid; they can make and sell mortgage loans on a regular basis. Fannie Mae and Freddie Mac also help investors who want to purchase MBS because investors know that these loans have met rigorous underwriting standards and are guaranteed by GSEs.

Fannie Mae was created by Congress in 1938 with the goal of keeping housing affordable. Before then, lenders required excessive down payment amounts, often 50 percent or more of the purchase price, and had excessively strict lending requirements. This meant that very few people could afford to finance a home purchase. Guaranteed mortgage loans through Fannie Mae meant that people could make lower down payments and qualify for a mortgage loan more easily because lenders knew that the loans would be backed, or guaranteed, by the federal government. By keeping the secondary market liquid, interest rates are kept lower and more money is available for loans to borrowers.

Freddie Mac was created in 1970 as a public enterprise. It was meant to expand the secondary market and allow public investors to compete with Fannie Mae. The **Financial Institutions Reform, Recovery, and Enforcement Act** made Freddie Mac a shareholder-owned company in 1989. However, in response to the mortgage crisis of 2008, the **Federal Housing Finance Agency** took over control of Freddie Mac, and now the federal government runs both agencies.

By making qualified mortgage loans, lenders help to guarantee that their loans can be sold to Fannie Mae or Freddie Mac. In doing so, the lender gets its capital back and is able to make more loans, and the lender is also protected from losing money in a foreclosure situation.

Conventional mortgage loans also have several aspects that make them attractive to homebuyers. Conventional mortgage loans can have down payment amounts as low as 3 percent and can be used to purchase primary residences, second homes, and even rental properties. Loans with 20 percent or higher down payments do not require private mortgage insurance (PMI), which is a type of insurance that helps to protect lenders in the event the borrower defaults on the mortgage loan. Loans that do require PMI have lower insurance costs than FHA loans. PMI can also be canceled once the principal balance reaches less than 80 percent of the value of the property.

Government Mortgages

While Fannie Mae and Freddie Mac buy mortgage loans on the secondary market, borrowers cannot obtain loans directly from those agencies. However, there are several government agencies that do offer mortgage loans directly to borrowers. Government-backed loans are offered through the Federal Housing Administration (FHA), the U.S. Department of Veterans Affairs (VA), and the U.S. Department of Agriculture (USDA). Because these loans are made and guaranteed by the federal government, the qualifications can sometimes be easier for borrowers to meet.

FHA Loans

The Department of Housing and Urban Development (HUD) oversees and insures FHA loans. FHA loans have easier qualification requirements than conventional mortgages, which allows more people to afford homes. FHA loans can be used to purchase a home as well as to refinance a primary residence. The FHA also has a program that allows homebuyers to purchase and renovate a home with a single loan.

Two of the key features of FHA loans are the lower down payment requirements and lower acceptable credit scores when compared to conventional mortgages. Down payments for an FHA loan can be as low as 3.5 percent with a credit score of at least 580. However, borrowers can have a credit score as low as 500 if they have a 10 percent down payment. FHA loans can also be approved even if the borrower has

severe credit delinquencies or a bankruptcy on their credit report. Additionally, FHA loans tend to have lower interest rates because they are backed by the federal government.

There are certain additional requirements for FHA loans. The property must be purchased as the borrower's primary residence, and the borrower must occupy the property within sixty days of closing. The property must also be appraised by an FHA-approved appraiser, and a home inspection is required as well (home inspections are recommended with any property purchase, but only FHA requires them).

Another requirement of FHA loans is mortgage insurance. Mortgage insurance protects the FHA lender in case the borrower defaults on the loan. The mortgage insurance is required for the life of the loan, or the first eleven years in the event of at least a 10 percent down payment. Borrowers must pay a **mortgage insurance premium (MIP)** of 1.75 percent of the loan amount at closing plus an annual amount between 0.45 percent and 1.05 percent of the loan amount, depending on the mortgage terms, down payment, and loan-to-value (LTV) ratio.

There are some limits on FHA loans, as well. The maximum FHA loan amount is $420,680 in low-cost areas and up to $970,800 in high-cost metropolitan areas. Borrowers also cannot exceed a mortgage payment of 31 percent of their gross monthly income and a maximum total debt-to-income ratio (DTI) of 43 percent.

VA Loans

VA loans are loans that are backed by the **U.S. Department of Veterans Affairs (VA)**. VA loans are a military benefit and are only made to eligible service members, veterans, and qualifying spouses. The loans are made by private lenders but are guaranteed by the VA, which offers certain protections to the lenders. Because of this, loans can be made with zero money down and with easier qualifying requirements than other types of mortgage loans. VA loans do not have a minimum credit score requirement, often have lower interest rates than conventional mortgage loans, and do not require mortgage insurance.

There are several kinds of VA loans, including home purchase, renovation loans, and jumbo mortgages. VA loans are intended to help borrowers purchase their primary residence; however, it is possible to use a VA loan to buy a second home or an investment property if certain requirements are met. The VA also offers several types of refinance loans, including rate/term refinances, cash-out refinances, and **Interest Rate Reduction Refinance Loans (IRRRL)**, which are used only to refinance into a new VA loan with a lower interest rate. VA loans are considered nonconforming mortgage loans on the secondary market because they do not conform to the conventional mortgage loan standards set by Freddie Mac and Fannie Mae. However, because they are backed by the federal government, they have greater flexibility and easier qualification for eligible borrowers.

USDA Loans

The **U.S. Department of Agriculture (USDA)** is involved in the development of rural and agricultural areas, including helping families in these areas purchase homes. USDA loans are designed to assist rural low- to moderate-income borrowers with purchasing homes. These loans are backed by the USDA, which means that these loans often have easier qualification requirements than conventional mortgage loans.

The USDA has three primary loan programs. USDA Direct loans are made by the USDA and have interest rates as low as 1 percent. Participating lenders can also offer USDA Loan guaranteed loans, which often have very low interest rates and down payments as low as zero. Lastly, the USDA offers home improvement loans to qualified borrowers.

USDA loans have specific requirements, particularly with regards to the geographic location of the property. The home must be in an eligible rural area as designated by the USDA. The website https://eligibility.sc.egov.usda.gov/eligibility/welcomeAction.do?pageAction=sfp allows potential homeowners to search for the property in question to see if it falls within one of the approved geographic areas.

Additionally, because the USDA loan is meant for low- to moderate-income borrowers, there is a maximum income limit based on the median income of the area where the property is located. A borrower's income cannot exceed 115 percent of the median income for their area. Potential borrowers can check their income on the same website where they can research the property being purchased.

Borrowers must demonstrate that they have stable, verifiable income and verifiable assets. Borrowers must also have a debt-to-income ratio (DTI) of less than 43 percent and a credit score of at least 640. Finally, USDA borrowers must be U.S. residents or permanent resident aliens.

Conventional/Nonconforming Mortgages

A **nonconforming mortgage** is any mortgage loan that does not meet the requirements of a conventional, conforming mortgage loan or of one of the government-sponsored enterprises (GSEs), such as Fannie Mae or Freddie Mac. These loans cannot, then, be sold to GSEs on the secondary market. These loans are not necessarily riskier than other types of mortgage loans, but they are harder for lenders to sell on the secondary market, which is an additional difficulty for the lender. As a result, nonconforming mortgage loans often have higher interest rates than conforming or government-backed loans. There are several types of nonconforming mortgage loans, including jumbo loans and subprime loans.

Jumbo and Alt-A Loans

Jumbo loans are one of the most common types of nonconforming mortgage loans. These mortgages are for higher amounts than the maximum limits allowed by Fannie Mae or Freddie Mac. The current maximum loan amounts for conventional or conforming mortgage loans are $647,200 in most areas and up to $970,800 in high-cost metropolitan areas. Mortgages that are above these limits are jumbo loans. While jumbo loans do not usually have higher interest rates, they do often have very strict qualification requirements, such as high credit scores and low debt-to-income ratios (DTIs).

Another type of nonconforming mortgage loan is called an **Alt-A loan**. These loans do not meet the requirements of conforming or government-backed loans but are not as risky as subprime loans, according to the lending industry's borrower classification scale. **Prime borrowers** are considered the most creditworthy and typically have higher credit scores and lower debt-to-income ratios (DTIs). While definitions vary between financial institutions, prime borrowers usually have credit scores of 660 and up, although some definitions of prime borrowers require credit scores of 670 or 680 and up. **Subprime borrowers** have lower credit scores and higher debt-to-income ratios (DTIs). They may have past credit problems, and they present the greatest risk to lenders with regards to their ability to repay the loan. Again, while definitions of subprime vary between financial institutions, borrowers with a credit score of 580 to 619 will typically be considered subprime borrowers. Alt-A loans are so named because they are typically for borrowers who are not considered prime borrowers but who are also not subprime borrowers, either. Alt-A loans fall somewhere in between.

Alt-A loans offer alternatives to the standard conforming mortgage loans. Alt-A loans allow for higher debt-to-income ratios (DTIs), lower incomes for borrowers, fewer required documents, lower credit scores, lower down payments, and higher loan-to-value (LTV) ratios. Alt-A loans are generally easier for borrowers to qualify for, but they also present greater risks to the lenders.

Subprime Loans

Subprime loans are the riskiest types of loans for lenders. These loans are made to borrowers who have low credit scores and have not demonstrated solid money management in the past. Borrowers with credit scores from 580-619 are generally considered to be subprime borrowers, although definitions do vary across financial institutions.

The interest rate on subprime loans is often very high to account for the risk to the lender. Lenders use four criteria to determine the interest rate on subprime loans: 1) the borrower's credit score, 2) the number of late payments or delinquencies showing on the borrower's credit report, 3) the types of delinquencies (such as 30-day, 60-day, or 90-day lates, for example), and 4) the size of the borrower's down payment. The higher the risk to the lender, the higher the interest rate on the loan. Of course, a higher interest rate means that the cost of the loan and the monthly mortgage payment are also higher, which makes affording a subprime loan harder for borrowers who may already have financial difficulties.

Guidance on Nontraditional Mortgage Product Risk

Due to the inherent risks of **nontraditional mortgage loans**, such as Alt-A and subprime loans, several federal agencies, including the Office of the Comptroller of the Currency, the Board of Governors of the Federal Reserve System, the Federal Deposit Insurance Corporation, the Office of Thrift Supervision, and the National Credit Union Administration, issued guidance to lenders on how to "offer nontraditional mortgage products in a safe and sound manner and in a way that clearly discloses the benefits and risks to borrowers." The guidance specifically addresses several types of nontraditional mortgage products, including interest-only mortgage loans, deferred-interest mortgage loans, and adjustable-rate mortgages (ARMs), because these types of loans often come with much higher payments later in the loan period, resulting in many borrowers being unable to afford the loan after the initial term.

The guidelines specify that lenders should employ sufficient underwriting standards to help ensure that borrowers are able to repay their loans. The guidelines also instruct lenders to make sure that borrowers are well-informed with regards to their loan terms and any potential risks before the borrowers make final decisions about their loans. Lenders should establish written policies and procedures that guide underwriting decisions as well as risk management and reporting systems.

State agencies are directed to oversee lenders to ensure that reasonable practices and precautions are being exercised.

One of the main components of some nontraditional loans is a low introductory payment that jumps to a much higher payment later in the loan period. For example, one type of nontraditional loan has an interest-only period, during which time the borrower is only making interest payments and is not required to pay on the loan principal. However, after this introductory period, the principal payment is added into the monthly mortgage payment, significantly increasing the monthly payment amount, referred to as **payment shock**. Some borrowers are able to easily afford the interest-only payment but struggle to pay the full mortgage and interest payment later, increasing the risk of default. Low introductory interest rates that increase later in the loan term are another type of loan that offers a lower initial payment that can then increase substantially after the initial period has ended. The guidance suggests that lenders qualify borrowers based on the higher interest rate and mortgage payment rather than the low initial payment amount.

Another common nontraditional loan involves a balloon payment at the end of a short loan term as a way to lower the monthly mortgage payment for the borrower. By amortizing only a small portion of the loan and requiring the full loan amount to be repaid in one lump sum later, borrowers are qualifying on a lower payment but do not have a ready way to pay the large balloon payment due at the end of the loan term. Borrowers often assume that they can just refinance the loan before the balloon payment becomes due, but that does not always work out, and then the borrowers are stuck trying to figure out a way to come up with an enormous sum of money to keep their home. The guidance suggests that lenders avoid making these types of **collateral-dependent loans**.

Non-Qualified Mortgages

Non-qualified mortgages are loans that do not meet the underwriting standards and requirements of the Consumer Financial Protection Bureau (CFPB) for sale on the secondary market, particularly for sale to Fannie Mae and/or Freddie Mac. Specifically, these loans do not follow the ability to repay rule.

Most nontraditional loans are also non-qualified mortgages. These loans include interest-only mortgage loans, loans with a balloon payment, and loans with longer-than-usual terms (the standard mortgage term is thirty years; some nontraditional loans can be financed for as long as forty years). **Negative amortization loans** are also considered non-qualified mortgages. These are loans in which the initial payment amount is less than the total interest charged, resulting in a negative amortization of the loan. The borrower can end up owing more than the initial loan amount.

While non-qualified mortgages cannot be sold to Fannie Mae or Freddie Mac, there are buyers on the secondary market that will purchase these types of loans. They are harder to sell, though, and lenders run the risk of being unable to sell the loan and having to carry the servicing for longer periods. The longer the lender has to carry the loan, the less money that lender has to make new loans to new borrowers.

Non-qualified mortgages can be beneficial to some borrowers, such as those with poor credit or difficult-to-verify income. However, the risks should be thoroughly evaluated before agreeing to this type of loan.

B. Mortgage Loan Products

There are various kinds of mortgage loans available to borrowers. Some have certain conditions for their use or repayment, so every borrower is likely to find a loan option that is best for their situation or preference. Some loans have special minimum qualifications depending on whether or not a federal agency is backing the loan and other factors, but most conventional mortgage loans share the same qualifications. These qualifications are a 3 percent down payment, a credit score of at least 620, private mortgage insurance (PMI) between 0.15 percent and 1.95 percent, a debt-to-income ratio (DTI) of 45 percent back-end, and a maximum limit of $647,200 specifically in low-cost areas. Almost all mortgages share either these same minimum qualifications or very similar qualifications, and this study guide will cover additional unique qualifications for specific loan types as they are relevant.

Fixed-rate Mortgages

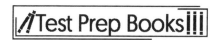

A **fixed-rate mortgage** is a loan with the same interest rate throughout the duration of the loan's repayment term. The fixed interest rate means that all payments are consistently the same amount, which makes it easier for borrowers to budget for their loan payments, though they are usually a little more expensive than adjustable-rate mortgages. This interest rate is usually at an advertised rate in increments of 0.25 percent or 0.125 percent and starts higher than an adjustable-rate mortgage, but because it is fixed, it cannot go up if interest rates go up over the course of the loan's repayment. The most common repayment durations are 15-year and 30-year mortgages, although both shorter and longer terms are available depending on the cost of the property. The Federal Housing Administration (FHA) standardized fixed-rate mortgage usage to make it one of the most common forms of loans for home purchases. Additionally, since it is one of the most common types of mortgages, it is usually also a qualified mortgage loan. Qualified mortgage loans are simply loans that meet the requirements of the Consumer Financial Protection Bureau's ability to repay rule, meaning lenders will examine the borrower's finances and ensure that the terms of the loan make it more likely that the borrower can pay the loan back.

Adjustable-rate Mortgages (ARMs)

An **adjustable-rate mortgage (ARM)** is a loan where the interest rate is adjusted periodically. The adjustments are always in reference to an index of information that describes the cost to the lender of borrowing on credit markets. These indexes may be published by the federal government, or they may be created and managed internally with the financial institution offering the loan. These types of loans are carefully regulated by the federal government to ensure they don't make too many changes to the interest rate and cause extreme financial issues for the borrowers. Adjustable-rate mortgages are typically advertised at an initial base interest rate, and then the interest rate is reviewed after specific periods of time (for example, annually) and adjusted. There are three significant limits on the changes that can be made (known in the industry as caps) to adjustable-rate mortgages. These are limits on:

- How much the interest rate can change the first time it is changed
- How much the interest rate can change on the second and all subsequent times it is changed (cumulatively across all periodic changes)
- The total change to the interest rate over the loan's entire lifespan

These limits typically are around 2 to 5 percent on each criterion, but financial institutions are the ones responsible for setting the values on those caps. Like fixed-rate mortgages, adjustable-rate mortgages are one of the most common types of mortgages and thus many meet the criteria to be considered qualified mortgages.

Purchase Money Second Mortgages

A **purchase-money mortgage** is a mortgage that is issued as part of a purchase transaction of a house. One of the major differences between it and other mortgages, however, is that it is not a mortgage made with a financial institution. Rather, it is a mortgage between the seller and buyer of a property. A down payment is provided, mortgage terms such as interest rate are agreed upon, and the terms are recorded in a security instrument document that is viewable in public records, in order to protect both parties from future arguments. Essentially, a purchase-money mortgage is a mortgage loan made between the buyer and seller of a property where both parties are private individuals and not financial institutions. A purchase-money second mortgage is a specific kind of purchase-money mortgage used when the property being sold already has a mortgage. In some cases, the purchase-money second mortgage is used to advance a portion of the down payment that is used on the primary mortgage.

Balloon Mortgages

A **balloon mortgage** is a type of mortgage where, at the end of the repayment period, there is still a balance due that requires a large payment. These types of mortgages are more common in commercial lending rather than residential, where the large payment at the end is more easily paid off by a business. In many cases, balloon mortgages are structured so the regular payments are from a longer-term mortgage while the actual period is shorter, such as regular payments from a thirty-year term when the actual mortgage is a seven-year loan. This keeps early payments lower in exchange for a large lump payment later, saving money in the long run. Balloon mortgages are part of a special group of mortgages called non-qualified mortgage loans, which do not meet the Consumer Financial Protection Bureau's (CFPB's) requirements for a qualified mortgage. This means that while it is still a valid mortgage, lenders have more control to set stricter requirements regarding repayment, making the mortgage riskier to both lenders and borrowers. It is more common for lenders to require higher credit scores and bigger down payments for balloon mortgages than conventional mortgages.

Reverse Mortgages

In a **reverse mortgage**, there are no regular mortgage payments. While borrowers are still responsible for dealing with homeowners' insurance and property taxes, the concept behind a reverse mortgage is that the borrower is essentially choosing to pay the mortgage, including interest, in the future in full. Rather than the borrower making monthly payments on interest and principal, the value of the monthly interest payments are instead added on to the total mortgage. The borrower therefore makes no monthly payments, and the amount owed on the loan steadily increases. When the borrower dies, sells the property, or moves out of their home, the full amount of the mortgage comes due. The heirs or estate managers of the person with the reverse mortgage may then either pay off the whole mortgage, sell the home and use the proceeds to pay off the mortgage, or allow the financial institution holding the mortgage to gain possession of the property through foreclosure to pay off the mortgage.

Reverse mortgages have several different and special requirements. They require the borrower to be at least sixty-two years old and have ownership in a significant amount of equity in the property (typically at least 50 percent). The Department of Housing and Urban Development (HUD) requires interested borrowers to complete a HUD-approved counseling session to ensure that the borrower fully understands the requirements and consequences of the mortgage. Lenders typically waive credit score and income requirements for reverse mortgages, only requiring borrowers to pay origination fees and mortgage insurance premiums (MIP). Finally, the borrower is expected to maintain property taxes and homeowners' insurance once they obtain the mortgage.

Reverse mortgages have a mixed reputation. They can be helpful for older, retired borrowers who don't want to deal with regular mortgage payments and instead want their estate to pay off their mortgage after their passing. Additionally, they carry the advantage of having no need to worry about the mortgage during the homeowner's life. However, a reverse mortgage leaves a massive obligation looming in the future, and authorities like the Consumer Financial Protection Bureau (CFPB) do not usually recommend them because they are often complex, misleading, and can carry a high risk of fraud.

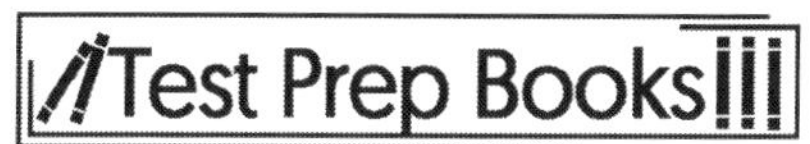

Home Equity Line of Credit (HELOC)

A **home equity line of credit (HELOC)** is a special type of loan that isn't directly a type of mortgage but does use the value of a property as collateral. Rather than giving the borrower the full amount of the loan up front, it is used as a line of credit kind of like a credit card, allowing the borrower to take out sums of money up to the maximum value of the loan. There are two periods of time during the loan—a draw period and a repayment period. **Draw periods** are typically ten years long and allow borrowers to freely draw and repay funds. During this time, borrowers are only required to make payments on interest that accrues on their balance. Once the draw period ends, the **repayment period** begins, and borrowers can no longer borrow more funds. Instead, the remaining outstanding balance must be repaid, either in a single lump sum or according to a loan repayment schedule.

HELOCs also have slightly different requirements from typical mortgages. They share the credit score and low debt-to-income ratio (DTI) requirements, but instead of the other typical requirements, they require the borrower to own a certain percentage of equity in their home as well as have sufficient income and a reliable payment history. If they meet these criteria, the borrower is eligible to borrow up to 85 percent of the value of the property, minus any amount they still owe on the primary mortgage.

A second-lien mortgage is a mortgage secured by both a property and a main mortgage. HELOCs are one form of second mortgages, but the name home equity line of credit typically has more positive connotations than the term second-lien mortgage.

Construction Mortgages

A **construction mortgage** is specifically lent out to finance the construction of a new home. The loan amount is given out in increments as construction progresses and only interest payments are required during this time. Once the house construction is finished, the loan amount either becomes due and must be repaid in full over time or rolls over into a typical mortgage. Since there is no currently existing property to refer to for value, construction mortgages are typically more difficult for borrowers to obtain due to the risks involved with building a new house. However, they can still be obtained if the borrower meets special criteria. The borrower must provide the lender with details of the qualified builder or construction team they have hired, a thorough construction plan for the house, an appraisal of the current plot of land and estimated value of the finished house, and a large down payment between 20 percent and 25 percent. The extra detail required is used to prove to the lender that the borrower is committed to the project's completion, since there is very high risk in giving out a loan for a property that doesn't exist yet and can only have an estimated value.

Interest-Only Mortgages

Most mortgages require that the regular payments pay off both accrued interest and a portion of the principal. However, sometimes payments are only required to cover the interest. In an **interest-only mortgage**, payments are only paying off accrued interest and are not going towards paying down the principal. Borrowers can still pay extra towards the principal, but it is not required. Since interest-only loans do nothing about the borrowed principal amount, they must either be regularly renegotiated, paid off in full later, or converted to an amortizing loan. It is not uncommon for a mortgage or loan to have a five- or ten-year-long interest-only period, then convert to a standard amortizing loan for the remaining years. This makes early payments slightly lower for borrowers since they don't have to pay a portion of the principal during this time. Interest-only mortgages also usually have higher interest rates since they are riskier for lenders to give and have slightly higher requirements. The minimum credit score requirement is increased to 700 or higher, the debt-to-income ratio (DTI) requirement is stricter at 43 percent, the down payment is much larger at 20 percent to 30 percent, and lenders often may scrutinize the borrower's assets and potential for future income to ensure the loan will be paid back in full later.

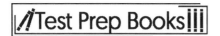

Different Mortgages, Different Advantages

All different types of mortgage products have their advantages and disadvantages. The two most common mortgages, fixed-rate and adjustable-rate, have very clear trade-offs. Fixed-rate mortgages typically start with a higher interest rate but are immune to fluctuations in the interest rate in the future, whereas adjustable-rate mortgages (ARMs) start with lower interest but could get much higher than a fixed-rate mortgage in the future. Purchase-money mortgages help homeowners who might not qualify for a typical mortgage be able to get a house, though because they are between two private individuals and no financial institution is directly involved, they are more informal and carry dispute risks between the individuals. Balloon mortgages are most appropriate for commercial property, since businesses can take advantage of the lower initial payments and pay off the rest later with saved profits. Reverse mortgages carry significant risk if the property's value becomes significantly less than the mortgage amount later, but they can be very useful for older homeowners who don't want to deal with mortgage payments and are willing to pay off the mortgage when they move or pass away. HELOCs are a unique way to get money for expensive purchases or projects by leveraging the value of an existing home. Construction mortgages help with building new homes, though they are risky to lend if there's not enough of a guarantee that the house will be completed. Interest-only mortgages can help low-income borrowers by minimizing the first few years of payments to allow borrowers to work up to a better income.

C. Terms Used in the Mortgage Industry

It is important for loan officers to be familiar with the vocabulary used in the business. These terms cover various aspects of the mortgage industry that play a role in providing loans to interested borrowers, including situations regarding the actual loan, disclosure, finance, and general mortgage knowledge. This allows loan officers to be knowledgeable on the various situations that affect both the lender and the borrower. Loan officers can also provide intelligent advice for clients that work in their best interest if the loan officer understands the differences between the various terms and when it is appropriate to use them.

Loan Terms: subordinate loans, escrow accounts, lien, tolerances, rate lock agreement, table funding

Borrowers are only given loans after careful assessment of the risk that comes with providing them the loan. Lenders need to have measures put into place that can protect their interests in providing borrowers a loan. One way to protect the interests of the lender is by using liens. **Liens** are agreements that allow lenders to seize various property for themselves if the borrower defaults on the loan. Liens are a way for borrowers to help secure a loan by promising to surrender the collateral, or something of value, to lenders if the borrower defaults on the loan. For example, the lien for purchasing real estate is the property itself. In the case of mortgage, liens are automatically placed on the property. This means that the bank has rights over the property until the mortgage is paid off.

Subordinate mortgage loans are related to liens because they are involved in how payment is made to lenders if a borrower defaults on a loan. Borrowers can have more than one loan issued to them, and subordination is a way for lenders to determine which loan is the primary or first-lien mortgage loan that is paid off first with the value of the collateral. Subordinate mortgage loans, such as an equity loan, are placed lower in importance and will be paid off after the primary or first-lien mortgage loan. Subordinate mortgage loan agreements make it easier to determine which loans to pay off first and are a way for a borrower to secure extra loans and money if necessary.

After closing on a mortgage, an option that could be available to borrowers is setting up a new escrow account. By doing this, a small portion of each mortgage payment is placed into the escrow account monthly. Escrow accounts ensure that payments made towards property taxes and insurance are made automatically and on time. This prevents consequences such as late fees from happening. The borrower does not manage the account. Instead, the lender will manage the account and make automatic payments on behalf of the borrower.

Escrow accounts have several benefits, including being easy to use, making automatic payments, and obtaining discounts for interest or closing fees. However, automatically placing funds in an escrow account means that borrowers may miss potential short-term investment opportunities.

One aspect of a mortgage that borrowers should be aware of is the Loan Estimate form, which estimates the charges and fees that need to be paid in order to close the loan. This includes closing costs, estimated interest rates, and monthly payments. For reverse mortgages, borrowers will receive a Good Faith Estimate (GFE) and a Truth in Lending (TIL) Disclosure instead of a Loan Estimate form.

Tolerance limits refer to how much the costs laid out in the Loan Estimate or GFE can increase at the time of closing compared to the original estimate. Final costs are laid out in a Closing Disclosure for most loans and in a **HUD-1 Settlement Statement** and a finalized Truth in Lending (TIL) Disclosure for reverse mortgages. There are three tolerance limits: no tolerance, zero tolerance, and 10 percent tolerance. No tolerance means that the lender may change these fees and not face any penalties. Zero tolerance fees are not allowed to change at all. 10 percent tolerance means that the fees listed may increase up to 10 percent of their value. Different fees are placed under each of these categories; the disclosure forms make it clear to borrowers which fees can increase and which cannot increase.

Borrowers sometimes have the option of entering a **rate lock agreement** with lenders, in which the current interest rate is locked in while the borrower is undergoing the homebuying process. This protects borrowers from rising interest rates that may happen while they are seeking a mortgage. The rate lock agreement lasts anywhere from thirty to sixty days, which gives borrowers time to finish the homebuying process and obtain a loan.

Table funding refers to a way of using another company's funds to provide funding for a loan. Lenders are able to offer borrowers a variety of different loan terms, which are then paid for by different investors. These investors will then take these mortgages and use them as investments. Most companies that offer table funding charge their own origination fees and service charges.

Disclosure Terms: yield spread premiums, federal mortgage loans, servicing transfers, lender credits

Yield spread premiums refer to the compensation that a mortgage broker receives for selling mortgage loans with a high interest rate to borrowers. Although the interest rate is higher than on a typical loan, borrowers can benefit from accepting a higher interest loan because the higher interest rate is accompanied by lower closing costs and origination fees, thus saving money upfront for the borrower. Yield spread premiums work best for short term loans or for borrowers who plan to refinance loans, because the money saved on fees will reduce the overall cost of the loan. Borrowers should carefully consider whether or not saving money on upfront fees is worth paying a higher interest rate overall. For example, if a borrower is unable to fully pay off a loan as quickly as they originally planned, they will be left with a loan that is more expensive because of the higher interest rate.

A related strategy to save money by accepting higher interest rate loans is with lender credits**. Lender credits** work similarly to yield spread premiums through reducing closing costs. If a borrower chooses to accept lender credits, the lender will pay for services such as home appraisal and pest inspection. The higher the number of credits that borrowers accept, the lower the upfront costs and the higher the interest rate. Borrowers need to determine whether or not the money saved on these various fees is worth paying a higher interest rate for the loan duration.

For some borrowers, securing a loan can be difficult due to low credit scores or low income. Federal mortgage loans are designed to help borrowers who typically have a difficult time securing a home mortgage loan by offering loans directly from the federal government. With the added protection from the federal government, banks are more likely to lend out money. Borrowers who accept these loans must pay a higher interest rate and add private mortgage insurance (PMI) to their monthly payments. PMI insures the loans of borrowers who are unable to put down the ideal 20 percent down payment on a home by offering additional protection to lenders if borrowers fail to repay their loan. Since borrowers who accept federal mortgage loans are typically riskier for investment, the added benefit of a higher interest rate and PMI allows lenders to successfully process loan requests from these borrowers. Borrowers must weigh the benefits of obtaining a loan against the costs of PMI and the higher interest rates associated with federal mortgage loans.

Service transfers refer to a change in who provides service to a borrower for a given loan. Service transfers are common in the mortgage loan industry and are typically not a sign of danger. However, borrowers must be made aware of any changes concerning their loan within fifteen days of a service transfer. These changes are outlined in a form that is given to borrowers detailing the information of the new company that will be handling their payments. This information includes the effective date of the transfer, the full contact information of the new company, when new payments will be accepted, and a written statement that explains that all loan terms remain unchanged despite the service transfer.

Financial Terms: discount points, 2-1 buy-down, loan-to-value (LTV) ratio, accrued interest, finance charges, daily simple interest

Discount points are a way for borrowers to customize their loan terms. These points trade higher upfront costs for lower interest rates. Using these points is best for borrowers who plan to keep a mortgage loan for a long time, because the lower interest rate will ultimately allow them to save money over the duration of the loan term. Borrowers who utilize both discount points and lender credits can customize their loan and create a payment plan that is most suitable for their needs.

In order for more potential borrowers to do business with a mortgage broker, a **2-1 buy-down offer** can be considered. This loan helps to attract new borrowers because the initial interest rate is lower than what the loan would normally cost. The interest rate is lower in the first year, increases in the second year, and settles into the permanent rate in the third year. By the third year, borrowers will need to pay for the loan at the new interest rate and also pay a fee for the interest not received during the first two discounted years. This deal is especially beneficial for new homebuyers, who may struggle to secure a loan for themselves. However, borrowers need to keep in mind that their income must support the eventual higher payments. Higher payments by the third year can be difficult to pay off if a borrower's income is not able to sustain it.

Placing a large down payment on a home can help borrowers receive better loan terms. This is because one of the many factors that underwriters consider when determining potential risk is the **loan-to-value (LTV) ratio.** An LTV ratio represents how much money is borrowed compared to the appraised property value. This ratio is calculated by dividing the mortgage amount by the appraised property value. For example, if a home has an appraised value of $100,000, and the buyer makes a 20 percent down payment on the home, the buyer will need to borrow $80,000. Dividing the borrowed amount by the appraised property value results in an LTV ratio of 80 percent. Borrowers will receive the lowest possible interest rate when the LTV ratio is at or below 80 percent. This is why the ideal down payment to make for a home is no less than 20 percent of the appraised value.

The **accrued interest** represents the amount of interest accumulated on a loan that has not been paid off. Every payment that a borrower makes will pay off some of the accrued interest and lower the principal. Interest usually begins to accumulate on a mortgage monthly. Some mortgages also accumulate interest daily. In order to calculate the amount of accrued interest for monthly terms, divide the annual mortgage interest percentage by twelve. This number is then divided by 100 to convert from a percentage to a decimal. This decimal is then multiplied by the mortgage balance. **Daily simple interest** is calculated similarly. In this case, the annual mortgage interest rate is divided by 365 instead of twelve.

For example, think of a borrower that has an annual mortgage interest of 12 percent and a mortgage of $100,000. The annual interest rate is 12 percent divided by 12, giving a 1 percent monthly interest rate. 1 percent of monthly interest converted into a decimal (e.g., divided by 100) is 0.01. Multiplying the decimal by the mortgage balance of $100,000 results in $1000 of accrued interest every month. To calculate simple daily interest, the 12 percent annual mortgage interest is divided by 365, giving a 0.033 percent interest rate. 0.03 percent interest converted into a decimal is 0.00033. Multiplying the decimal by the mortgage balance results in $33 of accrued interest daily.

The finance charge is the total amount of interest and loan charges that a person pays over the entire duration of the loan. This amount assumes that a borrower keeps the loan until the final payment is due. Loan charges include origination fees, mortgage insurance, and other associated fees.

General Terms: subordination, conveyance, primary/secondary market, third-party providers, assumable loan, APR

Lenders will usually include a **subordination clause** in the loan terms. Subordination is a way of ranking different loans in order of importance. The most important, or primary, loans will be paid off first and secondary loans will be paid off at a later time. This clause exists mainly to protect lenders if a borrower stops making payments on their loan. Typically, the most important loan to pay off is the primary mortgage. Any loan that is not placed first is referred to as a subordinate mortgage loan. Subordinate mortgage loans could include a second mortgage, home equity loans, and home equity lines of credit (HELOCs).

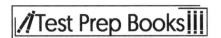

Conveyance is the act of transferring ownership of a property to another person. This process legally proves that a seller has transferred ownership to a new person. Conveyance can be done in a variety of situations, which usually involve a deed or a title. The deed of conveyance is a document that states the new owner of a property and protects the new owner from any issues regarding the ownership.

When an interested borrower first begins to look for a mortgage, they will begin their search in the primary market. The primary market is where new borrowers will engage with loan originators and find a loan that best suits them. The primary market provides the funds to borrowers and allows them to purchase property with a mortgage. After a borrower has secured a loan, the loan is then taken to the secondary market. The secondary market is where investors and lenders will profit off of generating mortgages by selling the mortgages to companies or private investors. The two biggest companies that buy mortgages on the secondary market are Fannie Mae and Freddie Mac. These two companies are sponsored by the United States government and were designed to compete with each other in different markets. Fannie Mae handles larger commercial banks, while Freddie Mac handles smaller banks and credit unions. The primary and secondary market work together to ensure that money is constantly flowing in the system and that the housing market continues to function.

Third-party providers are any entities that are not the main lender handling a loan. These third-party loan providers offer a variety of services, such as underwriting and marketing. Lenders use third-party providers to save money on underwriting and to speed up the origination process for borrowers. One criticism of utilizing third-party providers is that they do not have a long-term responsibility for the mortgage. After origination is finished, the mortgage is typically sold to investors or to companies like Fannie Mae on the secondary market.

One loan type that might appeal to certain buyers is an assumable mortgage loan. An assumable mortgage loan allows a buyer to take over a seller's existing mortgage. The assumable mortgage loan may have a lower interest rate than a new loan for borrowers. Another advantage that these loans offer is that appraisal is not required for the property. Loans sponsored by the Federal Housing Administration (FHA), Department of Veteran Affairs (VA), or other entities may be eligible for an assumable mortgage loan.

Loans will naturally generate interest yearly. Part of this interest is to cover the bank's cost of maintaining the loan. The annual percentage rate (APR) is the interest that is charged yearly to borrowers. Borrowers must be made aware of the APR before any loans can be distributed to them. APR can be expressed as either fixed or variable. A fixed APR has an interest rate that will never change throughout the life of the loan, while a variable APR does not have a stable interest rate and can fluctuate. Variable rates follow an index, such as a prime rate or Secured Overnight Financing Rate (SOFR). A **prime rate** is the interest rate that banks set to offer loans to other banks and customers. **Secured Overnight Financing Rate (SOFR)** is similar, but each transaction also includes a government bond used as collateral to finalize the loan.

Practice Quiz

1. Which of the following are the two primary government-sponsored enterprises (GSEs) that purchase loans on the secondary market?
   a. The Federal Nonconforming Mortgage Association and the Financial Home Loan Mortgage Company
   b. The Federal National Mortgage Association and the Federal Home Loan Mortgage Corporation
   c. The Financial National Mortgage Agency and the Federal Home Loan Mortgage Corporation
   d. The Financial National Mortgage Association and the Financial Home Loan Mortgage Company

2. FHA loan borrowers must pay a mortgage premium amount of what percent of the loan amount at closing?
   a. 0.45 percent
   b. 1.05 percent
   c. 1.75 percent
   d. 2.25 percent

3. Which of the following mortgage types is the riskiest for lenders?
   a. Fixed-rate mortgage
   b. Balloon mortgage
   c. Construction mortgage
   d. Adjustable-rate mortgage

4. What government organization has a system for classifying mortgages according to their ability to repay rule?
   a. Federal Housing Administration
   b. Department of Housing and Urban Development
   c. Federal Housing Finance Agency
   d. Consumer Financial Protection Bureau

5. How long does a rate lock agreement typically last?
   a. Ten to twenty days
   b. Thirty to sixty days
   c. Fifty to eighty days
   d. Ninety to one hundred days

See answers on the next page.

Answer Explanations

1. B: The Federal National Mortgage Association (Fannie Mae) and the Federal Home Loan Mortgage Corporation (Freddie Mac) are the two primary government-sponsored enterprises (GSEs) that buy loans on the secondary market. Mortgage loans that are designed for purchase by these agencies are called conforming mortgage loans because they conform to the guidelines set forth by the agencies. Choices *A, C*, and *D* are incorrect.

2. C: FHA loans require borrowers to pay a mortgage insurance premium (MIP) of 1.75 percent of the loan amount at closing. Choices *A* and *B* represent the range of the annual premium amount, which is between 0.45 and 1.05 percent of the loan amount. Choice *D* is also incorrect.

3. C: Construction mortgages are among the riskiest for lenders since they do not have a currently existing property to base value on, depending instead on the estimated value of a newly constructed house. Fixed-rate and adjustable-rate mortgages (ARMs) are two of the most common types of mortgages and typically have simple repayment rules, so they're not especially risky to lend, making Choices *A* and *D* incorrect. Balloon mortgages are potentially risky for lenders if the borrower cannot repay the final balloon payment, but the risks can be managed and mitigated by only lending such mortgages to businesses that have a higher likelihood of repaying the full payment later, making Choice *B* incorrect.

4. D: The Consumer Financial Protection Bureau has a system to classify common mortgages as qualified mortgages, following the criteria in their ability to repay rule. The Federal Housing Administration (FHA), Department of Housing and Urban Development (HUD), and Federal Housing Finance Agency all have other roles in the scope of homes and mortgages, so Choices *A*, *B*, and *C* are incorrect.

5. B: The rate lock agreement protects homeowners from increasing interest rates that may occur during the homebuying process. The rate lock agreement lasts anywhere from thirty to sixty days, which provides enough time for the borrower to finish obtaining a loan. Choices *A*, *C*, and *D* are not the correct duration for a rate lock agreement.

Mortgage Loan Origination Activities

A. Loan Inquiry and Application Process Requirements

The mortgage loan originator (MLO), loan officer, or mortgage broker is involved in each step of the mortgage process from inquiry to closing. There are many steps involved in obtaining a mortgage loan, and it is imperative that the loan originator ensures that each step is completed fully and accurately.

Loan Inquiry Process

The mortgage loan process begins with the **loan inquiry**, which is when a potential borrower approaches a loan officer or mortgage broker to inquire about applying for a mortgage loan. The loan originator and borrower will discuss the borrower's goals (e.g., whether they are seeking to purchase a home or refinance an existing property). If the borrower is purchasing a home, the originator will find out whether the borrower is a first-time homebuyer, if they want a shorter term loan (such as a 15-year loan versus a traditional 30-year loan), and how much money they intend to put as a down payment. If the borrower is seeking a refinance loan, the originator will find out the mortgage's current balance, interest rate, and payment amount and then discuss whether the borrower needs to cash out some equity in the home or if they are strictly hoping to reduce their interest rate and/or loan payment amount.

Most likely, the loan originator will also discuss the different loan programs available to the borrower as well as the current mortgage interest rates. If the borrower decides to proceed with the loan process, they will complete a formal loan application. Federal law requires that a formal Loan Estimate form be provided to the borrower within three days of the loan originator receiving six key pieces of information: the borrower's name, income, social security number, address, estimated value of the property involved, and the requested loan amount.

Borrower Application

While only six pieces of information are required to trigger a Loan Estimate, lenders often require much more detailed information on the loan application. It is the loan originator's responsibility to accept the application and to ensure that it is complete and accurate. The originator should also gather some initial documentation, including proof of the borrower's income (such as pay stubs, tax returns, and/or W-2 forms) and proof of any assets (such as bank and/or retirement account statements).

The loan originator is permitted to ask the borrower questions about their current employment situation, job history, income, assets, debts, and credit history. In addition, originators are required to ask about a borrower's ethnicity to remain compliant with HUD regulations; however, the borrower does not have to respond. In this case, the originator is permitted to make a visual assessment of the borrower's race. This is required so that HUD can prevent discrimination against minority borrowers.

There are some questions that mortgage originators are not legally allowed to ask. For example, loan originators may not ask the borrower any health-related questions or whether a borrower intends to start a family. These types of questions were used in the past to discriminate against women and people with disabilities and are not permitted under the Fair Housing Act and the Americans with Disabilities Act.

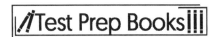

The loan originator will also inquire about the borrower's funds for the down payment if the loan is for the purchase of a property. If the borrower has been incrementally saving, a bank statement showing regular deposit amounts is usually sufficient. However, if the borrower has received any large sums of money, they will be required to document the source of those funds. For example, if the borrower received a large tax refund, they would need to show their tax return.

Borrowers may also receive **gift money** that they put toward a down payment. The rules for using gift money differ by loan program and even by lender. For example, conventional mortgage loans only allow gifts from immediate family members, while FHA loans allow gifts from more distant relatives as well as close friends, employers, and charities. VA and USDA loans allow gifts from anyone with whom the borrower has a relationship so long as the person does not have an interest in the property (e.g., the seller of the property).

In order for borrowers to use gift funds, they must submit a gift letter with their loan application. The gift letter must specify the dollar amount of the gift; date of the gift; donor's name, phone number, and address; donor's relationship to the borrower; the borrower's name; the address of the property the borrower is buying; and a statement the with the donor's signature indicating that no repayment of the monies is expected.

Loan originators are expected to protect the privacy of the borrower's personal information. **Regulation P, the Privacy of Consumer Financial Information rule**, dictates that all financial institutions must provide borrowers with written notice of their privacy policies, which must include the types of personal information collected and what information may be shared with affiliated and non-affiliated third parties. The disclosure must also include an explanation of the borrower's rights and information on how the borrower can opt out of having their information shared. In addition to the initial privacy policy disclosure, lenders must also provide borrowers with an annual privacy notice and notice of any revisions to their privacy policies.

Once the originator has this initial information, they can determine which loan product best suits the borrower's needs. The borrower may not qualify for some loan programs but may be perfectly suited for others. For example, some borrowers may not have a sufficient down payment to qualify for a conventional mortgage loan, but they could easily qualify for an FHA loan. VA loans are specifically designed for members of the military and are often the best option for military borrowers. Different loans also have varying interest rates and income or down payment requirements. The loan originator will take all of this into consideration and try to procure the best loan for the borrower's specific needs.

The loan officer will provide the borrower with a Loan Estimate that shows the borrower which loan program they are being offered and the estimated loan costs. The borrower can then choose to shop around for other offers, using the Loan Estimate as a comparison tool. The borrower may also try to negotiate the loan's terms, such as by asking for a reduction in the origination fee or paying points to lower the proposed interest rate.

Once the borrower and originator have agreed upon an acceptable loan product, the loan originator will complete a Loan Estimate disclosure that details the information about the loan. This estimate must be as precise as possible because there are firm limitations on how much it can vary from the Closing Disclosure at the end of the loan process.

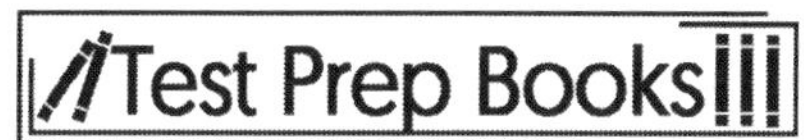

Verification

The lender must verify all of the borrower's information through the **underwriting** process. The borrower must sign authorization forms that allow the underwriter to verify their credit history, income, assets, employment, and other relevant information, such as homeowner's insurance.

To determine a borrower's credit score and history, the loan originator will pull the borrower's credit report, which indicates how the borrower handles debt obligations. Credit scores enable the originator to make a reliable assessment of the borrower's qualification for various loan programs.

The loan underwriter or mortgage loan processor (who helps get the submission package ready for underwriting) will call and verify the borrower's employment status. This entails confirmation that the borrower is employed at the job they indicated on the loan application and that their employment is likely to continue, meaning that they have not submitted a resignation notice or received a termination notice.

The underwriter will also review the borrower's income documentation and bank account assets. Some loan programs require that borrowers have a certain amount of **reserve money** left over after paying the down payment and closing costs. The required amount varies depending on the loan program. Required reserves can be as low as zero for a primary residence and as high as six to twelve months' worth of payments for second homes or investment properties.

Suitability of Products and Programs

One of the mortgage loan originator's (MLO's) main responsibilities is to determine which loan products and programs meet each borrower's specific needs and financial qualifications. The borrower's credit score, income, and down payment amount can affect which loan programs the borrower can qualify for and which programs might offer the best loan terms. For example, a borrower who does not have much money for a down payment but is a current or former member of the military would likely be best suited for a VA loan. A borrower with considerable assets and a high down payment amount could get a conventional mortgage, while a borrower with a low credit score might qualify for an FHA mortgage.

Accuracy

Loan originators are expected to provide borrowers with the most accurate Loan Estimate possible. The Loan Estimate form includes information about the type of loan, the loan amount, and the anticipated costs associated with the loan. The loan originator, acting on behalf of the lender, is expected to make a good faith effort to calculate the costs as closely as possible to the expected final costs of the loan. They should use exact figures when available and make reasonable estimations if exact figures are not available. Miscalculations or technical errors are not excuses for inaccurate Loan Estimate disclosures.

To prevent unscrupulous lenders from using bait-and-switch tactics on unsuspecting borrowers, there are limits to how much loan costs can vary between the initial Loan Estimate and the final Closing Disclosure. These variations are called tolerances, or tolerance limits. The TILA-RESPA Integrated Disclosure Rule (TRID) categorizes fees into three tolerances: zero tolerance, 10 percent tolerance, and no tolerance.

Zero tolerance fees cannot change from the initial Loan Estimate provided to the borrower. These are generally fees over which the lender has control (e.g., origination fees and fees paid to affiliated third parties such as contract loan processors or underwriters). Zero tolerance fees also include fees paid to unaffiliated third parties selected by the lender and for whom the borrower cannot shop, such as a lender-provided appraiser. Transfer taxes are another type of zero tolerance fee because those amounts are readily available and rarely fluctuate. Lenders should be able to quote these costs exactly, and they should have no reason to change them during the loan process.

10 percent tolerance fees are calculated cumulatively, meaning that the final fees cannot increase by more than 10 percent of the initial Loan Estimate. Fees in this category include recording fees and fees paid to unaffiliated third parties when the borrower was permitted to shop around but chose from a list provided by the lender. For example, if the lender provides the borrower with a list of appraisers, and the borrower selects an appraiser from that list, the lender should be able to make a reasonable cost estimate. However, the lender won't know the exact cost until the borrower chooses a specific appraiser. Settlement agent fees and notary fees can also fall under the 10 ten percent tolerance if the borrower was permitted to shop for these services but ultimately chose someone suggested by the lender.

No tolerance, or **unlimited tolerance**, fees can change so long as the initial estimate was provided in good faith. These are generally fees over which the lender has no control, including property taxes, homeowner's insurance premiums, homeowner's association fees, and prepaid interest. This category also includes fees for third-party service providers shopped for and selected by the borrower. For example, if the borrower selects a home inspector that is not on a list provided by the lender, the fee for that service falls under the no tolerance category because the lender cannot be expected to anticipate this cost. While no tolerance fees can change, the lender is expected to provide the borrower with the best information possible at the time of the initial Loan Estimate.

There are certain situations that would necessitate a new Loan Estimate, effectively resetting the fees for the loan. These situations are called changed circumstances. Changed circumstances generally affect the creditworthiness of the borrower or the value of the property. For example, if a borrower financed the purchase of a car after applying for a mortgage loan, the new debt would affect their debt-to-income ratio (DTI) and potentially impact their ability to repay the mortgage loan. This new debt would need to be considered, and a new Loan Estimate would need to be provided if the loan terms changed. The property's value could also change the loan terms. For example, if the appraised value of the property came in significantly lower than expected, the loan-to-value (LTV) ratio would change, which could affect the loan terms. This would also necessitate a new Loan Estimate.

If the loan originator does not abide by the expectations of these allowed tolerances, they would be in violation of the TRID rule. Any TRID violation incurs a fine of up to $5,000 per day that the violation goes uncorrected. Second-tier violations, which stem from recklessness, have fines of up to $25,000 per day. Third-tier violations, those of a deliberate nature, can have fines up to $100,000 per day.

Disclosure Timing

The TILA-RESPA Integrated Disclosure Rule (TRID) is also called the Know Before You Owe rule. TRID was implemented to simplify the loan disclosure process by consolidating several disclosure documents into two simplified forms. Those two forms—the Loan Estimate and the Closing Disclosure—provide the borrower with necessary, detailed information about the loan so that they can be fully informed of the loan terms. These disclosures must be provided to the borrower in a timely manner to allow the borrower time to review the information and compare loans from multiple lenders if they so choose.

Once the lender has the complete loan application and all required documentation from the borrower, the lender has thirty days to provide the borrower with a credit decision, referred to as a **Notice of Action Taken**. The action taken can be approval of the loan as submitted, counteroffer if the borrower does not qualify for the loan as applied, or an adverse action, such as denial of the loan application. The lender may also take adverse action, such as denial of the loan application or offering less favorable loan terms, if the loan application package is incomplete, additional information is required, or the borrower does not expressly accept the loan offer within ninety days.

When the lender takes adverse action, they must provide the borrower with a written notification. The notification must include the lender's name and address, a statement of the action taken, notice regarding the provisions of the Equal Credit Opportunity Act (ECOA), and the name and address of the federal agency that oversees compliance with ECOA. The notification must also include the specific reason for the adverse action or a disclosure informing the borrower of their right to obtain that information upon request.

The lender is also required to provide the borrower with certain early disclosure information. The Loan Estimate replaces the previous Good Faith Estimate (GFE) and Truth in Lending (TIL) disclosures and must be provided to the borrower within three days of application. The borrower must also be provided with an **Affiliated Business Arrangements (AfBA) Disclosure** notifying the borrower of business affiliations between the lender and any of the settlement services that may be part of the loan transaction. This disclosure must be made to the borrower at or prior to the time of referral. The borrower must also be notified that they can shop for services and are not required to use the affiliated providers.

Loan Estimate Timing

After receiving the six pieces of information that constitute the basic loan application, the lender must mail or deliver the initial Loan Estimate to the borrower within three business days. Generally, the Loan Estimate cannot be changed once it has been provided to the borrower except under specific changed circumstances or to reset tolerances in good faith. In addition, updating the Loan Estimate may be necessary if there are changes to the loan terms (such as locking an interest rate that was unlocked when the initial Loan Estimate was provided to the borrower). If revisions to the Loan Estimate become necessary, the lender must provide the new disclosure to the borrower at least four days prior to the loan closing date.

Each Loan Estimate does have an expiration date, which is listed at the top of the disclosure's first page and is usually ten business days from the date the disclosure was issued. The borrower must notify the lender of their intent to proceed with the terms provided in the Loan Estimate by the expiration date. Should the borrower decide to proceed after the Loan Estimate has expired, then the lender may create a new Loan Estimate under the changed circumstances provision of TRID. The lender must provide the new disclosure to the borrower within three business days of the borrower's indication that they wish to proceed with the loan.

If the Loan Estimate must be revised, the tolerances must be reset. The new Loan Estimate should reflect changes in interest rates or settlement fees.

In addition to the Loan Estimate, borrowers receiving a federally regulated mortgage loan must be provided with a **Homeownership Counseling Disclosure**. The Home Ownership and Equity Protection

Act (HOEPA) requires that borrowers be given a list of homeownership counseling services available in their area within three days of receiving either a loan application or the required information to complete a loan application. The list must include at least ten of the nearest counseling agencies approved by the U.S. Department of Housing and Urban Development (HUD). Additionally, the list may not be more than thirty days old, so the lender must ensure that all counseling agencies included on the list are still active and approved by HUD every thirty days.

Closing Disclosure

The Closing Disclosure replaces the old HUD-1 Settlement Statement and the Final Truth in Lending (TIL) disclosure. It is very similar to the Loan Estimate disclosure form, making it easy for borrowers to see if any changes were made between the initial disclosure and the closing.

The Closing Disclosure must be provided to the borrower at least three days prior to the consummation of the loan. Legally speaking, **consummation of the loan** refers to the date when the borrower becomes legally obligated to repay the loan. This is often, but not always, the loan closing date. Consummation dates are determined by state laws.

B. Qualification: Processing & Underwriting

Once the borrower's application is complete and the loan originator has collected the borrower's income and asset documentation, the loan package is ready for processing and underwriting. Some lenders employ loan processors to pre-underwrite the loan. The loan processor will ensure that all of the documentation is current and accurate and that the borrower appears to qualify for the loan before sending the loan package to the underwriter for approval. The processor is also often responsible for verifying the borrower's employment, ordering and reviewing the appraisal and title report, and obtaining insurance documentation. Whether or not the lender uses a loan processor in conjunction with an underwriter, the analysis of the borrower's creditworthiness and the strength of the loan application package is the same.

Borrower Analysis

Analysis of a borrower's creditworthiness and their ability to repay the loan rests on the strength of the loan application, including the borrower's assets, liabilities, income, credit report, and qualifying ratios. Lenders generally begin with the borrower's income, which can come from a wide variety of sources. The most common are wages, salary, tips, commissions, and bonuses from employment. How this income is calculated depends on several factors.

The first thing the processor or underwriter will do is verify that the borrower is still employed at the place they included on their loan application. They will call the employer and confirm that the borrower is still employed and the start date of employment. This is taken into consideration when determining if the borrower has stable, steady employment, which directly affects their ability to repay the loan. The lender will not ask any questions regarding the quality of the borrower's work or the likelihood of their remaining employed, as that is considered irrelevant to the loan application and an invasion of the borrower's privacy.

Income

Income that is paid by hourly wages or salary can be calculated based on the borrower's paystubs. The lender will require one month's worth of paystubs; weekly pay requires four paystubs, biweekly pay

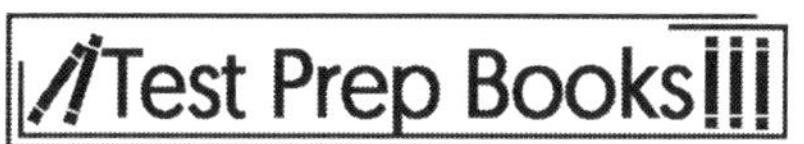

requires two, and monthly pay would require just one, for example. The lender will use those paystubs to determine the borrower's annual income. If the most recent paystub shows the year-to-date gross income (the total income before any tax or payroll deductions), the calculation involves simply dividing the gross income by the number of months in the year to that point. For example, if a borrower has worked for the same employer all year and the most recent paystub is from September 30 and shows a year-to-date income of $27,000, the lender will simply divide $27,000 by the nine months that have been paid so far that year, resulting in a monthly income of $3000. This is the simplest calculation, especially for borrowers who have varied work schedules or do not work the same number of hours or receive the same pay from paycheck to paycheck.

Not all calculations are that simple, of course. Adjustments must be made for borrowers who have not worked a full year at their current job, for instance. In this case, the lender will use the starting date of employment (determined from the verification of employment) in conjunction with the year-to-date amount shown on the paystub. For example, if the paystub from September 30 shows $27,000 but the borrower started the job on March 1 and has only worked for the employer for seven months, the monthly income is $3857 ($27,000 divided by seven months). If the pay calculation is not straightforward, the lender may require additional paystubs to verify that the income is steady and ongoing.

Fluctuating income that can have a wide variation, such as tips, commissions, and bonuses, is calculated based on the borrower's W-2s and tax returns. Because this type of income can vary greatly, from large amounts to nothing at all, paystubs are not usually an accurate representation. Lenders generally want to see two years of tax returns to verify that this type of income is regular, as opposed to a single bonus, for example, that will not be paid again. The lender will use the total income (before any tax deductions) from both tax returns and then divide that total by twenty-four months (two years) to arrive at an average monthly income for the borrower. For example, if the borrower's most recent tax return shows a total income of $35,000 and the prior year shows a total income of $28,000, the lender will add those together ($63,000) and divide the total by twenty-four months, arriving at an average monthly income of $2625. Tax returns are also used to calculate freelance or independent contractor income and income from self-employment.

Borrowers can also include other types of income to demonstrate their ability to repay. Other income sources include retirement and pension income, annuity payments, disability income, Veterans Affairs (VA) benefits, and child support and alimony payments. Bank statements, investment account statements, benefit statements, and court documents can all be used to verify these kinds of income sources.

Assets

Lenders will also want to verify any assets the borrower may have that could impact their ability to repay. Generally, borrowers will be asked to provide three months of bank, investment account, and retirement account statements. Lenders look for a few things when reviewing these documents, particularly bank statements. The first thing is, of course, the balance in the account. The balance should be in line with the borrower's income. A borrower who makes $3000 per month but has a bank account balance of $400,000 could create red flags for the lender.

This is not to say that people cannot save up money when they are purchasing a home, of course. However, large amounts of money must be explained. When a borrower has a significant amount of money in a bank account that does not seem in line with their income, the lender may ask to see additional bank statements and could require written explanations and documentation for any large deposits. Depending on the source of the funds, the lender may or may not consider that money when evaluating the borrower's ability to repay.

Credit Report and Liabilities

Once the lender has calculated and verified the borrower's income and assets, they will pull the borrower's credit report to verify liabilities and evaluate the borrower's credit usage and experience. Past credit performance is a good indicator of future credit performance. A borrower who manages debt well is likely to continue doing so and thus demonstrates strong creditworthiness.

In reviewing the borrower's credit report, the lenders will look for the number of open credit accounts and match these with what the borrower disclosed on their loan application. These accounts include credit cards and various types of loans, such as car loans, personal loans, student loans, and other mortgages. The credit report shows the most recent reported balance of all accounts; the payment history, including any late payments; and how long the account has been open. The credit report also shows the history of all closed accounts. In addition, the credit report shows any financial legal actions that have been taken against the borrower, such as accounts that have been sent to collections and any bankruptcy filings.

All of this information is boiled down into the borrower's credit score, which is a proprietary calculation used by each of the three major credit bureaus: Equifax, TransUnion, and Experian. The most common credit scoring models are **Fair Isaac Corporation (FICO)** and **VantageScore**. Credit scores are calculated based on the borrower's payment history, the amount of credit available versus how much is being used (known as credit utilization), the length of the borrower's credit history, and the mix of account types.

Although the borrower's credit score can determine their ability to qualify for any given loan program, lenders do not solely rely on the score when analyzing a borrower's creditworthiness. A borrower may have a high enough credit score while still demonstrating some undesirable credit usage, such as late payments or a past bankruptcy. Similarly, a single late payment is not likely to deter a lender from approving a mortgage loan, particularly if there are extenuating circumstances, such as an illness or a divorce. In these cases, the lender might simply request a letter from the borrower explaining the situation. A single period of poor credit management or financial difficulty does not necessarily preclude the borrower from qualifying for the loan.

A borrower who does not have an established credit history can still demonstrate the ability to manage debt. Paid utility bills, rent payments, and car insurance payments can all be used to determine whether the borrower reliably pays their debts in full and on time, if the lender allows such alternate credit information.

Qualifying Ratios

The borrower's income and debts are used to calculate their debt-to-income (DTI) ratio. This is the amount of debt the borrower must pay each month compared to their income. The ideal DTI ratios are 28 percent for housing and 36 percent for total debt. This means that the housing payment, including the mortgage payment, property taxes, and homeowner's insurance, should not equal more than 28 percent of the borrower's total monthly income, and the borrower's total debt payments, including the mortgage loan, car payments, loan payments, credit card payments, etc., should not equal more than 36 percent of the borrower's monthly income. For example, if a borrower has a monthly income of $3500, the housing payment should not total more than $980, and the borrower's total monthly debt obligations should not exceed $1260.

That said, different loan programs have different DTI allowances. Conventional mortgage loans can allow for a total DTI of up to 45 percent, and some lenders will even allow as high as 50 percent if the borrower has excellent credit, substantial savings, or other extenuating factors. Lenders may also make exceptions if the housing DTI ratio is high but the total DTI is below the maximum allowable, such as when a borrower has minimal monthly debt obligations outside of their housing expense.

Federal Housing Administration (FHA) loans allow a housing DTI ratio of up to 31 percent and a total DTI ratio of 43 percent, whereas U.S. Department of Agriculture (USDA) loans limit the ratios to 29 percent and 41 percent, respectively. VA loans do not have a maximum DTI ratio, but as with other loan programs, lower is generally better.

Ability to Repay

The borrower's income, assets, liabilities, credit history, and DTI ratios are used together to determine the borrower's ability to repay the loan. The better the borrower looks on paper, the higher the likelihood that the borrower will be able to repay the loan, which results in a lower risk to the lender. Borrowers with issues in any of these areas may present greater risk to the lender, making the lender less likely to approve the loan.

Appraisals

Appraisals are reports that detail the size, features, condition, and location of a property being used to secure a mortgage loan. The appraisal is a valuable tool for lenders to determine the fair market value of a home (how much it might sell for in the event of a surrender or foreclosure) and thus how much they should lend to a borrower wishing to purchase or refinance that property. Appraisals are done by certified, state-licensed appraisers who have training and have passed all of the courses and testing required for licensure. Appraisers must conduct their work in accordance with the **Universal Standards of Professional Appraisal Practice (USPAP)** and must be experts in their market area (an appraiser in Miami, Florida, should not do an appraisal in Jacksonville, Florida, for example, because they would not be familiar with the Jacksonville real estate market).

Approaches

Appraisers physically visit, inspect, measure, and photograph the property and conduct research into the market area in which the property is located to assess the property's value. There are three methods, or approaches, to doing an appraisal and calculating the fair market value of a property: sales comparison, cost approach, and income approach. The typical appraisal includes information and calculations for all three approaches that are then reconciled into the final determination of value.

The most common appraisal method is the **sales comparison approach**, sometimes also called a **market approach.** The appraiser determines the age, condition, and square footage of the home; the number of bedrooms and bathrooms; the total number of rooms; the lot size and features (such as whether the home is on a large lot or has water frontage); and other features of the property, such as the presence and type of basement and fireplace(s). The appraiser will then compare the property with recently sold properties in the area that are of similar size, age, and condition, known as comparable properties, or simply **comps**.

Very rarely are comparable properties available that are the exact same size, age, and condition as the subject property; however, the appraiser should use comps that are as similar as possible. The appraiser can make small adjustments to the property's value based on the available comps if necessary. These adjustments must be within reason, however, and cannot be excessive. For example, the appraiser will not use a six-bedroom, four-bathroom home as a comp for a two-bedroom, one-bathroom property. However, if a house just down the street has an extra half bath or a fireplace that the subject property does not have, that home would still be a reasonable comp, and adjustments can be made to that home's value to help determine the value of the subject property. Comps are expected to be in relatively close proximity to the subject property and should have sold within the last year. Exceptions can be made for unusual properties or properties that are in rural areas where the availability of comps is limited.

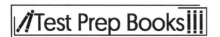

The **cost approach** involves determining the replacement cost of the property. It considers the cost of building a new home, including the cost of the land and construction, of the exact size and with the exact features of the subject property. The appraiser then determines the depreciation amount given the age and condition of the property and arrives at a value of the home. This is a less common approach, but it is factored into the final determination of value.

The last appraisal method is the **income approach**. This approach is used primarily for commercial properties or properties being used as investment properties, such as rental homes. The income approach includes a determination of the income-generating potential of the property, such as the rental amount a home might command given its size, features, and location. In addition, the income approach considers aspects such as vacancy rates, collection loss due to unpaid rents, and operating expenses in determining the income potential of a property. The income approach is a more complex calculation than the sales comparison or cost approach, and it generally is only used in conjunction with commercial property valuation.

Timing

Although the borrower is often responsible for the cost of the appraisal, the appraisal is usually ordered by the lender, and the lender will receive the appraisal directly from the appraiser. However, the lender is legally obligated to provide the borrower with a copy of the appraisal report upon its completion or at least three days prior to the consummation of the loan. In addition, the lender must provide a disclosure to the borrower within three days of receiving the loan application, informing the borrower of this right.

Independent Appraisal Requirement

Every effort is made to keep the appraiser, and thus the appraisal, as independent as possible. The appraiser is expected to be a disinterested third party to the transaction, meaning they do not have any involvement in the sale/purchase, loan process, etc. An appraiser who has a vested interest in the outcome of the transaction may be inclined to make valuations and calculations that favor their interest, which would be both unethical and illegal.

Purposes

The appraisal serves a couple of purposes with regard to the loan transaction. The appraisal tells the lender the specifics of the property, such as its square footage, the number of bedrooms and bathrooms, and other key features of the property. The appraisal also includes information about the property's construction (such as whether the home has vinyl siding or brick or what type of roof it has), its condition (if there appears to be damage to the roof or if the basement is unfinished, for example), and the property's value in the fair market.

The primary use of the appraisal is to assist the lender in determining how much money to loan against the property using the loan-to-value (LTV) ratio for the transaction. The ratio is calculated by dividing

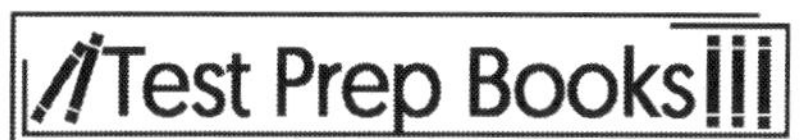

the loan amount by the appraised value of the property. For example, if a borrower is seeking a loan of $140,000 to purchase a property appraised at $175,000, the LTV would be 80 percent ($140,000 divided by $175,000). A lower LTV ratio is more desirable to lenders because it means that the borrower is putting more money down on the property and thus has more "skin in the game," as the saying goes. If the borrower has invested their own money into the purchase, they are more likely to repay the loan in order to retain ownership of the property. Borrowers who are more financially invested in a property are less likely to enter into foreclosure.

There are usually specific requirements for the maximum LTV for any given loan program. Conventional mortgage loans traditionally require at least a 20 percent down payment from the borrower and allow a maximum LTV of 80 percent. Some conventional mortgage loan programs, particularly subprime and Alt-A programs, allow higher LTVs but also come with higher interest rates. Federally backed loans through FHA allow for LTVs as high as 97 percent, requiring the borrower to only pay a 3 percent down payment. VA loans for military members and veterans often do not require any down payment and are financed at 100 percent LTV, meaning that the borrower can get a loan for the full value of the property.

Title Reports

Most lenders and mortgage companies require that a **preliminary title report** be completed prior to funding a loan on a property. A **title search** involves researching public records to verify the legal owner(s) of the property and to verify that there are no liens or claims against the property. Liens against the property can include things like unpaid property taxes or homeowner's association dues as well as liens created by contractors who were not paid for home improvements they made to the property. Once the records search is complete, a preliminary title report is provided to the lender showing whether or not the property has a **clear title**, meaning that there are no liens or encumbrances against it. Liens against the property stay with the property, not the owners, so when a buyer purchases the property, they also become responsible for any liens or encumbrances, making a title report uniquely important in the purchase and loan process.

Title reports are generally done by an attorney or a title company, and the person completing the research and report is called an **abstractor**. The abstractor reviews all of the public records on the property and completes a preliminary title report. The title report includes a listing of past owners (called the **chain of title**) as well as the legal description of the property and any encumbrances or liens. It may also include any easements across the property; any filed surveys; and any wills, lawsuits, or legal judgments that have involved the property. A title search generally takes a couple of weeks to complete, but it is definitely worth the wait to ensure that the borrower will hold clear ownership of the property upon completion of the purchase.

Once the preliminary title report has been generated, the borrower then purchases title insurance and obtains a title commitment. The **title commitment** document is the guarantee from the title insurer that the property is free and clear of any burdens, liens, or encumbrances. The title commitment and insurance protect both the borrower and the lender against any potentially undisclosed issues with the ownership of the property.

Insurance

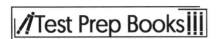

There are several types of insurance that can be required when obtaining a mortgage loan. Hazard insurance, also known as homeowner's insurance, is nearly always required. Some properties may also require flood insurance, and some loan programs require mortgage insurance as well.

Hazard and Homeowner's Insurance

Hazard insurance covers the property in the event of natural hazards such as fire, tornados, and other natural disasters. A hazard insurance policy covers the home or building and any other structures or improvements to the property in the event of damage or destruction from covered events. Not all hazard insurance policies cover every possible natural disaster, however, so it is important that homeowners review their policies carefully to ensure they have sufficient coverage for their area. For example, a policy may not cover damage from heavy snow or blizzards, but that is not likely to be necessary for a property in Miami. Hurricane damage would be an important coverage for a Miami property but would not likely be necessary for a home in Nebraska. Lenders will likely have specific requirements for what hazard insurance policies must cover based on the area where the property is located.

In addition to natural hazards and disasters, some hazard insurance policies cover other types of damage such as smoke damage, damage from falling trees, damage to vehicles on the property, and damages and loss from theft or vandalism. Some policies even cover damage resulting from malfunctioning systems within the home such as heating, ventilation, and air conditioning (HVAC); electrical; or plumbing issues, although these coverages vary from policy to policy.

Hazard insurance is a subset of the broader **homeowner's insurance** coverage. While hazard insurance protects the physical structures from hazards and natural disasters, homeowner's insurance covers personal property as well. Thus, if a property was destroyed by a tornado and the homeowner had hazard insurance coverage, the building would be repaired or replaced. The homeowner's insurance policy would cover any losses to personal property inside the building such as furniture, appliances, clothing, and other belongings. Homeowner's insurance also often covers any liability for injuries that are sustained on the property and may include coverages protecting the homeowner in the event of animal attacks as well. Not all policies are the same, and not all policies offer the same level of coverage, so it is important that homeowners review their policy carefully.

In the event of damage or loss of property, the insurance company usually pays for repair or replacement of the property less any deductible on the policy. For example, if the roof of a property is damaged by a hurricane, a covered event in the policy, the hazard insurance company will pay toward replacement of the roof. If the cost of the roof repair is $5000 and the policy has a $1000 deductible, the insurance company will pay $4000 toward the repair of the damaged roof, and the homeowner is responsible for the remaining $1000.

Lenders require that borrowers have hazard insurance because it protects the property that they are financing, similar to how auto finance companies require that financed vehicles be covered by full-coverage insurance policies. If a property is damaged or destroyed and is not repaired, the borrower may stop making payments on the mortgage loan. In addition, a damaged or destroyed property may no longer be sufficient collateral for the mortgage loan, resulting in a loss to the mortgage company.

The type of coverage and how much coverage is required is up to each lender. Some lenders will require that the insurance policy include **replacement cost**, which is enough coverage to replace the property in

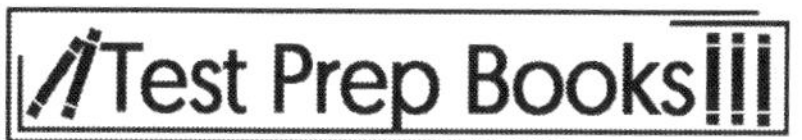

the event of total loss. Some lenders require extended replacement cost, which includes an extra 10 percent to 50 percent above the estimated replacement cost. This helps to account for increases in the price of materials or issues with replacement in the event of widespread loss, such as damage to an entire region. The lender could require guaranteed replacement cost, which means that the insurance company will pay for replacing the property regardless of cost. This, of course, is the most expensive type of hazard insurance policy.

Flood Insurance

Flood insurance coverage is a very specific type of hazard insurance. It protects homeowners (and subsequently lenders) in the event of flooding that damages or destroys the property. Flood damage is not generally covered under a standard hazard or homeowner's policy. It usually must be purchased as extra coverage when a property is located in a high-risk flood zone.

The Federal Emergency Management Agency (FEMA) designates some areas as high-risk, or flood-prone, areas, meaning that these areas have a greater likelihood of experiencing flooding or sustaining damage to property due to high water levels. Lenders will require flood insurance coverage for properties located in these areas.

Flood insurance policies are issued by private insurance companies, but discounts may be available for properties located within communities that participate in FEMA's **National Flood Insurance Program (NFIP)**. Communities participating in this program are required to "adopt and enforce floodplain management regulations that help mitigate flooding effects," according to FEMA's Flood Insurance website (https://www.fema.gov/flood-insurance).

Although homeowners may opt to have some flood coverage included with their hazard insurance policy, it is not required for every property, and the supplemental coverage offered by most insurers may not be sufficient. Lenders will likely require a specific flood insurance policy for properties that are located in flood hazard areas.

Mortgage Insurance

Mortgage insurance is not insurance that protects the property. Instead, mortgage insurance protects the lender in the event that a borrower defaults on a mortgage loan. Mortgage insurance is usually required on loans with a high LTV and/or for higher risk loans, such as Alt-A or subprime loans. There are two categories of mortgage insurance: private mortgage insurance (PMI) and government mortgage insurance, which requires borrowers to pay a mortgage insurance premium (MIP).

Lenders will usually require PMI on conventional mortgage loans in which the borrower puts down less than 20 percent, making the LTV greater than 80 percent. Depending on the loan, PMI can cost anywhere from 0.5 percent to 2 percent of the loan balance each year. PMI is usually paid either by up-front premiums, monthly premiums, or a combination of both. Any up-front premium will be shown on page two of the Loan Estimate Disclosure and the Closing Disclosure. Monthly payment amounts will be included in the total monthly payment that includes the principal, interest, taxes, and insurance (PITI). PMI can be canceled once the loan balance falls below 80 percent, and the lender is legally required to cancel PMI when the LTV ratio falls below 78 percent. Borrowers can also request cancellation of PMI once the loan is eleven years old.

Government mortgage insurance, known as **Federal Home Loan Mortgage Protection**, is provided by the Federal Housing Administration (FHA) on all FHA-backed mortgage loans with an LTV of 90 percent or more. Rather than paying for PMI, borrowers will instead pay a mortgage insurance premium (MIP). FHA loans allow for down payments as low as 3 percent and credit scores as low as 580, which means they also have a higher likelihood for default. As a result, MIP requirements are more stringent than PMI requirements.

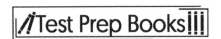

MIP requires both up-front premiums and monthly premiums that are paid throughout the life of the loan. The up-front premium, paid at closing, is 1.75 percent of the loan amount. The annual premium is between 0.45 percent and 1.05 percent of the loan balance, paid monthly. MIP cannot be canceled or removed like PMI. Options for cancellation depend on the loan origination date and the borrower's down payment amount. Loans that were originated before July 3, 2013, can have the MIP canceled once the loan amount reaches 78 percent LTV. Loans originating after this date and having less than 10 percent down will require MIP for the life of the loan. The only way to remove MIP payments in this case is to refinance the loan.

C. Closing

Once all necessary loan documentation has been submitted to underwriting and approved for financing, the loan can proceed to closing. For a purchase, closing is when the final documents are signed by both parties and property ownership transfers to the buyer(s). For a refinance, closing marks the new loan's acceptance and replacement of the old mortgage loan.

Title and Title Insurance

A property's **title** is not a physical document; instead, it refers to legal ownership, which encompasses ownership of the physical structure, the land the structure sits on, additional structures on the property, mineral rights, and additional rights, such as the use of neighborhood amenities. There are five specific rights (the **bundle of rights**) that are transferred when a buyer purchases a property:

- The Right of Possession: the owner has a right to possess the property
- The Right of Control: the owner can use the property as they see fit
- The Right of Enjoyment: the owner can enjoy the property as they see fit
- The Right of Disposition: the owner has the right to rent, sell, or transfer ownership of the property
- The Right of Exclusion: the owner can control permissions for property entrance

The **deed** is the physical document that transfers property ownership from one party to another. The selling party signs the deed, and the new owner is legally recorded by the county in which the property is located, making them the official holder of the property's title. There are several methods of holding title to a property, including sole ownership, joint tenancy, tenancy in common, tenancy by the entirety, and living trust. The most common is **sole ownership**, which occurs when the owner is a single person or a married couple who holds the title in their name(s) only and does not share the title with anyone else. **Joint tenancy** ownership occurs when two or more parties share ownership of the property. Married couples often use joint tenancy ownership because it gives each spouse equal share in the property, and that share carries its own right of survivorship, meaning that each spouse chooses who will own their share of the property upon their death. **Tenancy in common** is like joint tenancy; however, the parties may not necessarily each own an equal share of the property, though all owners have equal rights to access and use the property. With **tenancy by the entirety**, a couple is viewed as a single entity, so any transfer, sale, or encumbrance of the property must be agreed upon by both parties. Only married

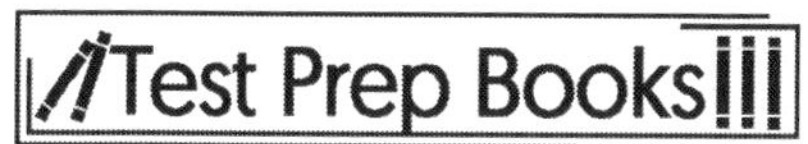

couples can hold title as tenancy by the entirety, and this option is not available in every state. Homeowners who hold title in a **living trust** act as both trustee and beneficiary for the property. Upon the homeowner's death, the property will be disbursed according to the instructions in the trust without need for probate.

Title insurance protects the lender's or homeowner's interest in the property by ensuring that there are no undisclosed liens, claims, or encumbrances to the property. A title company will conduct a title search to obtain and examine the property's records, including the chain of title (a list of past owners and the dates of ownership). Title records will also show unpaid liens, disputed wills, past-due taxes, or any other claims to the property. A clear title will have none of these encumbrances. Once the title is determined to be clear, the title company can issue title insurance.

A title insurance policy can be issued to the homeowner, the lender, or both. If there is a mortgage on the property, the lender will require a **lender's title insurance policy**. This type of policy protects the lender's interest in the property should the homeowner foreclose, forcing the lender to sell the property to recoup their mortgage loan investment. A **homeowner's title insurance policy** protects the homeowner in the event of outstanding liens, lawsuits, or encumbrances on the property; conflicting or disputed ownership claims; and even fraud or forgery. This type of policy is not required, but it can be a good investment to protect the homeowner.

Settlement/Closing Agent

The **settlement agent** oversees the closing transaction and ensures that all parties provide and receive the necessary information and documentation. They review all loan and closing documents with the buyer and seller, ensuring that the documents are fully executed, signed, and dated. Of particular importance is the **security instrument**, the document whereby the buyer agrees to repay the mortgage loan according to the terms set forth in the Closing Disclosure. The settlement agent will review this document with the buyer, ensuring that they fully understand and agree to the terms of repayment.

If a party to the transaction is unable to participate in the closing, a third-party designee may sign the closing documents in their place. **Power of attorney (POA)** is a legal document that assigns specific authority to the third party and allows them to act on behalf of another person. The settlement agent is responsible for ensuring that any power of attorney used in the transaction process is fully authorized and that the appropriate legal documentation is submitted with the closing package.

The settlement agent also ensures that funds for the closing transaction are processed and disbursed to the proper parties and that the necessary escrow accounts are established. Finally, the settlement agent confirms that the deed is signed by the seller and filed with the county or local jurisdiction where the property is located, officially transferring ownership to the buyer. The settlement agent is typically a representative of an escrow or title company, but some states require the settlement agent to be a licensed real estate attorney.

Explanation of Fees, Required Closing Documents, and Funding

A key document in real estate transactions is the Closing Disclosure, a five-page document that details the loan transaction, including monies owed and who is paying which costs. The disclosure also details the buyer's mortgage loan terms. The Closing Disclosure replaced the HUD-1 Settlement Statement that was used prior to October 2015.

Page one of the Closing Disclosure includes the names of the borrower(s) and seller(s), the property address, and the specific loan terms (including the loan amount, interest rate, and the monthly principal and interest amounts). Page two details the loan costs (including any loan origination fees), the appraisal fee, title insurance premiums, and other associated loan costs. This page also includes initial prepaid amounts that are used to establish the escrow account, which holds monthly insurance and tax payments and is used to pay annual insurance premiums. Page two also includes a chart indicating which party is responsible for paying which fees and costs. The third page of the Closing Disclosure shows the required cash to close for each party along with a detailed breakdown of the borrower's and seller's parts of the transaction. Page four includes the loan disclosures, such as rules regarding loan assumption, negative amortization, and late or partial payments. This page also includes information about the escrow account, any amounts that have been prepaid, and what costs are collected to establish the account. Finally, page five shows the total loan calculations and the contact information for the lender, the mortgage broker, the real estate agents, and the settlement agent. The Closing Disclosure must be provided to the borrower at least three business days prior to closing to allow the borrower adequate time to review and fully understand the transaction details.

Several other documents are also required for the loan closing transaction. A **promissory note** details the borrower's loan and repayment terms. The security instrument document explains the rights and responsibilities of the borrower and lender. In addition, the loan package will likely include proof of homeowner's insurance, the title report and title insurance, the property deed, the initial escrow statement, a certificate of occupancy, and a transfer of tax declaration. There may be additional state or local documents that are required parts of the mortgage transaction. The borrower and seller are provided with copies of any documents that include their signature.

The funding of a mortgage loan depends on the transaction type. With a purchase, funding happens on the day of closing. With a refinance, funding happens on the fourth business day after closing because the borrower has three days to change their minds. This is known as the three-day right of rescission. The **Notice of Right to Cancel form** explains the cancellation rules and provides information on how to cancel the loan should the borrower decide they do not want to proceed.

D. Financial Calculations

Mortgage loans require several financial calculations. The monthly loan payment amount depends on the down payment and the loan amount along with the interest rate and accrual period set by the lender.

Down Payment and Interest

The **down payment** is the amount of money that the borrower invests in the property upfront. Lenders want borrowers to have some vested financial interest in the property because this helps reduce instances of foreclosure. Different lenders and loan programs have varying down payment requirements. For example, FHA loans typically require between 3 and 10 percent down. Conventional mortgage loans can require at least 20 percent down, and subprime loans may require even more than that.

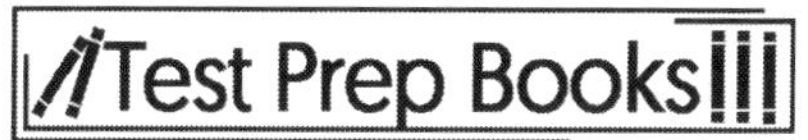

The down payment is calculated as a percentage of the property's sale price. To find the required down payment amount, multiply the purchase price by the down payment percentage, expressed as a decimal. For instance, if the purchase price of a property is $200,000, and the loan program requires a 20 percent down payment, multiply $200,000 by 0.20, which equals $40,000. Thus, the borrower must contribute $40,000 towards the purchase, and the lender will finance the remaining $160,000 (80 percent) of the purchase. A loan program that requires 3 percent down on a $150,000 purchase means that the borrower must contribute $4,500 (150,000 × 0.03), and the lender will finance the remaining $145,500.

Once the loan program and amount are established, the interest rate will be determined. The interest rate is the amount of money the borrower will pay in exchange for borrowing from the lender. In other words, it is the price of the loan. Interest rates can vary widely depending on current market rates, the type of loan, and the amount being financed. The lender must disclose the interest rate and accrual period within three business days of receiving the borrower's loan application. This information usually appears on the initial Loan Estimate disclosure.

Interest is quoted annually but compounds, or is calculated and added to a mortgage loan, periodically. Each loan earns a specific amount of interest each year; this is the annual interest rate. **Periodic interest** is the interest rate charged over a specific, smaller amount of time, or period. This rate allows the yearly annual interest to be broken down into periodic payments based on the loan principal, which are known as the **accrual rate**. Typically, mortgage interest accrues monthly, though for some loans, it can accrue daily. The annual interest rate is divided by twelve months to arrive at the monthly interest payment amount. For example, if the annual interest rate on a mortgage loan is 6 percent and is compounded monthly, then the monthly interest rate is 0.06 ÷ 12, or 0.005. If the principal balance on the loan is $150,000, then the monthly interest payment equals 0.005 × $150,000, or $750.

Monthly Payments

The monthly payment on a mortgage includes the principal (P) and interest (I). Lenders use a process called **amortization** to set fixed payment amounts for borrowers. Rather than changing the loan payment amount every month as the balance (and thus the interest payment) gets lower, borrowers pay the same amount each month. Initially, borrowers will pay more towards the interest and less towards the principal balance, but as the loan balance and interest amount decrease, more of the payment will apply towards the principal balance.

In addition to the principal and interest, most mortgage payments also include property tax payments and premiums for homeowner's insurance. These costs are quoted annually but paid monthly. If the property taxes are $3,600 per year, then the monthly payment is $3,600 ÷ 12, or $300. If the same borrower has an annual homeowner's insurance premium of $600, then the monthly insurance payment would be $600 ÷ 12, or $50. The complete monthly mortgage payment is known as **PITI** (principal, interest, taxes, insurance).

Closing Costs and Prepaids

Other key calculations in a loan transaction determine how much money is paid by and owed to both the borrower and the seller. The **closing costs** include fees for the appraisal, the credit report, title report and insurance, deed recording, application, and origination. Some of these costs are typically paid by the seller, but most of them are paid by the buyer/borrower. Closing costs generally total about 3 to 6 percent of the loan amount.

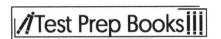

However, sometimes a purchase agreement includes **seller concessions**, which are costs (usually lump sums rather than specific fees) that the seller agrees to pay for the buyer at closing. Seller concessions can be helpful, particularly if the borrower is already paying a large down payment or if the borrower is short on funds for closing. There are limits, though, to how much a seller can pay towards the closing costs, and these limits depend on the loan type. Concession limits are based on either the appraised value or the purchase price of the property, whichever is lower. Seller concessions on conventional mortgage loans are limited to 3 percent for down payments less than 10 percent, 6 percent for down payments between 10 and 24.99 percent, and 9 percent for down payments of 25 percent or more. FHA concession limits are always 6 percent. VA loans have more specific rules for seller concessions that depend on which closing costs the seller is paying. The seller can pay up to 4 percent toward escrow accounts and any VA funding fees. The seller can contribute an unlimited amount towards other closing costs such as the appraisal, survey, and origination fees.

For example, if a buyer puts 15 percent down on a $200,000 property with a conventional mortgage loan, the seller concessions can be no more than 6 percent, or $12,000. It is important to note, however, that the seller concessions cannot be more than the borrower's total closing costs, regardless of whether they agreed to pay a higher amount.

The borrower will also be expected to pay prepaid costs at closing, which include the first six months to one year of homeowner's insurance, monies to set up the initial escrow account, and any prepaid mortgage interest. The escrow account is where the tax and insurance portions of the borrower's monthly mortgage payments are collected and held until they are paid to the local tax assessor or insurance company. Lenders will typically keep a **cushion** of a few months' payments in the account to ensure that there will be enough money to pay these bills when they come due and to account for any changes to the tax assessment amount or the annual insurance policy cost. That extra money is collected at closing and is used to set up the escrow account.

The homeowner's insurance is typically prepaid for a full year at closing. The lender will also collect at least two extra months of premium amounts to be held in escrow. As the borrower makes their monthly loan payments, any portion of the payment that is intended for insurance will be added to the escrow account. When the following year's premium is due, it will be paid from the escrow account.

Property taxes are also prepaid and held in escrow. At closing, the borrower and seller will usually split the property taxes according to who has (or will have) owned the property for how many months of the year. For example, if closing occurs at the end of October, the seller will have owned the property for ten months, and the new buyer will own the property for two months; each will be responsible for paying the taxes during their ownership periods. Depending on when taxes are due, this may be reflected as a credit to the seller (e.g., if the seller has already paid the taxes through the end of the year). In this case, the last two months of taxes would be shown as a credit to the seller on the Closing Disclosure. If the taxes are due soon or have not yet been paid, the seller's portion will be shown as a credit to the buyer on the Closing Disclosure. The monies credited to the seller are included in the total calculations for cash due to the seller at the transaction's finalization. Property tax monies that are credited to the buyer will be put into escrow and paid to the appropriate jurisdiction when the property taxes are due. As with the homeowner's insurance, the lender will also usually collect two months of property taxes to be held as a cushion in the escrow account, and any portion of the monthly mortgage

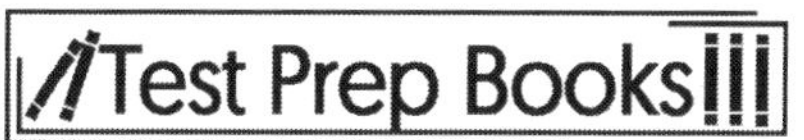

payment that is intended for taxes will be put into escrow and paid to the tax assessor the next time taxes are due.

The final prepaid amount involves mortgage interest. Mortgage interest is typically paid in arrears, meaning that the interest paid as part of October's mortgage payment was actually accrued in September. After closing, the borrower usually has at least thirty days before the first mortgage payment is due. In order to keep the mortgage payments consistent and prevent extra interest from being added to that first payment, the lender will collect prepaid interest at closing. Prepaid interest covers the time from the closing date to the first of the following month. For example, if closing occurs on August 20th, the borrower's first payment would typically be due on October 1st. The October payment will include the interest for the month of September, but the borrower also owes money for the interest from August 20th through the end of the month. So, the lender will calculate the daily interest rate, multiply the daily interest by the number of days between the closing and the end of the month, and collect that amount as prepaid interest at closing.

ARM Loans

Most mortgage loans are fixed-rate mortgages, which means the interest rate assessed at the start of the loan remains the same throughout the loan term. An **adjustable-rate mortgage (ARM)** is one in which the interest amount varies based on the current market conditions. If market rates increase, the interest rate on an ARM loan will also increase. Similarly, if market rates decrease, the interest rate on an ARM loan will decrease.

ARMs begin with a fixed-rate period, during which the rate will neither increase nor decrease. ARMs are usually fixed for the first five, seven, or ten years of the loan term. After this initial period, the ARM loan interest rate may be adjusted every year, meaning that the monthly loan payment will change every year after the initial fixed period. ARM loans are typically referred to as 5/1, 7/1, or 10/1 loans, indicating the fixed period (five, seven, or ten years) and the adjustment period (yearly).

ARMs can be appealing to borrowers because they often start with a lower rate than a fixed-rate mortgage, which means that the initial monthly payments are also lower. Borrowers also have a significant time during which their loan payments remain the same. Many borrowers will take out ARM loans to get the lower initial interest rate and then refinance their loans before the first adjustment period. However, ARM loans carry a certain amount of risk if the market rates increase significantly during the course of the loan. If borrowers find themselves unable to refinance for some reason or if the market rates are significantly higher when they refinance, borrowers can end up with a higher payment whether they keep the ARM loan or refinance into a fixed-rate mortgage loan.

Practice Quiz

1. Transfer taxes are classified as what type of tolerance?
   a. Zero tolerance
   b. 10 percent tolerance
   c. 20 percent tolerance
   d. No tolerance

2. What is the monthly income for a borrower who has worked for their current employer for eleven months and whose most recent paystub shows a weekly pay of $700 and a year-to-date income of $31,625?
   a. $2635
   b. $2875
   c. $1317
   d. $2800

3. If a borrower has a conventional mortgage loan with an initial loan amount of $175,000, at what loan balance can the borrower request to have private mortgage insurance (PMI) removed?
   a. $140,000
   b. $136,500
   c. It depends on the origination date of the loan.
   d. Only when the borrower refinances the loan

4. Which of the following includes a search of records to reveal any undisclosed liens, claims, or encumbrances on a property?
   a. Appraisal
   b. Home inspection
   c. Title report
   d. Property taxes

5. For how many days does a borrower have the right of rescission on a refinance loan?
   a. Three
   b. Five
   c. Ten
   d. Thirty

See answers on the next page.

Answer Explanations

1. A: Transfer taxes fall under the zero tolerance category. Zero tolerance means that these fees cannot change between the Loan Estimate and the Closing Disclosure because the lender either has control over these fees or should reasonably be able to provide the correct information without need for adjustments. Fees classified under 10 percent tolerance, Choice *B*, can change within a cumulated 10 percent from the Loan Estimate to the Closing Disclosure. This category includes fees that are paid to unaffiliated third parties that are on lists provided by the lender to the borrower. While the lender cannot control these fees, they should be able to estimate the costs reasonably. No tolerance fees, Choice *D*, include the costs of settlement service providers that are chosen by the borrower and over which the lender has no control nor any expectation of knowledge. There is no 20 percent tolerance category, so Choice *C* is a made-up answer.

2. B: Calculating the borrower's monthly income usually involves dividing the year-to-date income by the number of months the borrower has worked for the employer. In this case, $31,625 divided by 11 months equals $2875. The error on Choice *A* is dividing the year-to-date amount by a full 12 months, which is one month longer than the borrower has worked for their current employer. Choice *C* divides the year-to-date amount by 24 months, which is the time period used when calculating income with tax returns, not paystubs. Choice *D* was calculated by multiplying the weekly pay by four weeks per month, which is incorrect because there are more than four weeks per month (52 weeks per year divided by 12 months equals 4.3 weeks per month). In addition, the borrower does not always earn $700 per week, as evidenced by the year-to-date amount.

3. A: PMI on a conventional mortgage loan can be removed once the loan balance reaches 80 percent loan-to-value (LTV)—in this case, when the loan balance reaches $140,000. Choice *B* is 78 percent LTV, which is when the lender is required to remove the PMI. Choices *C* and *D* refer to mortgage insurance premium (MIP) requirements for Federal Housing Administration (FHA) loans.

4. C: The title report includes a search of the property's history, ensuring that there are no undisclosed liens, claims, or encumbrances to the property. The report will also include a chain of title and any information regarding unpaid liens or taxes, disputed wills, and any other claims to the property. The appraisal, Choice *A*, is a report on the property's value as compared to other properties in the area. A home inspection, Choice *B*, is optional for the buyer. The inspection can reveal the property's condition along with any immediate or future repair needs. Property taxes, Choice *D*, are required regardless of whether there are encumbrances or claims against the property.

5. A: The borrower has a three-day right of rescission on a refinance loan. During this period, the borrower can reconsider the loan and cancel the transaction if they so choose. The borrower must notify the lender in writing of their decision, and then the transaction becomes null and void. Choices *B*, *C*, and *D* present incorrect time frames.

Ethics

A. Ethical Issues

Prohibited Acts

Business professionals must treat everyone involved in a business transaction fairly and ethically. Everyone handling mortgages must conduct themselves in an ethical manner. A variety of ethical issues and prohibited acts that are unfair and jeopardize the integrity of various mortgage-related transactions are detailed below.

Redlining

Redlining is a discriminatory practice that involves the denial of services and protection based on certain factors, such as the financial status of where someone lives. This is commonly associated with mortgage lending, but this type of behavior can also be found in other situations involving loans, such as student loans and personal loans. The term was invented in the 1960s and involved physically drawing a red line around areas deemed to be poor financial risks. This discouraged investors from serving those areas.

Historically, if an area was deemed too risky or not worthy of attention, people living in that area would be at greater risk of exploitation. For example, if a resident lived in an undesirable part of the city, they would need to seek out unfair agreements with less trustworthy lenders because mainstream lenders viewed offering loans to them as an unacceptable risk. As a result, housing loans in the 1960s were expensive and risky.

The **Fair Housing Act of 1968** outlawed redlining by mandating that factors such as race, religion, and marital status are not allowed to be taken into consideration when deciding whether or not to provide loans. However, banks can legally consider factors such as credit history, income, condition of property, and lending portfolio.

RESPA Prohibitions

During any transaction involving mortgage and real estate, all information regarding the real estate transaction must be made clear to the borrower so they can make an informed decision. The Real Estate Settlement Procedures Act (RESPA) was passed in 1974 to provide borrowers with information about settlement costs, reduce and eliminate kickbacks, and reduce referral fees. RESPA prohibited acts including kickbacks, referral fees, disproportionate costs for advertising, and hiding relationships between an affiliated company and a business.

Kickbacks/Compensation

Kickbacks are a form of illegal payment for better services, offers, or treatment. A kickback can take many forms including money, gifts, privileges, or anything else that can be considered valuable. Kickbacks are looked down on in most business circumstances because they essentially act as a bribe. For example, a client may offer cash in exchange for accepting one company's services over another. It is the responsibility of the real estate agent and others involved in the business to perform to the best of their ability without expecting illegal bonuses.

Under RESPA, **referral fees** are also not allowed. Brokers are not allowed to provide compensation to other brokers or businesses who refer clients to them. With mortgages, extra fees and bonuses are not allowed to entice clients to choose certain loan products and services.

Businesses are not allowed to refer clients to an affiliated business or service without telling potential clients about this relationship. Terms and conditions must be made clear prior to recommending certain services. Clients do not have to listen to recommendations and have the freedom to choose another service not recommended by the person or business they are currently working with.

Permitted/Prohibited Duties

Loan originators collect consumer credit and financial information, assist consumers with obtaining or applying for credit, explain loan terms, negotiate rates, and submit applications to underwriters for review.

They are prohibited from receiving kickbacks from business referrals and compensation for services they did not provide. They must keep the best interest of the consumer in mind and are not allowed to steer them toward risky or unnecessary loan offers.

Fairness in Lending

Everyone has the right to mortgage terms that are fair and nondiscriminatory. Several topics, including referrals, coercion, conflict of interest, and discrimination, must be understood to gauge whether or not mortgage terms meet these criteria.

Referrals

Referrals are a way for loan officers to build their business and maintain a list of contacts. However, abusing the **finder's fees** and kickbacks associated with referrals have led to unsavory business practices that prioritize profit over the client. RESPA stringently regulates referrals and kickbacks to prevent this from happening.

When a lender provides a referral or recommendation to a borrower, the relationship between the service provider and the lender must be disclosed, as well as the list of charges and services offered, using an Affiliated Business Arrangements (AfBA) Disclosure form. These disclosures must be listed separately from the loan application and must be provided to the borrower as soon as the application is started. The client must always have the choice of whether or not to accept the services of a referred agent or loan officer.

Coercion

Coercion is the use of deception or intimidation to force someone to do something they would normally not do. With regard to mortgage loans, this changes the value of the property and influences the decisions of the borrower. For example, a bank that is refusing to approve a mortgage unless the borrower transfers their investments into a particular bank or its affiliates is engaging in coercion.

Appraiser Conflict of Interest

An **appraiser** will determine the value of the property and play an important part in the mortgage process. **Conflicts of interest** can arise when appraisers have a personal interest in making sure that certain outcomes happen during the transaction, such as referring the borrower to a specific agent or encouraging the buyer to accept certain terms. These conflicts of interest may be evident and occur openly, or they may be conflicts of interest that others perceive to be happening, even if the appraiser themselves do not believe so.

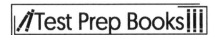

Discrimination/Fairness

The Fair Housing Act is a subsection of the landmark Civil Rights Act of 1968 that provides protection to people when they are renting or purchasing a home, seeking a mortgage loan, and other housing-related activities. It is illegal to discriminate and provide unfair terms to people based on their race, color, national origin, religion, marital status, gender, and disabilities. All who are involved in the real estate and housing business are responsible for providing fair treatment and terms regardless of these qualities. For example, they may not outright refuse to sell a house, provide different terms or housing services, or implement different sale prices and rental fees based on these criteria.

Fraud Detection

Fraud is hiding information or intentionally misleading others to obtain a service or benefit that would otherwise not have been received. For example, lying on a loan application in order to get underwriters to provide better terms than normal constitutes fraud. Fraud is mainly committed for either profit or to maintain ownership of a property. To combat fraud, loan officers, real estate agents, and others are required to follow strict licensing and educational guidelines. Organizations such as the Mortgage Bankers Association (MBA) and the Federal Trade Commission (FTC) also put forth guidelines and handle reports of fraud.

Asset/Income/Employment Fraud

Asset fraud occurs when borrowers represent themselves as having more assets than they actually have. This makes them seem more qualified to obtain a mortgage or to receive better loan terms. They may also engage in **asset rental**, in which they temporarily rent or borrow the assets of others and then repay these assets when the mortgage closes. **Income fraud** and **employment fraud** follow the same line of thinking as asset fraud. Details about income level, employment, debt, credit, and other information for mortgage approval may be intentionally omitted or misrepresented.

A related fraud is the use of straw buyers. **Straw buyers** purchase property for another person using false documents and credit reports. After falsely obtaining a mortgage, the straw buyer will pass the property to the actual buyer and relinquish their rights to the property. Investors will profit from this action through rental fees and will not need to pay for a mortgage themselves.

Sales Contract/Application Red Flags

Red flags signify dangerous situations that all borrowers and loan officers must be made aware of. Ignoring a red flag puts the borrower and the loan officer at risk. During business transactions, the contract and application are critical documents that explain the details of the mortgage and the property. This information must be accurate and disclosed before a mortgage can be approved.

The **sales contract** outlines the details of the transaction for everyone involved. The following are red flags that signal dishonest or dangerous situations involving a sales contract:

- A relationship exists between buyer and seller, such as being relatives, business partners, or very close friends. This is also known as a non-arm's length transaction. This relationship could lead to manipulated property values.
- The buyer is not listed on the contract or is deleted from the document.

- There is no involvement from a real estate agent.
- Commissions are extremely large or excessive.
- Dates and lists of transactions are incorrect.
- Names on checks and other forms of payment are incorrect.

The following are red flags involving the loan application:

- No signature or date is listed on the application.
- No employer address is available except for a post office box.
- Information is significantly different between typed and handwritten contracts.
- The buyer currently resides in the property to be bought.
- Extremely large payments are made, which may signify a straw buyer or misrepresented income.
- The telephone number of the applicant matches the telephone number of the employer.

Occupancy Fraud

Occupancy fraud is common because borrowers want to obtain better interest rates from lenders. In this form of fraud, the borrower lies about the occupancy status of a property. They state that the property is owner-occupied or that the person who owns the property also uses it as their primary residence. The opposite situation can also occur. **Reverse occupancy fraud** is when a borrower buys a home as investment property and lists it as part of their income, which increases their assets and value. However, instead of renting out the home, it is used as a primary residence.

General Red Flags

The following are general red flags to be wary of when conducting business:

- Social security numbers are incorrectly listed.
- Addresses are incorrectly listed.
- Different handwriting fonts and styles are used in a document.
- There is an excessive amount of automatic underwriting submissions.
- There are excessive alterations in a document, such as deletions and correction fluid.
- Verifications are completed too quickly, such as on the same day of the application or on a weekend or holiday.

Suspicious Bank and Other Activity, Information Not Provided to Borrower; Verifying Application Information

Both loan originators and consumers need to be aware of potential fraud and red flags. If basic information such as interest rates are not provided, borrowers need to exhibit due diligence and take caution. The Bank Secrecy Act (BSA) of 1970 required all financial institutions to monitor suspicious financial transactions and report them as soon as possible. The BSA specifically provides guidance on money laundering and identity theft. **Money laundering** is the act of making income obtained illegitimately appear to have come from a legitimate source. This illegal source of income could come from drug trafficking or terrorist funding. **Identity theft** involves stealing someone's personal information and using it for financial gain. The BSA requires all financial institutions to have onsite compliance officers who train staff for signs of suspicious banking activity and perform regular audits on the institution's adherence to industry standards.

Borrowers may request information, such as a receipt for payoff balance and details about the loan payment schedule. Companies are not required to provide borrowers repeated information, confidential information, or information not relevant to the loan. All provided information must be related to the mortgage account and cannot involve details such as the company's profitability and the personal information of employees servicing the borrower.

The normal process for verifying application information involves several steps. During the processing phase, underwriters will request documentation that verifies employment, assets, and income. This process ensures that all application information and loan terms are accurate.

Advertising

Advertising is a common way for businesses to make their services known in a public space. However, advertisements need to be carefully regulated in order to ensure that the information is true. The **National Association of Realtors (NAR)** states that advertisements need to include basic information such as the name of the realtor; the property value and tax; and accurate estimates of interest, costs, and payments for a mortgage loan. Similarly, the FTC states that advertisements must be fair, truthful, and evidence based. The FTC protects consumers from unfair and deceptive practices and pursues lawsuits against violators. Companies must comply with FTC guidelines and reports of false advertising are processed by the FTC.

Misleading Information

Misleading information on an advertisement misrepresents the reality of the situation. For example, an advertisement for a piece of property or loan may state that the interest rate on the loan is low and affordable. Therefore, more people would be more likely to seek out this particular loan from this business. However, there may be extra fees and payments associated with the loan before approval that are not listed in the advertisement. Buyers may enter an agreement that they are unable to afford if they are not given all of the necessary information.

Due Diligence Review

Due diligence applies to both loan originators and buyers. This is a process by which the quality of work done by loan originators is assessed and is also a chance for buyers to make sure they are getting a loan that is fair and truthful.

Loan originators must ensure that they are offering fair terms to borrowers based on the application information they have received. They need to verify the information and check each borrower's credit history and financial standing. Loan originators need to determine whether or not to actually dispense the loan, the correct amount of the loan, and the overall terms of the loan.

For buyers, due diligence is a chance for them to assess the property they are potentially looking to purchase and to verify the terms of their contract before it is closed. Buyers can inspect the property, conduct an appraisal, learn more about the homeowner's association in the area, check for titles, and define property lines.

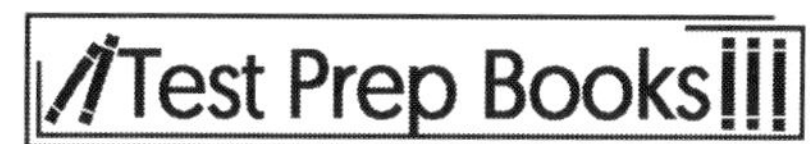

"Unfair, deceptive, or abusive acts and practices"

As a response to the financial crisis in 2007–2008, the Dodd-Frank Act was signed into law. This law addressed numerous areas within the financial sector that were a part of the crisis, such as the banking and real estate industries. One way it did so was by monitoring the financial stability of large companies. The law also protected consumers from risky financial transactions by identifying **unfair, deceptive, or abusive acts and practices (UDAAP)**.

The Dodd-Frank Act forbade acts that would coerce consumers into making unwise decisions. It also required full disclosure of all material relevant to the financial transaction and required lenders to make truthful statements. One example of UDAAP is advertising extremely low interest rates on a loan but not disclosing associated fees. Another example is a lender keeping a lien, or ownership, on a property even when the owner has already paid off the loan.

Federal Regulation

There are various regulatory bodies that protect consumers from unfair practices. The NAR and the FTC play similar roles in ensuring that all individuals are trained and licensed and can recognize unethical business practices. The Dodd-Frank Act provided federal regulation on large companies, predatory loans, and investing. These acts provided more stability to the economy by limiting risky financial transactions and ensuring that companies were able to recover from a financial crisis.

Predatory Lending and Steering

Lenders who encourage borrowers to take out risky loans that are not in their best interest are engaging in **predatory lending**. These risky loans have several characteristics that borrowers need to be aware of, such as excessive borrowing fees, high late fees, and seizure of collateral.

Steering is the act of persuading potential homeowners to either move to a certain neighborhood or to avoid it. This move is based on discriminatory factors that were outlined in the Fair Housing Act including race, religion, and national origin. For example, real estate agents are prohibited from persuading a Christian homeowner to move to a neighborhood with a large Christian population. They may make recommendations, but they may not influence or coerce a potential homeowner in any way. Steering can also refer to mortgage loan originators (MLOs) or lenders pushing borrowers to use particular service providers or accept particular loan terms, even if they provide less favorable terms for the borrower.

B. Ethical Behavior Related to Loan Origination Activities

Financial Responsibility

All lenders are responsible for working in the interest of their clients and providing the best possible service to them. They must be knowledgeable in various areas, such as how to handle fees and compensation, mortgage compliance, and personal information.

Permitted Fees/Compensation, Fee Changes, Closing Cost Scenarios, Referral Fees, Fee Splitting

Lenders must offer terms and rates that are fair and honest using the best information that is available at the time the Loan Estimate is made. These terms also include the topic of permitted fees, payments, and compensation, all of which are discussed and estimated with all information available at that time. Fees are detailed separately in the document and are provided to the borrower for review.

Fees can only be changed from the amounts presented to the lender in the Loan Estimate if there is a triggering event based on **changed circumstances**, such as job loss or retirement, that directly impacts a specific part of the loan. Other information that is not affected by a triggering event, such as transfer taxes and closing costs, remains the same. The Loan Estimate will be revised only with the affected information.

Closing costs are fees that are due at the end of a successful real estate or loan transaction and are included within the loan. They must be explained in detail and include the amount the borrower is responsible for, such as underwriting fees and taxes.

Referral fees and kickbacks are not allowed under RESPA, and full disclosure must be made regarding the relationship between one business and another to ensure that these practices are avoided.

Fee splitting is an even fifty/fifty split for joint marketing. This allows teams to work together and promote their services. However, fee splitting is unethical when any amount of payment is unearned. RESPA prohibits individuals from accepting payment for services that were not actually performed. For example, an individual who overcharges for the cost of another service without actually justifying the price increase through additional services or goods is in violation of RESPA.

Handling Borrower Complaints

Complaints made by a consumer toward a company or service is handled by the Consumer Financial Protection Bureau (CFPB). The CFPB will notify the company of the complaint, and the data and response from the company is submitted through a secure company portal. The CFPB makes complaint data available on their website so that other consumers can learn about what issues they may have when interacting with companies the CFPB is investigating. Companies usually respond to complaints within fifteen days.

Mortgage Company Compliance

Mortgage companies must be held to a high standard in order to ensure excellent, professional service and to protect consumers. Industry best practices and regulation must be followed and updated constantly. Normally, there is a compliance management system put in place within a company. This system is responsible for auditing the company and following laws, such as the Home Ownership and Equity Protection Act (HOEPA) and the Home Mortgage Disclosure Act (HMDA). HOEPA prevents buyers from overpaying on private mortgage insurance (PMI), and HMDA mandates that credit unions must retain all details about loans.

Discovery of Material Information, Information Supplied by Employers

Material information is any information that could influence the value of a property. For example, finding that a property has extensive structural damage and requires repairs is material information. Hiding material information intentionally is an act of fraud and punishable with fines and loss of licensure.

In order to assess the risk a borrower may present, the underwriter needs to obtain the borrower's employment information. They do this by sending employers a Request for Verification of Employment

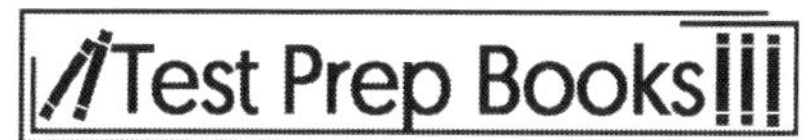

as well as requesting pay stubs and W-2 forms. This information will be used to verify the borrower's income and employment status.

Relationships with Consumers

Representing their company in a professional and ethical way is the responsibility of everyone involved in the mortgage loan business. Full disclosure needs to be given to clients, and transparency is key to a successful and honest transaction. There are particular ethical considerations that mortgage loan originators (MLOs) must be aware of in a variety of relationships with consumers.

Handling Personal Information/Cybersecurity, Disclosing Conflicts of Interest, Requesting Credit Reports

Mishandling personal information is a serious lapse in trust between a business and a borrower. Under the Gramm-Leach-Bliley Act (GLBA), any company that offers financial services must keep personal information confidential, make every effort to protect this data, and disclose the company's methods of protecting it. All consumers are able to decline sharing their nonpublic information with nonaffiliated third parties, or companies and services that are not directly controlled by the financial institution with which they are seeking a loan. All online records must be kept safe and confidential for five years, and all digital passwords must be secure and protected.

Any time a service provider refers a consumer to an affiliated service provider, an Affiliated Business Arrangement (AfBA) Disclosure must be provided either prior to or at the moment of referral. This makes the nature of the relationship between service providers clear and can avoid conflicts of interest.

The Fair Credit Reporting Act (FCRA) regulates the industry by controlling who is able to access credit reports and how this information may be used. For a mortgage, a credit report will be used to determine who is eligible for a loan and the loan terms. Companies are also required to notify consumers if there are any adverse actions taken based on their credit reports and to explain information found in the report.

Credit reports can be requested when a borrower is trying to obtain a mortgage. In a **tri-merge credit report**, information from the major credit bureaus Experian, Equifax, and TransUnion is combined into a single report and assessed for loan terms.

Changes in Down Payments or Offered Interest Rates, Powers of Attorney, Non-Resident Co-Borrowers

Changes made to the down payment or offered interest rates must be clearly conveyed to the consumers when a triggering event based on changed circumstances, such as job loss or retirement, occurs. Interest rates will be determined based on the initial down payment. A larger down payment means a lower interest rate. 20 percent of the property value is the ideal down payment. Borrowers who are unable to offer a 20 percent down payment will need to purchase private mortgage insurance (PMI). This insurance protects the lender if the borrower stops making loan payments.

It is important for an individual to designate another person to legally make decisions on their behalf if they are unable to do so. A power of attorney (POA) is a legal document that allows a chosen person to sign documents and to make decisions on behalf of someone who is incapacitated. A POA is also a very nice option to have if an individual is trying to buy or sell property while they are out of the country or in a location far away from where they live.

Anyone who is not living in a property but is co-borrowing on it is a **non-resident co-borrower**. These people, such as a parent who agrees to help pay for the property, can be added as a cosigner to help borrowers secure a mortgage loan. The non-resident co-borrower's income and debts will be combined with the borrower's assets to determine loan terms. They do not own the property but are financially responsible for paying for the loan if the borrower cannot.

Unreported/Fluctuating Income, Gifts/Unexplained Deposits, Appraiser Interactions, Multiple Applications

Some careers have a fluctuating income or unstable income. For careers that depend on tips, such as delivery drivers and bartenders, the total income that will be used to determine mortgage loans is calculated through a method that averages the amount made on tips over a two-year period. All tips must be reported to the Internal Revenue Service (IRS), or the worker will face penalties and will be required to be pay back the tax owed on any unreported tips. Borrowers are generally required to provide documentation showing two years of tip income as proof that their income is stable. There are some situations in which twelve months of documentation will be accepted, but that is at the discretion of the lender.

Gifts are not allowed to be given to influence the recipient's decision making. This could jeopardize the integrity of the business transaction. Small gifts, such as beverages or refreshments, are allowed.

Unexplained deposits can affect a borrower's chance to qualify for a loan. Underwriters will flag a large deposit and ask for clarification on where it came from. For example, underwriters will determine whether this deposit came from taking out a new loan or debt or if the borrower has additional income that was not previously stated. This is to ensure that underwriters have the necessary information to decide on loan terms. If a borrower has recently received gift money, it must be accompanied by a letter listing the gift giver's name, address, telephone number, and relationship to the borrower; the address of the property the borrower wishes to buy; the borrower's name; the date of the gift; the specific amount of the gift; and a statement signed by the gift giver that the gift is not a loan and does not need to be repaid. This prevents borrowers from hiding their true debt-to-income ratio (DTI) behind false gifts that are actually loans.

Appraisers treat everyone in the loan process fairly. Properties will be evaluated at the end of the appraisal process. If a property has already been appraised within the last three years, the appraiser must disclose this in order to avoid a breach in confidentiality. This is because the very act of a client requesting a property appraisal is confidential information.

Many borrowers submit multiple loan applications in order to find the best offer. During the **mortgage credit pull window**, a borrower is able to apply to as many lenders as they wish. To avoid having multiple hard inquiries from lending institutions negatively impact a borrower's credit score, the multiple applications will only count as one hard inquiry against the borrower's credit score. The time frame for applying ranges from seven to forty-five days.

Truth in Marketing and Advertising, Permissible Statements in Advertising

According to the FTC, any form of advertisement or marketing that a potential consumer might see online, in commercials, or in other ways must be factually true and, when possible, supported by scientific data. The FTC monitors advertisements regardless of where they appear and handles violations of marketing and advertising laws by handing out warnings and issuing lawsuits.

Every statement made on an advertisement must be truthful. The Fair Housing logo and/or the Equal Housing Opportunity slogan must also be visible on all advertisements. Information provided on the advertisement must actually be available, and rates must be written with all terms and specifications disclosed on the advertisement.

General Business Ethics

Everyone involved in the mortgage loan business must behave in a professional manner that puts the interests of the consumer first. They must treat all those who seek their services equally and fairly and provide the best possible service to them. Professionals must understand how to deal with situations, such as falsified information, giving advice, and speaking to outside parties, with wisdom and grace.

Falsified Information by Borrower or MLO

False information provided by a borrower can jeopardize the application and loan. Loan officers are allowed to deny the application if they are given false information and must report the information to their company's compliance officer.

On the other hand, mortgage loan officers (MLOs) are not allowed to fraudulently change information on an application to help a borrower receive a loan. False documents made by the loan officer can result in strict penalties and revocation of their license.

Giving Solicited/Unsolicited Advice

Loan officers should only provide advice that is in the best interest of the borrower in their current situation based on their professional opinion.

Advice can either be solicited or unsolicited. Solicited advice is when the borrower explicitly asks the loan officer for advice on what to do. In this case, the loan officer has a duty to respond honestly and offer their professional judgment. For example, they can review the loan terms in detail and also compare different loan terms in order to find the plan that would work best for the borrower.

Unsolicited advice is advice that was not asked for. This is an act of good faith and can build rapport and a better business relationship with borrowers. However, offering unsolicited advice can also be detrimental to the relationship between the loan officer and the borrower. It is best done with caution and only when it will significantly help the borrower.

Outside Parties Seeking Information

Care must be taken when parties that are not the borrower are requesting information. It is the responsibility of all loan officers to handle personal information safely and protect it from unsolicited use. For example, if a bank asked for credit scores before giving an offer, it would be best for the loan officer to refer them to the borrower themselves to disclose this information. The borrower has control over their own information and may share it with outside parties if they give permission.

Practice Quiz

1. Unfair, deceptive, or abusive acts and practices (UDAAP) were outlined in which of the following laws?
   a. Home Ownership and Equity Protection Act (HOEPA)
   b. Bank Secrecy Act (BSA)
   c. Home Mortgage Disclosure Act (HMDA)
   d. Dodd-Frank Act

2. A lender is eager to offer a particular loan to a consumer and pushes them to accept the terms. The consumer notices that the loan has excessively high late fees and borrowing fees. What is the lender guilty of doing?
   a. Due diligence
   b. Steering
   c. Redlining
   d. Offering unsolicited advice

3. A bank is requesting that a loan officer share a client's credit history so they can compare interest rates for different loans. What should the loan officer do in this situation?
   a. Refer the bank to the client directly.
   b. Report the bank to the proper authorities.
   c. Ignore the request.
   d. Share the information with the bank.

4. A delivery driver is seeking a mortgage for a new home. Due to the nature of their job, the lender informs the driver that they must determine their tip income in order to qualify for a loan. How will the total amount of tip income be determined?
   a. Dividing the total amount of tips earned in the last four years by twelve
   b. Adding the total tips earned in the last six months
   c. Multiplying one month of tip earnings by three
   d. Averaging the total amount of tips earned in the last two years

5. An Affiliated Business Arrangement (AfBA) Disclosure is given to consumers to prevent which of the following?
   a. Due diligence
   b. Solicited advice
   c. Conflict of interest
   d. Power of attorney (POA)

See answers on the next page.

Answer Explanations

1. D: The Dodd-Frank Act specifically outlined UDAAP as actions that would coerce or deceive consumers. Choice *A* (HOEPA) prevents buyers from overpaying on private mortgage insurance (PMI). Choice *B* (BSA) mandates that all financial institutions must monitor transactions for suspicious activities and report them. Choice *C* (HMDA) mandates that all credit unions must retain all details of a loan.

2. B: The lender is trying to persuade the consumer to agree to a loan with risky terms and is not thinking of the consumer's best interests; therefore, they are trying to steer the consumer. Choice *A* refers to a series of steps that lenders and consumers can take to ensure that the transaction is safe and works in the consumer's best interest. Choice *C* is discriminating against certain consumers. Choice *D* is providing advice to the consumer when they did not specifically ask for it.

3. A: Clients have control over their own personal information, and a lender may only disclose it to third parties if the client gives their permission. Choices *B*, *C*, and *D* do not involve the client giving their permission to share their personal information and are therefore incorrect answers.

4. D: Careers such as delivery drivers typically depend on tips for all or part of their income. Total tip income is determined by averaging the total amount of tips earned in the last two years. Choices *A*, *B*, and *C* are not the correct methods to determine total tip income for a loan.

5. C: An AfBA Disclosure details the nature of the relationship between certain businesses and services, which helps prevent a conflict of interest from forming. Choice *A* is a way for both lenders and consumers to protect themselves in financial transactions by verifying information. Choice *B* is advice that a consumer specifically asks for. Choice *D* is a legal document that gives another person the right to make decisions on behalf of a person who is incapacitated.

Practice Test #1

1. What is the first step in the loan process?
   a. Application
   b. Estimate
   c. Negotiation
   d. Inquiry

2. RESPA applies to which types of loans?
   a. Small business buildings
   b. Apartment buildings
   c. One- to four-family residential property loans
   d. Rental properties

3. Fannie Mae was created to help borrowers with what aspect of home purchase?
   a. Down payments
   b. Interest rates
   c. Appraisal values
   d. Loan amounts

4. Which of the following is NOT one of the six key pieces of information required for the basic loan application?
   a. Borrower's social security number
   b. Borrower's employer
   c. Property address
   d. Requested loan amount

5. How many days does the lender have to provide the borrower with a notification of actions taken once the full loan application package and documentation have been submitted by the borrower?
   a. Fifteen days
   b. Forty-five days
   c. Thirty days
   d. Sixty days

6. What is the name of the database that all mortgage loan originators (MLOs) must register with?
   a. Mortgage License Registry
   b. National Mortgage Licensing System and Registry
   c. National Financial Transaction Registry
   d. International Mortgage Licensing Verification Network

7. A client is seeking a loan for a new home and is denied by the loan officer due to the ethnic makeup of the client's neighborhood. What act is the loan officer committing?
   a. Referral
   b. Redlining
   c. Non-arm's length transaction
   d. Predatory lending

8. Which document can demonstrate the borrower's investment income?
   a. The daily NASDAQ report
   b. Investment account statements
   c. A letter from the borrower's financial advisor
   d. A check from the borrower in the amount of their investment income

9. Which types of loan are exempt from the ability to repay rule?
   a. Primary residence loans and HELOCs
   b. Construction loans, HELOCs, and reverse mortgages
   c. Subordinate mortgage loans and manufactured home loans
   d. Second mortgages and rental property loans

10. Which of the following situations is an example of an owner-occupied property?
   a. A property is seized as a collateral to secure a loan.
   b. A property is bought by a straw buyer and given to another person.
   c. A borrower buys a home as investment property and lives in it.
   d. A borrower owns a property and uses it as their primary residence.

11. A flipped property is defined by what two criteria?
   a. Condition of the property and cost of the renovations
   b. Length of ownership and increase in selling price
   c. Length of ownership and cost of the renovations
   d. Condition of the property and increase in selling price

12. A customer just moved into the area. They have a part-time job and enough savings to last them for a year or two, but expect to find a full-time job with a more stable income soon. They would ideally like early mortgage payments to be as low as possible so they can focus on settling down and finding work. What type of mortgage would be the best fit for this customer?
   a. Reverse mortgage
   b. Adjustable-rate mortgage
   c. Balloon mortgage
   d. Interest-only mortgage

13. Jim is in his thirties and his financial situation is a little shaky. He could use some help applying for a mortgage. What type of mortgage should he apply for?
   a. Interest-only mortgage
   b. Adjustable-rate mortgage
   c. Federal Housing Administration (FHA)-backed mortgage
   d. Reverse mortgage

14. Private mortgage insurance (PMI) is required on conventional mortgage loans with an LTV greater than what amount?
   a. 75 percent
   b. 80 percent
   c. 85 percent
   d. 90 percent

15. Which of the following laws ensured that consumers will be given full information on settlement costs?
    a. Community Reinvestment Act
    b. Civil Rights Act
    c. Real Estate Settlement Procedures Act
    d. Fair Credit Reporting Act

16. Which of the following is NOT something an MLO has to update online within thirty days of it changing?
    a. Legal name
    b. Current employer
    c. Legal action status
    d. Home address

17. If the annual interest rate on a $200,000 loan is 9 percent, what is the interest amount according to a monthly accrual rate?
    a. $1500
    b. $1600
    c. $1700
    d. $1800

18. Which of the following government agencies does NOT guarantee insurance for mortgages?
    a. Consumer Financial Protection Bureau
    b. Federal Housing Administration
    c. Rural Housing Service
    d. Department of Veterans Affairs

19. Which of the following is NOT a considered factor in determining a borrower's ability to repay a loan?
    a. The borrower's employment status
    b. The monthly payment on the loan
    c. The borrower's income and debts
    d. The borrower's marital and familial status

20. A borrower is planning to use gift money as their down payment. They have submitted a gift letter to the loan originator that includes the amount and date of the gift along with the donor's information and their relationship to the borrower. What information is missing?
    a. A statement of repayment expectations
    b. The sale price of the property
    c. The amount of the mortgage loan
    d. The reason for the gift

21. Which law mandates that MLO identifiers be publicly and easily available?
    a. SAFE Act
    b. MLO Act
    c. HIPAA
    d. CMP Act

22. Which of the following factors is not allowed to be taken into consideration when approving a loan?
    a. Income
    b. Credit history
    c. Employment history
    d. Race

23. The ability to repay rule is part of which congressional act?
    a. Dodd-Frank Wall Street Reform and Consumer Protection Act (Dodd-Frank Act)
    b. Real Estate Settlement Procedures Act (RESPA)
    c. Consumer Financial Protection Bureau (CFPB)
    d. Equal Credit Opportunity Act (ECOA)

24. What is the punishment for the crime of concealing over $10,000 inside luggage?
    a. Up to two years prison and forfeiting property up to twice the smuggled amount
    b. Up to seven years prison without bail
    c. Up to eight years prison without bail or parole
    d. Up to five years prison and forfeiting property up to the smuggled amount

25. After closing a loan, a lender offers to open a new account for a borrower that will automatically make monthly payments towards property taxes and insurance. What is the name of this account?
    a. Table funding
    b. Good Faith Estimate
    c. Escrow
    d. Finance charges

26. Income fraud is misrepresenting which of the following in someone's portfolio?
    a. The total amount of income received in a given time period
    b. The total value of all personal properties owned
    c. Employment history
    d. Criminal history

27. How often do lenders need to provide borrowers with a privacy disclosure?
    a. At the start of the loan process and if any changes are made to the policy
    b. At the start of the loan process and annually
    c. Annually and if any changes are made to the policy
    d. At the start of the loan process, annually, and if any changes are made to the policy

28. Historically, which unethical act originated from physically drawing a line around certain areas or neighborhoods?
    a. Redlining
    b. Kickback
    c. Referral
    d. Coercion

29. Which type of loan is considered the riskiest for lenders?
    a. Subprime loans
    b. Prime loans
    c. Alt-A loans
    d. Jumbo loans

30. What is considered the ideal debt-to-income (DTI) ratio for housing and for total debt?
    a. 0 percent and 0 percent
    b. 31 percent and 43 percent
    c. 30 percent and 50 percent
    d. 28 percent and 36 percent

31. Which of the following types of fraud is misrepresenting the amount of personal property that someone has in order to receive better terms on a loan?
    a. Straw buyer
    b. Asset fraud
    c. Income fraud
    d. Employment fraud

32. Which of the following is NOT a factor in determining the interest rate for a mortgage loan?
    a. The current market rates
    b. The type of loan
    c. The amount being financed
    d. The title company acting as settlement agent

33. What is an IRRRL?
    a. VA Interest Rate Reduction Refinance Loan
    b. FHA Interest Rate Reduction Refinance Loan
    c. VA Interest Rate Residential Relocation Loan
    d. FHA Initiative Residential Relocation and Recovery Loan

34. The Department of Housing and Urban Development contains which of the following organizations?
    a. Federal Mortgage Protections Bureau
    b. Federal Housing Administration
    c. Consumer Financial Protection Bureau
    d. U.S. Treasury

35. Fannie Mae refers to which government agency?
    a. Federal Home Loan Mortgage Corporation
    b. Federal Housing Administration
    c. Federal National Mortgage Association
    d. Department of Veterans Affairs

36. Which of the following situations is an example of appraiser conflict of interest?
    a. The appraiser denies service due to religious factors.
    b. The appraiser asks the borrower's bank for a credit report.
    c. The appraiser is a business partner of the borrower.
    d. The appraiser intimidates a client into making a decision they would not normally make.

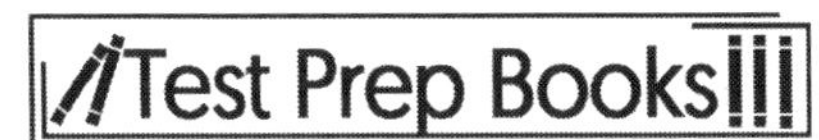

37. There are three primary credit bureaus used to determine a borrower's creditworthiness. Which of the following is NOT one of these?
    a. Equifax
    b. TransUnion
    c. VantageScore
    d. Experian

38. What key feature separates FHA loans from conventional mortgage loans?
    a. FHA loans can have a lower loan-to-value ratio than conventional mortgage loans.
    b. FHA loans do not require home inspections.
    c. Borrowers can have a lower credit score than what is required for conventional mortgage loans.
    d. Qualification for FHA loans is more difficult for borrowers.

39. Who is responsible for compensating an MLO for their work?
    a. The lender only
    b. The borrower only
    c. The lender AND the borrower
    d. The lender OR the borrower

40. Which of the following is NOT one of the primary provisions of the Real Estate Settlement Procedures Act (RESPA)?
    a. Eliminate referral fees and kickbacks
    b. Disclose financing and settlement costs
    c. Regulate and limit escrow account costs
    d. Define the duties of the mortgage broker

41. A loan officer is very good friends with a real estate agent and has promised to refer clients to them when possible. This situation may be viewed as which of the following?
    a. Conflict of interest
    b. Discrimination
    c. Income fraud
    d. Asset fraud

42. Which of the following describes a changed circumstance that would require the lender to provide the borrower with a new Loan Estimate disclosure?
    a. The borrower requests a new disclosure.
    b. The appraised value of the property is significantly lower than originally expected.
    c. The borrower's selected home inspector has gone out of business and a new inspector must be chosen.
    d. The borrower decides to close the loan in the middle of the month rather than at end of the month, thus changing the amount of prepaid interest that will be due at closing.

43. For USDA loans, the borrower's income cannot exceed what percent of the median income for their area?
    a. 90 percent
    b. 100 percent
    c. 115 percent
    d. 125 percent

44. How many times can someone fail the MLO test before having an extended retake waiting period?
    a. One time
    b. Two times
    c. Three times
    d. Four times

45. Under the HMDA, all loans must have a special string of characters that is unique to each loan known as a what?
    a. Credit score
    b. Lien status
    c. Universal loan identifier
    d. Monetary instrument log

46. If an MLO misses the renewal window and their license becomes inactive, when can they next renew their license?
    a. Immediately
    b. After 30 days
    c. After 90 days
    d. After 180 days

47. What is used as collateral from the borrower in a home equity line of credit (HELOC)?
    a. Their property
    b. Their insurance coverage
    c. Their credit score
    d. Their possessions

48. If a borrower started working for their employer on March 1 and they are applying for a loan using their most recent paystub from November 30, how many months are used in calculating their monthly income using the year-to-date showing on the most recent paystub?
    a. Three
    b. Six
    c. Nine
    d. Twelve

49. How long does a financial institution have to retain copies of its advertisements in the event the institution comes under investigation for deceptive mortgage advertising?
    a. Six months
    b. Twelve months
    c. Eighteen months
    d. Twenty-four months

50. When a mortgage is assumed, who is responsible for paying it off?
    a. The former borrower
    b. The new homeowner
    c. The lending institution
    d. The local government

51. If a borrower puts down less than 10 percent on a new FHA loan, how long will they be required to pay government mortgage insurance?
    a. Five years
    b. Ten years
    c. Until the loan balance is less than 80 percent LTV
    d. For the life of the loan

52. Which of the following is an example of a kickback?
    a. An appraiser offers borrowers a discount for any appraisal order in the current month.
    b. A mortgage broker provides a borrower with a list of suggestions for service providers.
    c. A mortgage company drives business towards a particular title company in exchange for financial compensation.
    d. A borrower chooses to use a family friend who is a licensed pest inspector.

53. The Fair Housing Act is a subsection in which of the following laws?
    a. Community Reinvestment Act
    b. Civil Rights Act
    c. Truth in Lending Act
    d. Consumer Credit Protection Act

54. Which of the following tasks is NOT something an MLO can have another person assist them with or do for them?
    a. Performing assessments
    b. Filing and distributing paperwork
    c. Writing emails to borrowers
    d. Discussing loan negotiation terms

55. Several federal agencies have issued guidance to lenders on how to handle nontraditional mortgage risk. Which of the following agencies did NOT participate in issuing this guidance?
    a. Office of the Comptroller of the Currency
    b. Department of Housing and Urban Development
    c. Board of Governors of the Federal Reserve System
    d. Office of Thrift Supervision

56. What is the purpose of the Loan Estimate form?
    a. To provide a breakdown of the expected costs of the loan
    b. To provide a list of the required application documentation
    c. To provide a list of settlement service providers
    d. To provide details about the loan transaction process

57. What legal document gives a third-party designee the authority to sign closing documents on behalf of someone else?
    a. HUD-1
    b. Promissory note
    c. ECOA
    d. Power of attorney

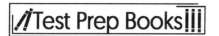

58. What organization conducts background checks on prospective MLOs?
    a. Federal Bureau of Investigation
    b. National Mortgage Loan Registry
    c. Mortgage Loan Originator Security Bureau
    d. Department of Housing and Urban Development

59. When adjusting the interest rate of an adjustable-rate mortgage (ARM), lenders will consult an index of information that describes what?
    a. Competitors' interest rates
    b. Cost of borrowing on credit markets
    c. Current state of the national housing market
    d. Risk to interest rate stability

60. Which tolerance category does not permit changes between the initial Loan Estimate and the Closing Disclosure?
    a. No tolerance
    b. Zero tolerance
    c. 10 percent tolerance
    d. Good faith tolerance

61. What was another common name for the Homeowners Protection Act of 1998?
    a. Front Lawn Act
    b. Home Mortgage Disclosure Act
    c. PMI Cancellation Act
    d. AML Home Act

62. The act of intentionally hiding information or intentionally misleading others for profit is known as which of the following?
    a. Conflict of interest
    b. Fraud
    c. Discrimination
    d. Kickback

63. What is the key feature of an ARM?
    a. An adjustable interest rate
    b. An annual mortgage payment
    c. An assessed rate of mortgage
    d. A fixed interest rate

64. An MLO is working with a borrower to secure a mortgage for them. Before the deal can be finalized, the state she works in changes the state-level requirements for MLOs, and the MLO needs to update her registration. However, the MLO can continue to work for a few days to keep business moving smoothly. What is the name of this situation?
    a. Origination grace period
    b. Temporary authority
    c. Situational forgiveness
    d. Business authority

65. Which of the following is NOT a changed circumstance that allows the lender to revise the Loan Estimate form?
   a. The lender can't verify part of the borrower's income; as a result, the buyer now has a higher debt-to-income ratio (DTI) and no longer qualifies for the original loan product.
   b. The borrower requests a change in the loan terms, reducing the loan from a 30-year fixed loan to a 15-year adjustable loan.
   c. The lender increases the origination fee for the loan.
   d. The appraised value of the property is lower than originally expected.

66. Finance charges are the monies that lenders make on the loan; these include which of the following?
   a. Appraisal fee
   b. Homeowner's insurance premiums
   c. Origination fee
   d. Deed recording fees

67. A borrower with a low credit score may be best suited for which type of loan program?
   a. Secondary
   b. Conventional
   c. VA
   d. FHA

68. The practice of conducting oneself in a professional and moral way is known as which of the following?
   a. Ethics
   b. Edicts
   c. Credibility
   d. Goodwill

69. Which of the following is NOT a way that an interest-only mortgage develops?
   a. Repaying the loan in full
   b. Doubling the interest rate of the loan
   c. Converting the loan to an amortizing loan
   d. Renegotiating the loan terms

70. RESPA includes six specific pieces of information that constitute a borrower's loan application. Which of the following is NOT one of the six pieces of information specified by RESPA?
   a. Borrower's birthday
   b. Borrower's income information
   c. Property address
   d. Property value

71. Which appraisal method uses information from recently sold properties to determine the value of the subject property?
   a. Cost approach
   b. Income approach
   c. Sales comparison approach
   d. Loan-to-value approach

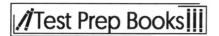

72. A transaction that takes place between a buyer and seller who have a personal connection, such as being family members, is referred to as which of the following?
   a. Non-arm's length transaction
   b. Arm's length transaction
   c. Fraud
   d. Redlining

73. What information is included in the chart at the top of the Truth in Lending (TIL) Disclosure form?
   a. The APR, the interest rate, the amount financed, and the monthly payment
   b. The interest rate, the finance charge, the total payments, and the monthly payment
   c. The APR, the finance charge, the amount financed, and the total payments
   d. The interest rate, the APR, the amount financed, and the total payments

74. Which of the following is NOT information obtained from a borrower's credit report?
   a. Credit score
   b. Credit history
   c. Borrower's income information
   d. How the borrower handles debt

75. If the borrower of a reverse mortgage passes away, who is responsible for seeing that the reverse mortgage is repaid?
   a. A designated secondary borrower
   b. The borrower's relatives
   c. The city government
   d. No one—the obligation is cleared.

76. Once the lender has received a completed loan application and all required documentation from the borrower, the lender has how many days to provide a credit decision?
   a. Three
   b. Ten
   c. Thirty
   d. Ninety

77. Where on the Closing Disclosure can the borrower find a detailed breakdown of the costs of the loan and the total amount each party is paying?
   a. The first page
   b. The second page
   c. The third page
   d. The fourth page

78. As a house is being built, how much of a construction mortgage must be paid off?
   a. Interest plus full regular principal payments
   b. Interest plus 50 percent of the regular principal payments
   c. Only interest
   d. Nothing

79. Who is the person who collects all of the documentation and pre-underwrites the loan?
    a. Loan originator
    b. Loan broker
    c. Lender
    d. Processor

80. Before signing off on a loan, a potential borrower notices that the commission the agent will receive is unusually high. Which of the following statements is true?
    a. This is a red flag.
    b. This is an example of material information.
    c. This is standard procedure for all loan terms.
    d. This is not a concern as long as the agent is a close friend.

81. What would be the monthly income for a self-employed borrower who provided two years of tax returns that showed annual incomes of $45,000 and $65,400?
    a. $4600
    b. $3750
    c. $5450
    d. $9200

82. What does an underwriter do for an MLO?
    a. Physically writes in the necessary information on paperwork
    b. Examines the risk of providing a loan to a borrower
    c. Delivers communication between the MLO and the lender
    d. Speaks with the borrower on behalf of the MLO

83. The Equal Credit Opportunity Act (ECOA) was primarily designed to prevent lenders from doing what?
    a. Receiving kickbacks and illegal referral compensation
    b. Requiring unreasonable amounts of monies for escrow accounts
    c. Hiding or misconstruing the loan terms
    d. Discriminating against borrowers based on factors unrelated to loan repayment

84. What are the allowable DTI ratios (for housing and for total debt) for Veterans Affairs (VA) loans?
    a. 28 percent and 36 percent
    b. 31 percent and 43 percent
    c. 35 percent and 50 percent
    d. There are no DTI ratios for VA loans.

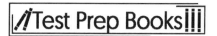

85. Which of the following demonstrates a violation of ECOA?
   a. The borrower discloses that they are married, so the lender denies the loan application pending receipt of the spouse's credit information.
   b. The borrower is self-employed and has provided a profit and loss statement; however, the lender decides to also request the borrower's tax returns.
   c. The borrower claims to have $20,000 available for the down payment and closing costs, but does not wish to provide bank statements to the lender, so the lender denies the loan application.
   d. The borrower is purchasing a home in a lower-income neighborhood, and the appraiser determines that the home will need a new roof in the next six months. The lender decides to deny the loan based on the property's condition.

86. Which type of insurance protects against fire, tornados, and other types of natural disasters?
   a. Homeowner's insurance
   b. Flood insurance
   c. Hazard insurance
   d. Mortgage insurance

87. What is a balloon payment?
   a. A first scheduled payment that is much higher than the other payments
   b. A type of payment schedule that gets rapidly more expensive
   c. A type of payment schedule where payments get delivered further up the chain of authority in a financial institution
   d. An alternate name for sending payments by mail instead of delivering them in person

88. Which of the following best represents the prohibited act of an MLO using bait-and-switch tactics?
   a. Colluding with a real estate agent on a property sale
   b. Attempting to conceal their NMLS identifier
   c. Advertising different mortgage terms than those the borrower actually receives
   d. Hiding documents from a Consumer Financial Protection Bureau (CFPB) investigation

89. Borrowers who agree to a federal mortgage loan must also purchase what?
   a. Yield spread premiums
   b. Private mortgage insurance
   c. Rate lock agreements
   d. Lender credits

90. What is the title as it relates to property ownership?
   a. A document that proves property ownership
   b. A group of rights that define property use
   c. Legal property ownership
   d. A document that transfers property ownership

91. The Consumer Financial Protection Bureau generally does not recommend borrowers obtain reverse mortgages for which of the following reasons?
   a. They can have misleading terms and risk being fraudulent.
   b. They don't further economic growth through regular payments.
   c. They are only offered by irresponsible lenders.
   d. They are not covered by most instances of homeowners insurance.

92. When was the Consumer Financial Protection Bureau established?
    a. 2013
    b. 2008
    c. 2001
    d. 2010

93. An agent who does not disclose their relationship with a service provider before recommending them to a potential borrower is in violation of which act?
    a. Community Reinvestment Act
    b. Civil Rights Act
    c. RESPA
    d. Fair Housing Act

94. What form explains the borrower's right of rescission on a refinance loan?
    a. Notice of Cancellation
    b. Notice of Right to Rescind
    c. Notice of Right to Cancel
    d. Notice of Rescission

95. What does the acronym HOEPA stand for?
    a. Home Ownership and Equal Proceeds Act
    b. Home Occupancy and Equitable Protections Act
    c. Home Ownership and Equity Protection Act
    d. Household Occupancy and Equity Proceeds Act

96. What does the balloon in balloon mortgage refer to?
    a. The rising cost of payments over the mortgage's term
    b. The high interest rate the mortgage begins with
    c. The large lump payment at the end of the mortgage's term
    d. The high property value the mortgage is covering

97. Currency transaction reports are often sent to which agency?
    a. Central Intelligence Agency
    b. Financial Crimes Enforcement Network
    c. Federal Bureau of Investigation
    d. Consumer Financial Protection Bureau

98. A loan officer is unhappy with the decision of a borrower and attempts to use deception and intimidation to make them change their mind. This is known as which of the following?
    a. Redlining
    b. Referrals
    c. Finder's fees
    d. Coercion

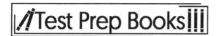

99. What is the maximum allowable amount of seller concessions on a $150,000 conventional mortgage loan with a 15 percent down payment and total closing costs of $3000?
    a. $3000
    b. $4500
    c. $9000
    d. $13,500

100. Financial institutions collect information about consumers such as bill repayment and bankruptcies in a type of report called a what?
    a. Currency transaction report
    b. Financial accuracy report
    c. Identity report
    d. Credit report

101. Which of the following is NOT a responsibility of the settlement agent?
    a. To confirm that the property constitutes suitable security for the mortgage loan
    b. To ensure that the transaction funds are processed and disbursed
    c. To verify that the necessary escrow accounts are established
    d. To file the signed deed with the county or local jurisdiction

102. What did the second subtitle of Title III of the Patriot Act do?
    a. Made it easier for law enforcement to pursue money laundering
    b. Added requirements for financial institutions to record any transactions in any global areas of concern
    c. Increased the penalties for other currency crimes like smuggling cash
    d. Expanded the definition of money laundering

103. Fixed-rate mortgages are one of the most common forms of home loans thanks to the standardization efforts of what organization?
    a. Federal Housing Administration
    b. Federal Reserve
    c. Treasury Department
    d. National Mortgage Lenders Association

104. Which type of loan typically has the lowest down payment requirement?
    a. Conventional
    b. Subprime
    c. FHA
    d. VA

105. Which statement about electronic signatures is correct?
    a. Electronic signatures must be written via a touchscreen interface.
    b. Oral communication or recordings are not accepted as electronic signatures.
    c. Electronic consent can be assumed if the consumer does not deny it.
    d. Electronic agreements prior to October 1, 2000, had to be rewritten to follow new guidelines within three months.

106. A kickback can take the form of which of the following?
   a. A fairly earned commission
   b. Properly disclosing the relationship between a recommender and a service
   c. The promise of expensive gifts if clients are referred to a service
   d. Denying service based on ethnicity or race

107. The term finder's fees refers to which of the following?
   a. Lying on an application to receive better terms
   b. Commission received from referring a customer to another business or service
   c. Having a close, personal relationship with an agent
   d. Intimidation and deception

108. If a borrower defaults on a loan, what happens to the lien listed in the loan?
   a. A variable APR will be placed on the lien.
   b. The lien will be transferred to another person using a deed of conveyance.
   c. The lien will accrue simple daily interest.
   d. The lien will be surrendered to the lender.

109. Which of the following is NOT a closing cost for a mortgage loan?
   a. Origination fee
   b. PITI
   c. Credit report fee
   d. Deed recording

110. The Good-Faith Estimate (GFE) was replaced by what form beginning in 2015?
   a. Closing Disclosure form
   b. HUD-1 Settlement Statement
   c. Truth in Lending form
   d. Loan Estimate form

111. Some borrowers may intentionally commit fraud and hide information on an application for a loan in order to:
   a. Keep ownership of a property
   b. Obtain a higher mortgage interest rate
   c. Surrender a property
   d. Receive finder's fees

112. The process of determining which loans are paid off first if a borrower defaults on a loan is referred to as what?
   a. Subordination
   b. Conveyance
   c. Servicing transfers
   d. Tolerances

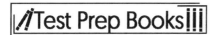

113. Which of the following conveys the right to sell, rent, or transfer property ownership?
    a. Right of Control
    b. Right of Possession
    c. Right of Exclusion
    d. Right of Disposition

114. A straw buyer is someone who:
    a. Has a personal relationship with a realtor or loan officer
    b. Receives payments for referrals
    c. Purchases property for someone else using fraudulent documents
    d. Approves loans

115. Which organization created the Red Flags rules?
    a. Office of Housing Counseling
    b. Consumer Financial Protection Bureau
    c. Federal Trade Commission
    d. Supreme Court

116. A borrower misleads a loan officer and states that a certain property is an investment and adds it to their total assets. However, the borrower also uses this property as their primary residence instead of renting it out. This action is known as which of the following?
    a. Income fraud
    b. Occupancy fraud
    c. Reverse occupancy fraud
    d. Asset fraud

117. Sometimes when lending a mortgage, a portion of the down payment is loaned in advance and repaid as an additional component of the primary loan. What is this known as?
    a. Good faith mortgage
    b. Down payment loan
    c. Line of credit loan
    d. Purchase-money second mortgage

118. Title insurance ensures that the property is free from what?
    a. Undisclosed encumbrances on the property
    b. Damages to any structures on the property
    c. Joint tenancies
    d. Undiscovered minerals on the property

119. When a financial institution first establishes a business-consumer relationship, it must explain to the consumer what information it collects about them and how it uses and shares it. What is this document called?
    a. Privacy policy
    b. End-user license agreement
    c. Data collection policy
    d. Safeguard agreement

120. When are closing fees due?
    a. After property appraisal
    b. After a successful referral
    c. After obtaining a Verification of Employment
    d. After securing a loan

Answer Explanations #1

1. D: The loan process begins with an inquiry. If the loan originator thinks that the borrower could qualify for a mortgage loan, they will have the borrower complete an application, Choice *A*. The Loan Estimate, Choice *B*, is the first disclosure form that is provided to borrowers. Negotiation, Choice *C*, is when the originator and the borrower work to come up with a suitable loan option that is agreeable to all.

2. C: RESPA applies to loans for purchases, home improvements, assumable mortgage loans, refinances, and home equity lines of credit involving one- to four-family dwellings. RESPA does not apply to commercial properties or properties purchased for investment purposes, such as those listed in Choices *A, B*, and *D*.

3. A: Prior to the creation of Fannie Mae, lenders regularly required excessive down payment amounts for home purchase, often 50 percent or more. Fannie Mae was created to keep housing affordable by guaranteeing loans that met certain loan down payment requirements. Choices *B, C*, and *D*, while subject to other oversights in later years, were not originally governed by Fannie Mae.

4. B: The borrower's employment information is not one of the six key pieces of information. The six pieces of information are the borrower's name, the borrower's social security number (Choice *A*), the borrower's income, the property address (Choice *C*), the property's value, and the requested loan amount (Choice *D*).

5. C: The lender has thirty days in which to notify the borrower of actions taken on the borrower's loan application. Choices *A, B*, and *D* are either too short or too long.

6. B: All MLOs must be licensed and registered with the NMLS (National Mortgage Licensing System and Registry). The other three names are fake names, so Choices *A, C*, and *D* are all incorrect.

7. B: Discriminating based on the ethnic makeup of where someone lives is an example of redlining. Choice *A* allows a service provider to recommend an affiliated service provider to a client. Choice *C* refers to a situation in which the buyer and seller have a personal relationship, such as being family members or close friends. Choice *D* refers to lenders who offer loans with unfavorable terms to people who would not normally be approved for these loans.

8. B: Investment account statements can be used to show how much money a borrower has in an account; these statements often show any payments that are made to the borrower as well. Choice *A* would be insufficient because it would not show specific accounts or investment amounts that the borrower owns. Similarly, a check, Choice *D*, does not show available funds or proof of regular deposits. A letter from a financial advisor, Choice *C*, is not considered verifiable proof of income or assets.

9. B: Construction loans, HELOCs, and reverse mortgages are exempt from the ability to repay rule, along with timeshares and bridge loans. Most other types of mortgage loans, including primary residential loans (Choice *A*), subordinate mortgage loans and manufactured home loans (Choice *C*), and second mortgages and rental property loans (Choice *D*), are all required to follow ability to repay guidelines to be considered qualified mortgages.

10. D: The reason people list a property as owner-occupied is because lenders offer better interest rates for these kinds of property. Choice *A* is an example of coercion. Choice *B* is incorrect because straw

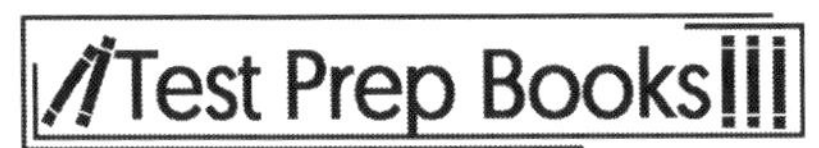

buyers typically are not interested in the property and will relinquish it to the actual person who wants it. Choice *C* is reverse occupancy fraud.

11. B: A flipped property is defined based on how long the seller has owned the property (less than 180 days) and the difference between the selling price and the seller's original purchase price (an increase of more than 10 percent or 20 percent, depending on how long the seller has owned the property). Choices *A, C,* and *D* are made-up answers. The condition of the property and the cost of the renovations are not factored into the definition of a flipped property.

12. D: In this situation, an interest-only mortgage would be the most appropriate for this customer. It would keep initial payments as low as possible and allow for a transition into a typical mortgage in the future. Choice *A* is incorrect because a customer must already own property or have a mortgage to set up a reverse mortgage. Additionally, while reverse mortgages can prevent regular payments entirely, they often create problems for the customer in the future. Choice *B* is incorrect because an adjustable-rate mortgage (ARM) carries the risk of interest rates significantly increasing in a year or two and making regular payments difficult for the customer. Choice *C* is incorrect because the customer is unlikely to have saved enough money by the time the balloon payment of a balloon mortgage comes due if they are currently looking for a job to gain an income stream.

13. C: The FHA offers support for many people to get mortgages when they do not meet the qualifications for traditional loans, so the best mortgage type Jim could apply for here is an FHA-backed mortgage. Interest-only and adjustable-rate mortgages (ARMs) might start fine but could incur even more financial strain later, so Choices *A* and *B* are incorrect. Reverse mortgages are only available to homeowners who are at least sixty-two years old, and since Jim is in his thirties, Choice *D* is incorrect.

14. B: PMI is typically required on loans with an LTV greater than 80 percent, meaning that the borrower has put down less than 20 percent. Choice *A* is an LTV that would not require PMI. Choices *C* and *D* are both situations that would require PMI, but they are not the cutoff percentage for which PMI is required, so they do not answer the question as well as Choice *B*.

15. C: The Real Estate Settlement Procedures Act (RESPA) ensures that consumers have full access to terms and settlement costs at the very beginning of a transaction. Choice *A* was passed to reduce the occurrence of redlining. Choice *B* was a landmark act that outlined discriminatory practices that are not allowed. Choice *D* protects consumer information from being accessed by third parties without permission.

16. D: MLOs changing home addresses is not something that has to be updated within thirty days as part of procedure. Legal name changes, employment changes, and legal action taken against them are all things that an MLO needs to update in the NMLS database, so Choices *A*, *B*, and *C* are all incorrect.

17. A: 9 percent annual interest divided by 12 months equals an interest rate of 0.0075 per month ($9 \div 12 = 0.75 \div 100 = 0.0075$). Multiplying the monthly interest rate by the loan balance of $200,000 results in an interest payment of $1500 per month. Choices *B, C,* and *D* represent improper calculations.

18. A: The Consumer Financial Protection Bureau offers advice and help with the mortgage process, but does not guarantee mortgage insurance itself. The Federal Housing Administration (FHA), Rural Housing Service, and Department of Veterans Affairs (VA) all have procedures for guaranteeing mortgage insurance, so Choices *B*, *C*, and *D* are incorrect.

19. D: While the guidelines require verifying any alimony or child support obligations, whether the borrower is married or has children is not a consideration with regards to the borrower's ability to repay and using the borrower's family status as a factor for loan approval could actually be a violation of ECOA. Choices *A, B*, and *C* are important factors in evaluating a borrower's eligibility for the mortgage loan.

20. A: The gift letter must include a statement indicating that no repayment is required or expected. Choices *B, C*, and *D* are not necessary pieces of information.

21. A: The SAFE Act (Secure and Fair Enforcement for Mortgage Licensing Act) requires MLO identifiers to be made easily available to the public for reference. The MLO Act is a fake name, so Choice *B* is incorrect. HIPAA (Health Insurance Portability and Accountability Act) is a health care act that has nothing to do with mortgages, so Choice *C* is incorrect. The CMP Act is a fake name, so Choice *D* is also incorrect.

22. D: Factors such as race, religion, and marital status are not allowed to be taken into consideration for the approval of a loan. Choices *A, B*, and *C* are acceptable criteria to be used for loan consideration.

23. A: The ability to repay rule is part of the Dodd-Frank Wall Street Reform and Consumer Protection Act (Dodd-Frank Act) that was implemented in January 2014. Choice *B*, RESPA, is legislation that protects homebuyers and sellers by creating transparency in mortgage transactions. Choice *C*, the Consumer Financial Protection Bureau, is the body that oversees the Dodd-Frank Act. Choice *D*, ECOA, is the act that prevents discrimination in mortgage transactions.

24. D: This particular crime is punishable by up to five years of prison time and forfeiture of property up to the amount smuggled. Choices *A, B*, and *C* are all incorrect because they are not the correct punishment and are either too extreme or too lenient.

25. C: An escrow account is managed by a lender and applies a part of each monthly mortgage payment to property taxes and insurance. Choice *A* is the process of using another company's funding to offer loans to borrowers. Choice *B* is given to borrowers to estimate the charges and fees to close a loan. Choice *D* is a summary of the total interest and loan charges that a borrower pays across the duration of the loan.

26. A: Income fraud is a common type of fraud in which the total income for a time period is misrepresented. Choice *B* is asset fraud. Choice *C* is employment fraud. Choice *D* is a part of application fraud.

27. D: Lenders are required to provide a privacy disclosure to borrowers at the start of the loan process, annually thereafter, and whenever policy changes are made. Choices *A, B*, and *C* are each missing one of the requirements.

28. A: Redlining is a historical term that originated from the 1960s and was named as such because of the physical red markings that were drawn on a map to signal areas that were dangerous for investment, resulting in unfair terms and an unwillingness to do business there. Choice *B* is an illegal gift or payment for services. Choice *C* is the act of recommending a service to someone. Choice *D* is using intimidation or deception to influence a client to make a decision that is not in their best interest.

29. A: Subprime loans are the riskiest loans for lenders because they are typically made to borrowers who have lower credit scores, unverifiable income, or other factors that make them less creditworthy

than other borrowers. Prime loans, Choice *B*, are the least risky loans for lenders because the borrowers usually have strong credit ratings and solid, verifiable income. Choice *C*, Alt-A loans, fall somewhere between prime and subprime loans. Jumbo loans, Choice *D*, are classified as such due to the high loan amount. While they have some risks, lenders generally reserve jumbo loans for very creditworthy borrowers to minimize that risk.

30. D: An ideal debt-to-income ratio (DTI) is 28 percent for housing and 36 percent for total debt, although lower is typically better. A DTI ratio of 0, Choice *A*, would suggest that the borrower has no debts or housing payments and therefore cannot demonstrate creditworthiness and an ability to repay. Choice *B* is the maximum allowable ratios for FHA loans. Choice *C,* although sometimes permissible, is higher than the ideal.

31. B: Asset fraud is a type of fraud in which someone lies about the total assets (personal property) they have, therefore receiving better loan terms. Choice *A* is a person who buys property for someone else illegally. Choice *C* is a type of fraud in which total income is not accurate. Choice *D* is lying about employment status and employment history.

32. D: Who acts as the settlement agent has no bearing on a mortgage loan's interest rate. Choices *A, B,* and *C,* along with the borrower's creditworthiness, can all impact the interest rate.

33. A: An IRRRL is a VA Interest Rate Reduction Refinance Loan, used to refinance an existing loan into a new loan solely to lower the interest rate. Choices *B, C,* and *D* are incorrect.

34. B: The only organization here that's a part of the Department of Housing and Urban Development is the Federal Housing Administration (FHA). The U.S. Treasury is a separate department, so Choice *D* is incorrect. The Consumer Financial Protection Bureau is part of the Department of the Treasury, so Choice *C* is also incorrect. The Federal Mortgage Protections Bureau is a made-up name, so Choice *A* is incorrect.

35. C: The Federal National Mortgage Association (Fannie Mae) is one of the two GSEs that purchase mortgages on the secondary market. The other is Choice *A*, Federal Home Loan Mortgage Corporation, or Freddie Mac. Choice *B*, the Federal Housing Administration (FHA), and Choice *D*, the Department of Veterans Affairs (VA), both guarantee loans but do not purchase them on the secondary market.

36. C: Appraisers must perform their duties professionally and fairly. If they are business partners with the borrower, they may be unable to perform their duties ethically due to a conflict of interest. Choice *A* is an example of discrimination. Choice *B* is prohibited by the Fair Credit Reporting Act (FCRA) and may be released only with the borrower's permission. Choice *D* is an example of coercion.

37. C: VantageScore is one of the two credit scoring models. It is not one of the three main credit bureaus, which are listed in Choices *A, B,* and *D.*

38. C: One of the key features of FHA loans is that borrowers can have much lower credit scores than with conventional mortgage loans, as low as 500. This makes qualifying for an FHA loan easier rather than more difficult, as in Choice *D*. FHA loans also sometimes allow a higher loan-to-value (LTV) ratio than conventional mortgage loans, not lower, as in Choice *A*. FHA loans do require home inspections (Choice *B*).

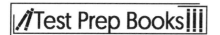

39. D: Depending on who is employing the services of the MLO, either the lender or the borrower will pay the MLO. It is not the sole responsibility of one of those parties, so Choices *A* and *B* are incorrect. An MLO should never be paid by both the lender and the borrower, as a conflict of dual compensation might arise, so Choice *C* is incorrect.

40. D: RESPA does not specifically define the duties of mortgage brokers. It does, however, eliminate referral fees and kickbacks, regulate the disclosure of financial and settlement costs to borrowers, and regulate and limit escrow accounts, Choices *A, B*, and *C*, respectively. In addition, RESPA also updated recordkeeping requirements for land title information.

41. A: Appearances of conflict of interest can exist even if there really is no conflict of interest between two parties. Business professionals must be wary of involving close, personal relationships in their business transactions. Choice *B* uses information such as race and marital status to provide unfair terms. Choice *C* involves lying about earned income to receive better terms. Choice *D* involves lying about total assets on an application.

42. B: A difference in property value changes the loan-to-value (LTV) ratio, which in turn can change the interest rate, loan program, or other terms of the mortgage. This necessitates a new Loan Estimate. The borrower cannot simply request a new disclosure, though they can request a new copy of a disclosure they were previously given; therefore, Choice *A* is incorrect. Choices *C* and *D* both fall under "no tolerance," and changes to these fees would not require a new Loan Estimate.

43. C: USDA loans are meant for low- to moderate-income borrowers; thus, the borrower's income cannot exceed 115 percent of the median income for their area. Choices *A, B*, and *D* are incorrect.

44. C: After the third consecutive failure of the MLO test, the mandatory retake waiting period is extended from 30 days to 180 days to give applicants more time to study and refocus themselves. One or two failures only have the normal 30-day waiting period, so Choices *A* and *B* are incorrect. If someone failed the test a fourth time, it would be the start of a new cycle, and they would also only have to wait 30 days, so Choice *D* is incorrect.

45. C: A universal loan identifier (ULI) is a special string of characters that acts as a unique identifier for any given loan. A credit score is a general measure of how likely someone is to repay their obligations on time, so Choice *A* is incorrect. Lien status refers to which entity retains rights to a piece of property, so Choice *B* is also incorrect. Monetary instrument logs (MILs) are reports that are filed if cash purchases of monetary instruments between a value of $3,000 and $10,000 are made, so Choice *D* is incorrect.

46. A: MLOs don't have to wait to renew an inactive license; they may do so immediately online. Because there is no need to wait, Choices *B, C,* and *D* are all incorrect.

47. A: HELOCs use the borrower's property as collateral for the loan. Insurance coverage has little effect on a HELOC and isn't used as collateral, so Choice *B* is incorrect. While their credit score may be at risk if they don't handle the loan properly, it isn't collateral for the loan, so Choice *C* is also incorrect. Using other possessions as collateral isn't uncommon in some life situations, but for a proper home equity line of credit (HELOC) it must be the borrower's property used, so Choice *D* is incorrect.

48. C: The borrower has worked for nine months, so the year-to-date income should be divided by nine to determine the monthly income amount. Choices *A, B*, and *D* are either too few months or too many months.

49. D: 12 CFR Part 1014 Regulation N requires all financial institutions to retain copies of their commercial communication for at least twenty-four months from the last date it was used. Any shorter is illegal, so Choices *A*, *B*, and *C* are all incorrect.

50. B: When a mortgage is assumed, payment liability is transferred from the home's seller to the buyer. The former borrower is removed from the mortgage, and the new homeowner becomes responsible for seeing the mortgage to amortization. Because the former borrower is removed, Choice *A* is incorrect. The lending institution wants the loan repaid, but they do not become responsible for making payments to themselves, so Choice *C* is incorrect. Choice *D* is incorrect because with the exception of making sure the transaction is in order, the local government has nothing to do with a private mortgage between an individual and a financial institution.

51. D: Loans originated after 2013 and having less than a 10 percent down payment will require MIP for the life of the loan. Private mortgage insurance (PMI) on a conventional mortgage loan can be canceled once the LTV reaches 80 percent, Choice *C*, but that does not apply to government mortgage insurance. Choices *A* and *B* are made-up answers.

52. C: A kickback is any payment or compensation given to a company in exchange for preferential treatment. Choice *A* is acceptable marketing practice because the appraiser is offering a discount to any borrower who uses their service in a given month. Mortgage brokers are permitted to offer borrowers suggestions for service providers, as in Choice *B*, as long as they do not give preferential treatment to any one of them. Borrowers are able to choose their own service providers for some mortgage services, and there is no requirement or rule against using someone they know, as in choice *D*.

53. B: The Fair Housing Act is a subsection of the larger Civil Rights Act. Choices *A*, *C*, and *D* are therefore incorrect.

54. D: MLOs are the only entity licensed to perform negotiations of mortgage terms; they cannot receive assistance or have someone else perform this for them, even if only as a mouthpiece. MLOs can, however, get assistance with any kind of clerical work. Assessments, filing paperwork, and writing emails are all tasks that others are allowed to perform for an MLO in their line of work, so Choices *A*, *B*, and *C* are all incorrect.

55. B: The Department of Housing and Urban Development did not participate in issuing this guidance. The guidance was issued by the agencies listed in Choices *A*, *C*, and *D*, along with the Federal Deposit Insurance Corporation.

56. A: The Loan Estimate form provides the borrower with a breakdown of the expected costs of the mortgage loan to compare with the Closing Disclosure. Choices *B*, *C*, and *D* are made-up answers.

57. D: A power of attorney document gives a third party the legal authority to sign documents on behalf of an individual who is incapacitated or otherwise unable to be physically present to sign the documents. Choice *A*, the HUD-1, is an old closing document that was replaced by the Closing Disclosure in 2015. Choice *B*, promissory note, is the document that borrowers sign as a commitment to repay the loan according to the agreed-upon terms. Choice *C* refers to the Equal Credit Opportunity Act (ECOA).

58. A: The Federal Bureau of Investigation conducts background checks on prospective MLOs to ensure they have not committed any felonies or other criminal activities. The National Mortgage Loan Registry sounds similar to the National Mortgage Licensing System and Registry, but is a fake name, so Choice *B* is incorrect. The Mortgage Loan Originator Security Bureau is a fake name, so Choice *C* is incorrect. The Department of Housing and Urban Development does not have anything to do with background checks on MLOs, so Choice *D* is incorrect.

59. B: Lenders consult an index of information that describes the cost to the lender of borrowing money on credit markets in order to determine the adjustments to be made to an adjustable-rate mortgage (ARM). They don't consult indexes of competitors' interest rates, the current state of the housing market, or the risk to interest rate stability, so Choices *A*, *C*, and *D* are all incorrect.

60. B: Zero tolerance fees cannot change between the initial Loan Estimate and the Closing Disclosure, except under very specific circumstances. Choice *A*, no tolerance fees, can change within reason as long as the lender disclosed the fees in good faith and made an effort to provide accurate information to the borrower. Choice *C*, 10 percent tolerance fees, can cumulatively change within 10 percent of the originally disclosed figures. Choice *D* is a made-up answer.

61. C: The focus of the act was setting clear rules about how to cancel private mortgage insurance (PMI), so it is also called the PMI Cancellation Act. The Home Mortgage Disclosure Act (HMDA) is a different act that was passed in 1975, so Choice *B* is incorrect. Both Choice *A* and Choice *D* are made-up act names, so they are incorrect.

62. B: Fraud, or lying and providing misleading information, is commonly committed for profit. Choice *A* refers to a situation in which close, personal relationships may jeopardize the integrity of a transaction. Choice *C* uses information such as race and marital status to provide unfair terms or deny service. Choice *D* is an illicit payment received after providing services to someone.

63. A: An adjustable-rate mortgage (ARM) is one in which the interest rate varies based on current market conditions. A fixed-rate mortgage, Choice *D*, is one in which the interest rate does not change throughout the course of a loan. Choices *B* and *C* are made-up answers.

64. B: Temporary authority is a situation in which an MLO can continue to perform MLO-related duties for up to fourteen days while updating or addressing state-specific registration requirements. Origination grace period, situational forgiveness, and business authority are all false terms, so Choices *A*, *C*, and *D* are all incorrect.

65. C: The loan origination fee is a zero-tolerance fee, meaning that is cannot be changed once it is disclosed on the Loan Estimate form, and it cannot be changed from the Loan Estimate form to the Closing Disclosure. Choices *A, B*, and *D* all represent acceptable changed circumstances that would require a revised Loan Estimate form.

66. C: The origination fee is considered a finance charge for the loan. The homeowner's insurance premiums, Choice *B*, are collected on behalf of the borrower and are paid to the insurance company. Choices *A* and *D* are both closing costs, but they are not considered finance charges since they are not money the lender makes on the loan.

67. D: FHA loans are generally designed for borrowers with lower credit scores and/or lower down payment amounts. Secondary mortgages, Choice *A*, are loans that hold a secondary lien position on the title; these are generally more difficult to get. Borrowers with higher credit scores and/or larger down payments can usually qualify for conventional mortgage loans, Choice *B*. VA loans, Choice *C*, are specifically for military borrowers.

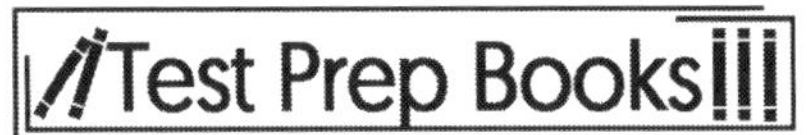

68. A: Ethics is a guiding principle that all professionals in the mortgage industry must follow. Choices *B*, *C*, and *D* are not the terms used to signify the ethical business practices that professionals must follow.

69. B: If you double the interest rate of an interest-only mortgage, the situation of the loan's repayment has still not really changed. Repaying the principal in full, converting to an amortizing loan, or renegotiating the loan's terms are the only ways of developing an interest-only mortgage to eventual maturity, so Choices *A*, *C*, and *D* are all incorrect.

70. A: RESPA specifies six pieces of information that make up a borrower's loan application. Those six items include the borrower's name, monthly income, social security number, the address and value of the property, and the requested loan amount. The borrower's birthday is not a required piece of information under RESPA. However, lenders often require additional information, which is permitted but is not specified under RESPA. Choices *B, C*, and *D* are all part of the required information per RESPA guidelines.

71. C: The sales comparison approach uses recently sold properties as comparable properties, or "comps," to determine the value of the subject property. The cost approach, Choice *A*, involves determining the replacement value of the property, and the income approach, Choice *B*, determines the income potential of a commercial property as part of the property valuation. Choice *D* is a made-up answer.

72. A: Non-arm's length transactions are business transactions between people who have a close connection and may cause others to believe there is a conflict of interest, even if there is not. Choice *B* is the opposite, in which unrelated parties engage in business. Choice *C* is lying during the business transaction. Choice *D* is a method of refusing to do business with someone due to discrimination.

73. C: The top of the TIL includes the APR, the finance charge, the amount financed, and the total payments. The chart also includes brief explanations of each figure, such as the APR being "the cost of your credit as a yearly rate." Choices *A, B*, and *D* are made-up answers. The chart does not include the interest rate nor the monthly payment amount, though the monthly payment information can be found in another section of the TIL.

74. C: A credit report provides the lender with the borrower's credit score and credit history, and it shows how the borrower handles their debt (Choices *A*, *B*, and *D*). The report does not include income information, making Choice *C* the correct answer.

75. B: If the borrower of a reverse mortgage passes away, the executors of the borrower's estate or the borrower's relatives are responsible for seeing the obligation of the reverse mortgage fulfilled. There is not necessarily a secondary borrower named in advance, so Choice *A* is incorrect. The city government is not responsible for a private citizen's financial obligations, so Choice *C* is also incorrect. The mortgage obligation is not simply forgiven or ignored, so Choice *D* is incorrect.

76. C: The lender must inform the borrower of the credit decision with a Notice of Action Taken within thirty days. Three days, Choice *A*, is the required time for providing the borrower with the initial Loan Estimate. The lender may take adverse action if the borrower does not expressly accept the loan offer within ninety days, Choice *D*. Choice *B* is also incorrect.

77. B: The second page of the Closing Disclosure shows a breakdown of all of the costs of the loan, broken down into three columns: "Borrower-Paid," "Seller-Paid," and "Paid by Others." The first page of the document, Choice *A*, is very similar to the Loan Estimate form and shows the borrower's information, the property, the type of loan, and the terms of the loan, as well as payment information. Page three, Choice *C*, shows the calculations used to arrive at the borrower's cash to close and a summary of the transaction. Page four, Choice *D*, includes additional disclosures and contact information for the loan parties.

78. C: During a house's construction, only the interest on a construction mortgage must be paid. Afterwards, the principal is either paid in full or converted to a standard mortgage. Principal payments don't have to be made as the house is being built, so Choices *A* and *B* are incorrect. Payments do still have to be made on interest, however, so Choice *D* is incorrect.

79. D: The loan processor collects all of the documentation, verifies employment, orders the title and appraisal, and pre-underwrites the loan before it is sent to the underwriter for approval. The loan originator and loan broker, Choices *A* and *B*, take the borrower's initial application and collect their documentation, but they do not usually pre-underwrite the loan. The underwriter and sometimes the processor work for the lender, Choice *C*.

80. A: Unusually high commission rates are a red flag that clients need to be wary of. Choice *B* is any information that could influence the value of a property, which is not the case for an agent's commission. Choice *C* does not recognize that this is a red flag. Choice *D* is a conflict of interest.

81. A: Calculating income from tax returns involves adding up the total income from each return and dividing by the total months (twenty-four months when using two years of returns). In this case, the total income is $110,400, divided by twenty-four equals an average monthly income of $4600. Choice *B* includes a twelve-month calculation based on the first-year income ($45,000), and Choice *C* includes a twelve-month calculation based on the second year income ($65,400). Choice *D* adds both years but then only divides by twelve rather than twenty-four.

82. B: Underwriters perform risk assessment on potential borrowers to give an analysis to the MLO. They aren't in charge of paperwork outside of that, so Choice *A* is incorrect. They don't communicate with either the lender or borrower on behalf of the MLO, so Choices *C* and *D* are also incorrect.

83. D: ECOA was primarily designed to prevent discrimination against borrowers based on factors unrelated to their ability to repay the loan. Choices *A* and *B* are both addressed under RESPA, and Choice *C* is prevented by the Truth in Lending Act (TILA).

84. D: VA loans do not have maximum DTI ratios, although lower is generally considered better. Choice *A* includes the ideal DTI ratios. Choice *B* is the maximum DTI allowed for FHA loans, and Choice *C* is a made-up answer.

85. A: Lenders cannot require that a borrower include their spouse on a loan application. Choices *B, C,* and *D*, however, are permitted in the lender's evaluation of the creditworthiness of a borrower and the value of the property being financed.

86. C: Hazard insurance covers the property in the event of a natural disaster, such as fire, tornado, or hurricane. Homeowner's insurance, Choice *A*, offers a wider range of coverage, including personal property and liability. Flood insurance, Choice *B*, specifically covers the property in the event of flood damage. Mortgage insurance, Choice *D*, protects the lender in the event of default on the mortgage loan.

87. B: A balloon payment is a type of scheduled payment that becomes rapidly more expensive and was prohibited under the Dodd-Frank Act. There isn't an alternate name for payments by mail, so Choice *D* is incorrect. Both Choices *A* and *C* also have rising action to them in a sense, but balloon payments don't start high, nor do they move around a financial institution's authority, so they are both incorrect.

88. C: The act of bait-and-switch sale tactics with regard to mortgages involves advertising mortgage products in a different way than what the borrower receives as the final product, such as advertising at a lower interest rate than the final mortgage will actually have. Colluding with a real estate agent is a prohibited act, but it is not representative of bait-and-switch tactics, so Choice *A* is incorrect. Choices *B* and *D* both involve concealing information either from the borrower or from the CFPB, both of which are prohibited, but because neither has to do with bait-and-switch tactics, they are both incorrect.

89. B: People who agree to federal mortgage loans typically have poor income or credit. They must purchase private mortgage insurance (PMI) on the loan, which is an extra fee added to each monthly payment that protects lenders if the borrower defaults. Choice *A* is compensation that lenders receive for offering high-interest-rate loans. Choice *C* is an agreement to guarantee that the interest rate will not increase until a borrower has finished applying for a loan. Choice *D* refers to a way for borrowers to lower the upfront costs of a loan in exchange for a higher interest rate.

90. C: The title refers to the legal property ownership. It is not a physical document showing ownership, Choice *A*, or transfer of ownership, Choice *D*. Choice *B* refers to the bundle of rights, which includes the five specific rights that are transferred when a buyer purchases a property.

91. A: The Consumer Financial Protection Bureau warns against reverse mortgages due to a high risk of misleading language and the possibility of fraud against the borrower. There is no mention of the impact to economic growth, so Choice *B* is incorrect. Many verified lenders will still offer reverse mortgages, so claiming they are only offered by irresponsible lenders is wrong, making Choice *C* incorrect. Homeowners insurance is required for all mortgages, so Choice *D* is also incorrect.

92. D: The Consumer Financial Protection Bureau was established in 2010 as part of the Dodd-Frank Act. 2001 is when several terrorist attacks in the U.S. took place, which led to the Patriot Act, but that act didn't create the CFPB, so Choice *C* is incorrect. 2008 is when the financial crash that led to the Dodd-Frank Act happened, but the CFPB wasn't created until the act passed two years later, so Choice *B* is also incorrect. 2013 is too late, so Choice *A* is incorrect.

93. C: RESPA ensures that all settlement costs are disclosed prior to any transaction and also requires all relationships between any service providers to be made clear. Choice *A* was passed to provide guidance on redlining. Choice *B* outlined and prohibited discriminatory business practices. Choice *D* provides protection to people for housing-related activities.

94. C: The Notice of Right to Cancel form explains the cancellation rules and provides information on how to cancel the loan should the borrower decide they do not want to proceed with refinancing during the three-day right of rescission. Choices *A, B*, and *D* are made-up answers.

95. C: HOEPA is the Home Ownership and Equity Protection Act. It protects consumers from high interest rates and fees on refinance and home equity mortgage loans. Choices *A, B*, and *D* are made-up answers.

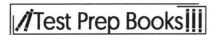

96. C: Balloon in balloon mortgage refers to a single large lump payment made at the end of the mortgage's term. It doesn't refer to the payment costs, interest rate, or property value, so Choices *A*, *B*, and *D* are all incorrect.

97. B: Currency transaction reports are filed with the Financial Crimes Enforcement Network (FinCEN). The Consumer Financial Protection Bureau (CFPB) may become involved depending on the situation, but it is not who the reports are primarily sent to, so Choice *D* is incorrect. The Central Intelligence Agency (CIA) and Federal Bureau of Investigation (FBI) likewise may only become involved depending on the crime or situation, so Choices *A* and *C* are also incorrect.

98. D: Coercion is a relatively recent addition to RESPA and is forcing the borrower to make decisions that are not in their best interest. Choice *A* is discrimination based on ethnicity or race. Choice *B* is recommending certain services to others. Choice *C* is compensation received for referrals.

99. A: Seller concessions cannot exceed the total closing costs of a loan, regardless of loan type or down payment amount. Conventional mortgage loans do allow seller concessions of 3 percent, Choice *B*; 6 percent, Choice *C*; and 9 percent, Choice *D*; but only if those amounts do not exceed the total closing costs.

100. D: Credit reports compile financial information about consumers, such as their bill repayment history, liens, and bankruptcies to use as an indicator of how likely they are to repay obligations. Choice *A* is incorrect because a currency transaction report is filed anytime a cash transaction exceeds $10,000 in a single day. Financial accuracy report and identity report are both made-up terms, so Choices *B* and *C* are incorrect.

101. A: It is not the settlement agent's responsibility to determine whether the property is acceptable collateral for the mortgage loan. The underwriter and/or lender would have already made that determination before approving the mortgage loan. The settlement agent is responsible for the tasks listed in Choices *B, C*, and *D*.

102. A: The second subtitle of Title III of the Patriot Act made it easier for law enforcement to receive information about and pursue money laundering cases. Choices *B* and *D* are both results of the first subtitle, and Choice *C* is a result of the third subtitle, so they are all incorrect.

103. A: The Federal Housing Administration (FHA) is the organization that sets many mortgage standards and is responsible for making fixed-rate mortgages the most common choice of home loan. Neither the Federal Reserve nor the Treasury Department has anything to do with mortgages, so Choices *B* and *C* are incorrect. The National Mortgage Lenders Association is a false term, so Choice *D* is incorrect.

104. D: VA loans are often financed at 100 percent LTV, meaning that they do not require any down payment. Conventional mortgage loans, Choice *A*, usually require 20 percent down, although subprime loans, Choice *B*, can sometimes be less than that. FHA loans, Choice *C*, usually require at least 3 percent down.

105. B: Oral consent or recordings are not accepted as a form of electronic signature for consent. Choice *A* is incorrect because electronic signatures may take the form of any sound, symbol, or process that is associated with the contract and adopted with the intent to sign. Choice *C* is incorrect because all electronic signatures must be a form of affirmative consent; assuming consent at any point is not valid. Choice *D* is incorrect because electronic agreements made prior to October 1, 2000, are grandfathered in under the E-Sign Act and are accepted.

106. C: Kickbacks are similar to bribes or gifts for services and referrals. Choice *A* is the compensation that agents and officers fairly receive for their services. Choice *B* is required by RESPA. Choice *D* is the act of redlining.

107. B: Finder's fees are rewards for referring clients to certain services, which is under heavy regulation by RESPA. Choice *A* is a fraudulent activity to receive unfair terms. Choice *C* is a potential conflict of interest. Choice *D* is using coercion to unfairly influence decision making.

108. D: The lien is collateral listed on a document to protect lenders if a borrower defaults on loan payments. If the borrower defaults, the lien is then seized by the lender. Choices *A*, *B*, and *C* do not have anything to do with defaulting on a loan. Choice *A* refers to the annual interest generated on a loan. Choice *B* is the act of conveyance. Choice *C* is an option for some loans, where interest is accrued daily.

109. B: PITI stands for principal, interest, taxes, and insurance. It represents the total amount of money that the borrower will pay each month towards the principal balance and interest on the loan as well as the monthly tax and insurance payments. It is not part of the closing costs for a mortgage. Choices *A, C,* and *D* are all typical closing costs involved in obtaining a mortgage loan.

110. D: The Good-Faith Estimate (GFE) was replaced by the Loan Estimate form for loans after 2015. Choice *A*, the Closing Disclosure form, is a form that is provided to borrowers just prior to closing. It replaces the HUD-1 Settlement Statement, Choice *B*. The Truth in Lending (TIL) form, Choice *C*, is still a required disclosure.

111. A: Those committing fraud usually do so for profit or to maintain ownership of a property. Choices *B*, *C*, and *D* are factors that do not typically lead to a decision to commit fraud.

112. A: Subordination is the process of determining which loans are paid off first if a borrower defaults on a loan. Choice *B* refers to the act of transferring ownership of property from one person to another. Choice *C* is when the service provider for a borrower changes. Choice *D* is included with a Good Faith Estimate (GFE) or Loan Estimate and determines which fees may or may not increase.

113. D: The Right of Disposition gives the property owner the right to rent, sell, or transfer ownership of the property. The Right of Control, Choice *A*, means that the owner can use the property as they wish. Choice *B*, the Right of Possession, gives the owner the right to possess the property, and the Right of Exclusion, Choice *C*, allows the owner to control who is permitted to enter the property.

114. C: Straw buyers buy property for others and then relinquish the property to the actual owner. Choice *A* is an example of a conflict of interest. Choice *B* is an example of a finder's fee. Choice *D* is the job of a loan officer.

115. C: The Federal Trade Commission (FTC) created the Red Flags rules to push financial institutions into creating Identity Theft Prevention Programs. The Office of Housing Counseling, Consumer Financial Protection Bureau, and Supreme Court have nothing to do with the creation of the Red Flags rules, so Choices *A*, *B*, and *D* are all incorrect.

116. C: Instead of renting out the property as an investment, this property is used as a primary residence. Choice *A* is lying about total income in a given time frame. Choice *B* occurs because people want to receive better interest rates from lenders by stating that the property is owner-occupied or that the person who owns the property also uses it as their primary residence when they are using it as a rental property instead. Choice *D* is lying about the total assets in a person's portfolio.

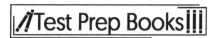

117. D: Loaning a portion of the down payment for a larger loan is one form of what's called a purchase-money second mortgage. It isn't related to a line of credit loan, usually called a home equity line of credit (HELOC), so Choice *C* is incorrect. Choices *A* and *B* are both false loan names, so they are incorrect.

118. A: Title insurance ensures that there are no undisclosed encumbrances, liens, or claims to a property. It is most commonly issued to lenders who hold the mortgage loan for the property, though homeowners can obtain their own title insurance policies as well. Choice *B*, damages to structures on the property, may sometimes (but not always) be disclosed on the appraisal. Joint tenancies, Choice *C*, indicates one possible means of holding title. Choice *D* is an irrelevant answer because it has nothing to do with title insurance and is therefore incorrect.

119. A: A privacy policy dictates what information about their consumers a financial institution collects and how it uses that information. End-user license agreements are a related policy document specifically for computer software, so Choice *B* is incorrect. Data collection policy and safeguard agreement are made-up terms, so Choices *C* and *D* are also incorrect.

120. D: Closing fees are due after a loan is secured for the borrower. Choices *A* and *C* do not require closing fees. Choice *B* requires finder's fees after a successful referral.

Practice Test #2

1. What are tolerances?
    a. The number of debts a borrower can have compared to their income
    b. The ratio of the loan amount compared to the property value
    c. The maximum loan amount permitted by the loan program
    d. The limitations on cost variations between the Loan Estimate and the Closing Disclosure

2. What does the acronym HELOC stand for?
    a. Home Equity Line of Credit
    b. Housing Equity Loan or Credit
    c. Home Equity Loan or Credit
    d. Household Expenses Line of Credit

3. What is due diligence for a loan originator?
    a. Verifying application information and understanding the terms of the loan
    b. Learning about the local homeowner's association and defining property lines
    c. Encouraging consumers to sign up for loans with high interest rates and borrowing fees
    d. Sharing borrower information with third parties without their permission

4. At what point can the borrower in a HELOC no longer borrow more money?
    a. As soon as they make their first repayment
    b. After they have borrowed the full amount
    c. Until the end of the repayment period
    d. As soon as the repayment period begins

5. What is annual interest that is broken down into smaller, regular amounts of time?
    a. Accrual rate
    b. Periodic interest
    c. APR
    d. Amortization

6. What is the absolute minimum penalty for a single violation of compliance with MLO rules?
    a. One year of prison time
    b. $50,000 fine plus six months of prison time
    c. $10,000 fine plus necessary remedial action
    d. $5000 fine plus license probation

7. RESPA can be found under which section of the Code of Federal Regulations?
    a. Title 12, Chapter 10
    b. Title 12, Chapter 2
    c. Title 12, Chapter 6
    d. Title 12, Chapter 15

8. Which of the following are the two credit scoring models used by the three main credit bureaus?
    a. FICO and Experian
    b. FICO and VantageScore
    c. VantageScore and TransUnion
    d. TransUnion and Equifax

9. When a borrower falls behind on making mortgage loan payments, the lender is required to contact the borrower within what time frame following the first delinquency?
    a. Thirty days
    b. Forty-five days
    c. Sixty days
    d. Ninety days

10. USDA loans are designed to help borrowers purchase homes in what areas?
    a. Urban and metropolitan areas
    b. Rural and agricultural areas
    c. Suburban areas
    d. Overseas

11. What organization enforces rules regarding MLOs and mortgages?
    a. Department of the Treasury
    b. Department of Housing and Urban Development
    c. Consumer Financial Protection Bureau
    d. Federal Housing Administration

12. A consumer is able to decline to share their personal information with third parties because of which law?
    a. Fair Housing Act
    b. Dodd-Frank Act
    c. Civil Rights Act
    d. Fair Credit Reporting Act

13. Per ECOA rules, how long must lenders keep loan applications on file?
    a. Twelve months
    b. Twenty-five months
    c. Thirty-six months
    d. Sixty months

14. What are the two key topics that a loan originator may NOT ask a borrower about during the loan application process?
    a. Race and ethnicity
    b. Family planning and ethnicity
    c. Health and family planning
    d. Health and employment

15. Which organization implements the ability to repay rule?
    a. Department of Housing and Urban Development
    b. Consumer Financial Protection Bureau
    c. Federal National Mortgage Association
    d. Federal Home Loan Mortgage Corporation

16. What is the time period for the annual MLO license renewal with the National Mortgage Licensing System and Registry (NMLS)?
    a. December 1 through January 31
    b. November 1 through December 31
    c. August 1 through September 30
    d. March 1 through April 30

17. Tony is purchasing a home from Jasmine. The annual property taxes are $3000, and the closing is happening at the end of May. How much will each of them pay in taxes at closing?
    a. Jasmine will pay $1500; Tony will pay $1500.
    b. Jasmine will pay $1250; Tony will pay $1750.
    c. Jasmine will pay $1750; Tony will pay $1250.
    d. Jasmine will pay $1000; Tony will pay $2000.

18. What type of interest rate calculation is based on the current rates, points, and loan pricing being offered for low-risk mortgage loans?
    a. Annual percentage rate
    b. First-lien mortgage rate
    c. Subordinate mortgage rate
    d. Average prime offer rate

19. A borrower becomes incapacitated during a car crash and is unable to make their own decisions. Prior to this accident, he signed a document that allowed another person to act on his behalf. What is this document known as?
    a. Steering
    b. Fee splitting
    c. Due diligence
    d. POA

20. Which of the following is a crime that, if convicted, will cause an MLO to immediately and permanently have their license revoked?
    a. Fraud
    b. Aggravated battery
    c. Driving under the influence of alcohol
    d. Burglary

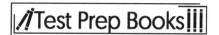

21. If a lender has a maximum allowable debt-to-income (DTI) ratio of 45 percent and a borrower has a total monthly income of $4000, how much can the borrower have in total monthly debt, including housing?
    a. $1800
    b. $89
    c. $890
    d. $2000

22. Steering refers to which action taken by a mortgage broker?
    a. Directing a borrower towards a more favorable loan with lower costs
    b. Suggesting a certain title company that has lower costs than another
    c. Directing a borrower towards a less favorable loan in order to gain additional compensation
    d. Requiring that the borrower use a specific homeowners insurance company in exchange for additional compensation

23. After a service transfer, within how many days must a company inform a borrower of changes concerning their loan?
    a. Five days
    b. Ten days
    c. Fifteen days
    d. Twenty days

24. Why are licensing requirements for MLOs taken very seriously?
    a. To protect lenders and their capital
    b. To catch criminals trying to conduct money laundering
    c. To ensure a fair transaction between borrowers and lenders
    d. To make the licensing process more rigorous

25. One of the key concerns with regards to issuing nontraditional loans is the large increase in payment that happens when introductory loan terms, such as interest-only payment periods, expire. This is commonly referred to as what?
    a. Interest rate hike
    b. Payment shock
    c. Balloon payment
    d. Negative amortization

26. Consumers are able to request a free credit report every year thanks to which act?
    a. Fair and Accurate Credit Transactions Act
    b. Fair Credit Reporting Act
    c. Gramm-Leach-Bliley Act
    d. Public Credit Information Act

27. What is amortization?
    a. The monthly periodic interest payments on a loan
    b. The process lenders use to maintain a fixed monthly loan payment amount
    c. The amount of money a borrower pays in exchange for a loan
    d. The money a borrower invests towards purchasing a property

28. When an MLO has been inactive for five years, they will need to retake the Secure and Fair Enforcement (SAFE) test to reactivate their license. What percentage of questions will they need to answer correctly to be eligible to reactivate their license?
    a. 55 percent
    b. 60 percent
    c. 75 percent
    d. 90 percent

29. How large of a down payment would be expected for a construction mortgage?
    a. 5–10 percent
    b. 20–25 percent
    c. 10–15 percent
    d. 30–35 percent

30. An appraiser must disclose if a certain property has already been appraised within how many years?
    a. One
    b. Three
    c. Five
    d. Seven

31. Which of the following is NOT included in a title search?
    a. A list of past owners and the dates of ownership
    b. Any unpaid liens or taxes on the property
    c. Contested ownership, including disputed wills
    d. A clear title insurance policy

32. Before obtaining consent to use electronic signatures from a consumer, what information do financial institutions have to disclose?
    a. That electronic signatures are superseded by pen-and-paper signatures by law
    b. Whether or not consent will be assumed if they do not answer
    c. What an electronic signature is
    d. If the approval of electronic signatures applies only to one transaction or to several over time

33. If the borrower of an interest-only mortgage loan also wants to start repaying the principal with their monthly payments, what is the best option for them to use?
    a. Contact the lender and inform them of additional payments.
    b. Wait until the interest-only period ends and then make payments on the principal.
    c. Pay the principal off in one lump sum.
    d. Add more to what they pay in the interest-only monthly payment.

34. An MLO changes jobs, moving from one financial institution to another. If they leave their job on a Monday, what is the last day of the week they can report the employment change to the NMLS without being penalized for late reporting?
    a. Friday
    b. Wednesday
    c. Sunday
    d. Saturday

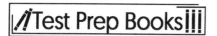

35. What is the date of final termination for private mortgage insurance (PMI)?
    a. The seventh day of the ninth month after loan repayment begins
    b. The seventh day of the month that the midpoint of the loan's repayment period occurs in
    c. The first day of the month after the first year of the loan repayment period
    d. The first day of the month following the midpoint of the loan's repayment period

36. What is the purpose of a cushion in an escrow account?
    a. To ensure that there is enough money in the account to pay the annual property taxes and homeowner's insurance premiums
    b. To protect the lender if the borrower does not make one of the monthly mortgage payments
    c. To pay any unforeseen liens or claims against the property
    d. To finance any additional charges not listed on the Closing Disclosure

37. The Dodd-Frank Act was passed as a result of a major economic downturn in what year?
    a. 2008
    b. 1929
    c. 1990
    d. 2001

38. Federal law prohibits advertisements that may be perceived as discriminatory due to the passing of which law?
    a. Fair Housing Act
    b. Dodd-Frank Act
    c. Real Estate Settlement Procedures Act
    d. Gramm-Leach-Bliley Act

39. How much is the minimum down payment on the most common mortgages?
    a. 5 percent
    b. 3 percent
    c. 10 percent
    d. 8 percent

40. In order for a mortgage loan originator (MLO) to impose force-placed insurance on a borrower, the MLO must be reasonably certain of what behavior from the borrower?
    a. An intent to refinance a mortgage with a different servicer
    b. Attempted identity theft or money laundering
    c. Failing to comply with property insurance or loan obligations
    d. An outstanding arrest warrant for criminal activity

41. If a revised Loan Estimate is required, the disclosure must be provided to the borrower within which timeframe?
    a. At least four days prior to closing
    b. At least one week prior to closing
    c. Within five days of the change in terms
    d. Within three days of the loan application

42. Which of the following is NOT one of the possible actions a lender can take on a loan application?
    a. Approval
    b. Making a counteroffer
    c. Adverse action
    d. Requiring a co-signer

43. Sally, a borrower requesting a home purchase mortgage loan, has provided her loan officer with her name, social security number, income, and the address of the property she wishes to buy. When will she receive her Loan Estimate from the loan officer?
    a. Within three business days
    b. When she submits a request in writing
    c. When the property appraisal is done
    d. When she tells the loan officer the estimated property value and a requested loan amount

44. If a borrower pays 5 percent down on their FHA home mortgage, how long will they be required to pay mortgage insurance?
    a. Five years
    b. Eight years
    c. Eleven years
    d. The length of the loan term

45. Which of the following is NOT something a prospective mortgage loan originator (MLO) needs to provide during their initial registration?
    a. Their birth city and country
    b. Employment history
    c. Civil lawsuit history
    d. Fingerprints

46. Before finalizing mortgage terms, a lender discovers that a property the borrower listed as purely an investment property is actually their primary residence. This is an example of which type of fraud?
    a. Asset fraud
    b. Reverse occupancy fraud
    c. Employment fraud
    d. Occupancy fraud

47. Violations of the TILA-RESPA Integrated Disclosure Rule (TRID) can incur fines in which of the following ranges?
    a. $1,000 to $50,000 per day
    b. $1,000 to $50,000 per month
    c. $5,000 to $100,000 per day
    d. $5,000 to $100,000 per month

48. Escrow accounts hold funds that will be used to pay for what?
    a. Missed mortgage payments
    b. Extra interest paid by the borrower
    c. Extra principal paid by the borrower
    d. Taxes and insurance

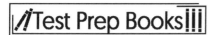

49. The acronym GSEs refers to which agencies?
    a. Government-sponsored enterprises
    b. Government-subsidized enterprises
    c. Government-sponsored entities
    d. Government-subsidized entities

50. Which of the following types of state-level organizations is most likely to hire an MLO?
    a. Benefits distributor
    b. Court system
    c. Infrastructure planning
    d. Financial regulator

51. Which document transfers ownership of a property from one party to another?
    a. Title
    b. Deed
    c. Closing Disclosure
    d. Purchase Contract

52. What is phishing?
    a. Using a fake website or email to illegitimately obtain private information
    b. The act of violating the National Do Not Call Registry
    c. Breaking into a financial database to steal private information
    d. Impersonating someone else to take advantage of their credit

53. What is the title of a staff member who assists an MLO by verifying information and collecting all the necessary paperwork for the loan application?
    a. Underwriter
    b. Loan processor
    c. Mortgage clerk
    d. Bank teller

54. What is the normal fee splitting rate for joint marketing?
    a. Ten/ninety
    b. Twenty/eighty
    c. Thirty/seventy
    d. Fifty/fifty

55. Which loans are designed for members of the military?
    a. USDA loans
    b. FHA loans
    c. VA loans
    d. Conventional mortgage loans

56. Which of the following actions is part of taking a loan application that ONLY the MLO is legally allowed to perform?
    a. Verifying the accuracy of information on the application
    b. Determining if the applicant qualifies for a mortgage based on the information provided
    c. Explaining what information is required for the application
    d. Assisting the consumer through the application submission steps

57. If a borrower closes on a refinance loan on a Thursday, which day is the end of the right of rescission period?
    a. Saturday
    b. Sunday
    c. Monday
    d. Tuesday

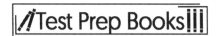

58. Why would someone list a non-resident co-borrower on a mortgage loan?
    a. To receive a commission from referrals
    b. To help secure a mortgage loan
    c. To illegally maintain continued ownership of a property
    d. To obtain a higher mortgage interest rate

59. What does a PITI mortgage payment include?
    a. Principal, interest, taxes, insurance
    b. Payment, interest, taxes, insurance
    c. Principal, insurance, total, incidentals
    d. Principal, insurance, taxes, incidentals

60. Loans that qualify for purchase by Fannie Mae or Freddie Mac are called what?
    a. Secondary loans
    b. Federal loans
    c. Government loans
    d. Conforming loans

61. The borrower must be given the Closing Disclosure document at least how many days before the loan closing?
    a. One day
    b. Three days
    c. Seven days
    d. Four days

62. Nonconforming mortgage loans that exceed the maximum limits allowed by Fannie Mae or Freddie Mac are called what?
    a. Alt-A loans
    b. Jumbo loans
    c. Prime loans
    d. Subprime loans

63. How many rights are included in the bundle of rights that is transferred to a buyer upon purchase of a property?
    a. Three
    b. Four
    c. Five
    d. Six

64. A mother plans to purchase property on behalf of her son due to his poor credit history. After the purchase, she will transfer property rights over to her son. What is the mother guilty of doing?
   a. Redlining
   b. Steering
   c. Straw buying
   d. Asset fraud

65. Subprime borrowers are generally borrowers with credit scores below what?
   a. 500
   b. 580
   c. 620
   d. 700

66. Which of the following is NOT a topic of discussion during the loan inquiry?
   a. Whether the borrower intends to start a family
   b. Where the borrower is employed
   c. How much money the borrower will have for a down payment
   d. Whether the borrower has credit card debt

67. What is the most popular repayment term for a fixed-rate mortgage?
   a. 15 years
   b. 10 years
   c. 30 years
   d. 20 years

68. An initial escrow statement must be provided to the borrower within how many days of the loan closing?
   a. Ten days
   b. Thirty days
   c. Forty-five days
   d. Ninety days

69. Which of the following is a person who assists with gathering and verifying the borrower's information and preparing the loan package for submission?
   a. Processor
   b. Underwriter
   c. Lender
   d. Loan originator

70. Adjustable-rate mortgages (ARMs) have three limits on how much the interest rate can be changed. Which of the following is NOT one of those limits?
   a. How much the interest rate can change in the second half of the loan's term
   b. How big all changes after the first change to the interest rate can be
   c. How much the interest rate can change in total
   d. How big the first change to the interest rate can be

71. Which of the following is NOT something you can find on the Department of Housing and Urban Development's website?
    a. A step-by-step list on the process of becoming a homeowner
    b. A list of information necessary to comply with the Home Mortgage Disclosure Act
    c. FAQ lists for consumers and businesses for how to interact with their insurances, funds, and claims
    d. A list of approved lenders that accept FHA mortgage insurance

72. An appraiser is a family member of the person seeking a loan. This relationship may be perceived as which of the following?
    a. Power of attorney
    b. Conflict of interest
    c. Non-resident co-borrower
    d. Straw buyer

73. What does a 7/1 adjustable-rate mortgage (ARM) mean?
    a. The interest rate stays fixed for seven years and then adjusts every year after that.
    b. The monthly payment stays the same for the first seven years of the loan and then adjusts every month after that.
    c. The interest rate cannot change more than 1 percent over the first seven years of the loan.
    d. The interest rate can change by a maximum of 7 percent over the course of the loan, adjusted annually.

74. A customer comes to you looking to get a mortgage to finance the construction of a new house. Which of the following is NOT something you would need to see as part of their construction plan?
    a. A timeline for when they will move into the finished house
    b. Detailed blueprints and plans for construction
    c. The builder or construction team the customer has hired
    d. An estimated appraisal of the finished house

75. Which of the following aspects of loan information must be reported under the HMDA?
    a. The amount of the loan, if it is above a certain amount
    b. The loan's interest rate, if it is above a certain percentage
    c. The name of the borrower
    d. How many months until the interest rate may change

76. When considering the loan-to-value (LTV) ratio, what is the ideal initial down payment for a loan?
    a. 5 percent of the appraised property value
    b. 10 percent of the appraised property value
    c. 15 percent of the appraised property value
    d. 20 percent of the appraised property value

77. How should a lender handle a borrower who has a fluctuating income due to tips?
    a. Deny them service.
    b. Average the total amount of tips they have earned in the last two years.
    c. Request assistance from the Mortgage Bankers Association.
    d. Verify their employment with the Internal Revenue Service.

78. Which federal regulation dictates how loan originators and lenders protect the privacy of the borrower's information?
    a. Regulation X
    b. Regulation B
    c. Regulation Z
    d. Regulation P

79. Prior to December 2020, the debt-to-income ratio (DTI) was capped at what percent?
    a. 25 percent
    b. 28 percent
    c. 43 percent
    d. 50 percent

80. What type of loan is obtained when a borrower seeks to get a new loan against a property that they already own?
    a. Refinance loan
    b. Balloon mortgage loan
    c. Adjustable-rate mortgage
    d. Subordinate lien

81. What was the primary purpose of the Gramm-Leach-Bliley Act (GLBA)?
    a. To disclose the ways that financial institutions are protecting customer data
    b. To prevent buyers from overpaying on private mortgage insurance (PMI)
    c. To require all financial institutions to monitor suspicious financial transactions
    d. To outline what constitutes unfair, deceptive, or abusive acts and practices (UDAAP)

82. When the borrower chooses an appraiser from a list provided by the lender, which type of tolerance applies to the appraisal fee?
    a. No tolerance
    b. Zero tolerance
    c. 10 percent tolerance
    d. 15 percent tolerance

83. What is the purpose of making qualified mortgage loans for lenders?
    a. They will be guaranteed by FHA.
    b. They will be guaranteed by VA.
    c. They can be sold to private insurers.
    d. They can be sold on the secondary market.

84. Finders' fees are obtained after which of the following actions?
    a. Discrimination
    b. Income fraud
    c. Redlining
    d. Referrals

85. How many paystubs would be required to verify income for a borrower who is paid weekly?
    a. One
    b. Two
    c. Four
    d. Eight

86. An MLO wants to advertise their services to attract potential borrowers and get work. According to the CFPB, which of the following pieces of information is required to be present on all copies of the ad?
    a. The MLO's NMLS identifier
    b. The company the MLO works for
    c. The results of the MLO's last ten mortgage offers
    d. The MLO's phone number

87. What is the Consumer Financial Protection Bureau's stance on mortgages?
    a. Set rules regarding mortgage practices, but otherwise remain uninvolved.
    b. Heavily monitor financial institutions for any violations and enforce standards of behavior.
    c. Inform consumers and monitor institutions for abusive behavior.
    d. The CFPB focuses on other areas of financial interest and has no stance on mortgages.

88. RESPA specifically prohibited which of the following?
    a. Kickbacks
    b. Straw buying
    c. Non-resident co-borrowers
    d. Occupancy fraud

89. A mortgage agreement made between two private individuals is called what?
    a. One-on-one mortgage
    b. Private mortgage
    c. Cash mortgage
    d. Purchase-money mortgage

90. What documentation is required for borrowers who earn income from tips, commissions, and/or bonuses?
    a. Paystubs
    b. Tax returns
    c. Employment verification
    d. Statement of income

91. Which of the following could constitute a red flag on a borrower's asset documentation?
    a. A recent deposit of $10,000 into the account of a borrower who earns $2500 per month
    b. A deposit of $3000 into the account of a borrower who earns $2700 per month
    c. A $100,000 deposit into the account of a borrower who recently sold their home
    d. A gift letter from the borrower's mother explaining a deposit of $20,000 into the borrower's savings account

92. If a customer seems to be dodging reporting requirements when making cash transactions, what report should be filed?
    a. Pretexting report
    b. Suspicious activity report
    c. Currency transaction report
    d. Customer investigation report

93. Which of the following laws was passed as a direct result of the 2008 financial crisis?
    a. Gramm-Leach-Bliley Act
    b. Civil Rights Act
    c. Dodd-Frank Act
    d. Fair Housing Act

94. MLO applicants who have been convicted of a felony may have their application denied if that conviction was within how many years of application?
    a. One year
    b. Three years
    c. Five years
    d. Seven years

95. What happens to monthly interest in a reverse mortgage?
    a. It is paid off every month as normal.
    b. Half of the interest is paid off every month, and the other half is added to the balance of the mortgage.
    c. It is added onto the total balance of the mortgage.
    d. There is no monthly interest in a reverse mortgage.

96. What is the primary purpose of an appraisal?
    a. To show the borrower how much they should pay for a property
    b. To help the borrower negotiate a lower purchase price for a property
    c. To determine what repairs and maintenance a property needs
    d. To determine the fair market value of a property

97. Which Title of the Patriot Act focuses on money laundering crimes?
    a. Title IX
    b. Title VII
    c. Title III
    d. Title IV

98. Which appraisal method is used primarily for investment properties?
    a. Income approach
    b. Sales comparison approach
    c. Loan-to-value approach
    d. Cost approach

99. A financial institution has an automated system that triggers a warning on an account if it transfers too much money in a single day without prior notice. Which of the four basic elements of an Identity Theft Prevention Program is at work here?
    a. Identifying relevant red flags
    b. Updating the red flags detection program with ongoing training
    c. Detecting red flags during daily operations
    d. Preventing identity theft once red flags are detected

100. Before signing off on a loan, a consumer inspects the property, conducts an appraisal, and learns about the local homeowner's association. This consumer is displaying which of the following practices?
    a. Steering
    b. Fee splitting
    c. POA
    d. Due diligence

101. Which of the following describes the amount of money that a borrower is investing in the property?
    a. Down payment
    b. Investment funds
    c. Closing costs
    d. Loan amount

102. A loan offer that has a low interest rate for the first and second years before increasing to its permanent rate by the third year is referred to as what?
    a. Escrow
    b. FHA mortgage loan
    c. Assumable mortgage loan
    d. 2-1 buy-down

103. When advertising mortgage products, there is certain information you cannot misrepresent or be misleading about. Which of the following is NOT mentioned by 12 CFR Part 1014, Regulation N?
    a. The existence of fees associated with the mortgage
    b. How many mortgages the institution has approved
    c. The variability of the interest rate of the mortgage
    d. The type of mortgage

104. A lender determines that they are not able to provide service to a client because their neighborhood has a history of being financially risky. What prohibited act does this behavior display?
    a. Coercion
    b. Steering
    c. Conflict of interest
    d. Redlining

105. A real estate company demands payment from another company for referring a client to their service. This real estate company is in violation of which law?
   a. RESPA
   b. Bank Secrecy Act (BSA)
   c. Dodd-Frank Act
   d. Civil Rights Act

106. Which phrase best describes the types of financial institutions that are exempt from reporting loan information required by the HDMA?
   a. Any financial institution that applies for exemption
   b. State-chartered financial institutions that have a similar state reporting law
   c. All state-chartered financial institutions regardless of whether or not they apply for exemption
   d. No financial institution is exempt

107. Which document verifies that there are no liens or claims against a property?
   a. Property appraisal
   b. Homeowner's association report
   c. Preliminary title report
   d. Title commitment

108. A borrower is applying for a mortgage to purchase a nine-unit apartment building that they will use as a rental income property. Can the borrower apply for a residential mortgage loan for this purchase?
   a. No, because the building is being purchased as a business enterprise.
   b. No, because a mortgage loan cannot be used for commercial purposes.
   c. Yes, because the property consists of residential units.
   d. Yes, because the borrower will be renting the units for tenants' primary residences.

109. What is the main difference between straw buying and listing a non-resident co-borrower?
   a. RESPA prohibits straw buying but allows listing a non-resident co-borrower.
   b. The Fair Housing Act prohibits listing a non-resident co-borrower but allows straw buying.
   c. Straw buying is considered fraud, but listing a non-resident co-borrower is legal.
   d. Listing a non-resident co-borrower will result in higher interest rates, but straw buying will result in lower interest rates.

110. What are the costs that the seller agrees to pay for the buyer at closing?
   a. Settlement costs
   b. Origination fees
   c. Concessions
   d. Conventional costs

111. Which type of insurance protects a property damaged by water from a hurricane?
   a. Homeowner's insurance
   b. Flood insurance
   c. Hazard insurance
   d. Mortgage insurance

112. Which government agency is tasked with enforcing Regulation B?
   a. Consumer Financial Protection Bureau
   b. Federal Reserve
   c. Department of Banking and Finance
   d. Securities and Exchange Commission

113. If a borrower is unable to offer a 20 percent initial down payment for a house, what must they do?
   a. Purchase PMI.
   b. Obtain a tri-merge credit report.
   c. Ask their straw buyer for assistance.
   d. Request an Affiliated Business Arrangement (AfBA) Disclosure.

114. How much is the allowable seller concession for escrow accounts and funding fees on a VA loan?
   a. Unlimited
   b. 6 percent
   c. 5 percent
   d. 4 percent

115. What typically happens after closing to a loan that a third-party provider helps originate?
   a. The loan is sold to investors or the secondary market.
   b. The Federal Housing Administration sponsors the loan.
   c. Lender credits are used to decrease the closing costs.
   d. Private mortgage insurance is purchased alongside the loan.

116. The borrower's expected cash to close can be found in which two places on the Loan Estimate form?
   a. The top of page one and the bottom of page two
   b. The bottom of page one and the bottom of page two
   c. The bottom of page two and the bottom of page three
   d. The top of page one and the bottom of page three

117. What is the purpose of the Closing Disclosure?
   a. It provides details about the loan transaction, including the loan terms and the closing costs.
   b. It notifies the borrower of their right to cancel the loan.
   c. It protects the borrower in the event of any undisclosed liens or encumbrances on the property.
   d. It transfers ownership of the property from one party to another.

118. When must an AfBA Disclosure be given to a borrower?
   a. After informing the Federal Trade Commission (FTC)
   b. Fifteen days after the referral is made
   c. At the time of the referral
   d. Disclosure for a referral does not have to be given within a certain time period.

119. Which of the following is a common requirement for balloon mortgages that differs from normal requirements?
    a. A higher credit score
    b. A smaller debt-to-income ratio
    c. A lower maximum limit
    d. A greater percentage of private mortgage insurance

120. Which organization handles borrower complaints?
    a. RESPA
    b. NAR
    c. CFPB
    d. FTC

Answer Explanations #2

1. D: Tolerances refer to the allowed variations in fees between the initial Loan Estimate and the Closing Disclosure. Choice *A* refers to the borrower's debt-to-income ratio (DTI), and Choice *B* is the loan-to-value (LTV) ratio. Choice *C*, the maximum loan amount, varies according to loan program and geographic area.

2. A: HELOC refers to a home equity line of credit. Choices, *B, C*, and *D* are made-up answers.

3. A: A loan originator should ensure that all loan application information is correct and be prepared to explain the terms to the borrower. Choice *B* is due diligence from the borrower. Choice *C* is steering borrowers to make unwise decisions that are not in their best interest. Choice *D* is an unethical action for a loan originator to take.

4. D: HELOCs have two periods, a draw period and a repayment period. Once the draw period ends and the repayment period begins, borrowers can no longer withdraw any money through the line of credit. They are required to make payments on interest, so they can still borrow money after the first payment during the draw period, making Choice *A* incorrect. If they have borrowed the full amount, they can still repay a portion of it during the draw period and withdraw again afterwards, so Choice *B* is incorrect. They cannot borrow any money after the repayment period begins, so Choice *C* is incorrect.

5. B: Periodic interest is the annual interest rate divided into smaller, regular periods. The periodic payments based on the periodic interest are known as the accrual rate, Choice *A*. APR, Choice *C*, refers to the total cost of the loan, including all fees, loan charges, and interest. Amortization, Choice *D*, is the method of calculation that lenders use to keep the loan payments consistent throughout the loan term.

6. C: Even in the lightest case, a violation of MLO compliance rules results in a minimum civil fine of $10,000 plus any action required to remedy the violation. One year of prison time is also included if it is an intentional violation, but it is possible for the violation to not be intentional, so Choice *A* is incorrect. Choice *B* has too high a fine and includes a prison sentence, so it is incorrect. Choice *D* is incorrect because the fine amount is too low, and although any violation is a risk factor for an MLO losing their license, the minimum possible penalty would not include license probation.

7. A: RESPA is detailed under Title 12, Chapter 10, part 1024 of the Code of Federal Regulations. Chapter 2 of Title 12, Choice *B*, governs the Federal Reserve. Chapter 6, Choice *C*, is the Farm Credit Administration, and Choice *D*, Chapter 15, is the Department of the Treasury.

8. B: FICO and VantageScore are the two most common credit scoring models used by the credit bureaus. The three main credit bureaus—Experian, TransUnion, and Equifax—are included in Choices *A, C*, and *D*.

9. B: Lenders are required to contact borrowers within forty-five days of the first delinquency. Choices *A, C*, and *D* are time frames that are either too short or too long.

10. B: USDA loans help borrowers purchase property in rural and agricultural areas. Choices *A, C*, and *D* are incorrect.

11. C: The Consumer Financial Protection Bureau (CFPB) has the authority to enforce all rules relating to mortgages and MLOs. The Department of the Treasury has nothing to do with MLOs or mortgages, so

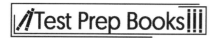

Choice *A* is incorrect. Both Choices *B* and *D* sound plausible, but the Department of Housing and Urban Development (HUD) and Federal Housing Administration (FHA) only assist with consumers getting information about mortgages, not enforcement of rules, so they are both incorrect.

12. D: The Fair Credit Reporting Act (FCRA) allows borrowers to control who sees their personal information. Choices *A* and *C* prohibit discrimination from housing deals. Choice *B* outlines what constitutes unfair, deceptive, or abusive acts and practices (UDAAP).

13. B: Lenders must keep loan applications on file for twenty-five months after the date of the last action taken and for twenty-five months after the date of an adverse action for existing accounts. Choices *A, C*, and *D* are made-up answers.

14. C: The originator may not ask the borrower any questions related to health or family planning. The originator is legally required to make a determination about the borrower's race and ethnicity even if the borrower chooses not to disclose this information; therefore, Choices *A* and *B* are incorrect. The borrower's employment partially determines their ability to repay the loan and therefore must be disclosed, making Choice *D* incorrect.

15. B: The ability to repay rule is implemented and overseen by the Consumer Financial Protection Bureau. Choice *A*, HUD, creates and implements policies and programs around the housing needs of American citizens. Federal National Mortgage Association (Fannie Mae) and Federal Home Loan Mortgage Corporation (Freddie Mac), Choices *C* and *D*, are entities that buy mortgage loans on the secondary market.

16. B: The annual license renewal period is always at the end of a calendar year, from November 1 through December 31. It doesn't cross over the new year, so Choice *A* is incorrect. It isn't in August or September, so Choice *C* is incorrect. It isn't in March or April, although that is when many organizations file tax returns, so Choice *D* is incorrect.

17. B: If the annual property taxes are $3000, that equates to $250 per month ($3000 total annual tax divided by twelve months). By closing on the purchase at the end of May, Jasmine will have owned the property from January through May (five months), and Tony will own the property for the remaining seven months. Thus, Jasmine's tax responsibility is $1250 ($250 times five), and Tony's is $1750 ($250 times seven). Choice *A* has them each paying half of the annual tax bill, which would only happen through a seller concession not indicated in the question. Choice *C* has Jasmine paying a greater amount than Tony, even though she will have owned the property for less of the year than Tony. Choice *D* is based on incorrect calculations where Jasmine pays for one third of the yearly taxes (four months) and Tony pays for two thirds of the yearly taxes (eight months).

18. D: The average prime offer rate is an interest calculation based on current market conditions for mortgage loans made to low-risk borrowers. It is used in the determination of whether a mortgage is considered high cost. Choice *A*, the annual percentage rate (APR), is calculated using the interest rate plus any fees or finance charges on the loan. Choice *B*, a first-lien mortgage, means any primary mortgage loan made on a property that will be paid off first in the event of a foreclosure. Choice *C*, a subordinate mortgage, is any mortgage loan that will be paid off after the first mortgage in a foreclosure situation.

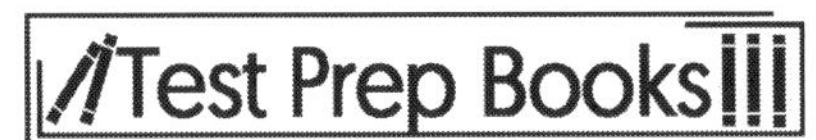

19. D: Prior to their incapacitation, the power of attorney (POA) document was signed, allowing someone else to make decisions for this person. Choices *A*, *B*, and *C* are not legal documents that grant this authority.

20. A: Fraud, along with crimes of dishonesty, breach of trust, and money laundering, is a crime that will cause an MLO to have their license permanently revoked, becoming barred from ever obtaining one again. Although any other crime will reflect poorly on an MLO and must be reported to the NMLS, fraud is the only choice that will immediately result in having a license revoked, so Choices *B*, *C*, and *D* are incorrect.

21. A: To find the allowable DTI, the monthly income is multiplied by the maximum allowable percentage. In this case, $4000 multiplied by 45 percent (0.45) equals a monthly debt amount of $1800. Choice *B* resulted from an incorrect calculation of dividing by forty-five. Choices *C* and *D* are made-up answers.

22. C: A mortgage broker who directs a borrower towards a particular lender in order to gain additional compensation, even though the loan terms are less favorable, is guilty of steering. Choices *A* and *B* would be appropriate for the mortgage broker because the suggestions would benefit the borrower. Choice *D*, while not steering by definition, does constitute an illegal action by the mortgage broker.

23. C: Borrowers must be informed of changes to their loan due to a service transfer within fifteen days. Choices *A*, *B*, and *D* are not the correct timeframe for informing a borrower of changes to their loan.

24. C: MLO licensing requirements are strict to make sure that both borrowers and lenders are protected when an MLO works to negotiate a mortgage offer. It isn't just to protect lenders and their money, so Choice *A* is incorrect. Catching criminals conducting money laundering is not the point of the licensing system, so Choice *B* is incorrect. The strict requirements do make the process more rigorous, but that is more of a side effect and not the reason for the requirements, so Choice *D* is incorrect.

25. B: Borrowers often experience payment shock when the low-payment introductory period expires and their loan reverts to the full monthly payment amount. While not called a hike, an increase in interest rate, Choice *A*, can be one of the causes of payment shock. A balloon payment, Choice *C*, refers to a large pay-off amount that is due at the end of a low-payment period. Negative amortization, Choice *D*, occurs when the borrower is making monthly payments that are lower than even interest-only, resulting in an increase in the loan balance over time rather than a decrease.

26. A: The Fair and Accurate Credit Transaction Act (FACTA) allows consumers to annually request a credit report. The Fair Credit Reporting Act (FCRA) sets rules regarding credit reports and their usage, but is not what allows consumers the right to request a report of their own credit, so Choice *B* is incorrect. The Gramm-Leach-Bliley Act (GLBA) sets other privacy-related rules for financial institutions, but is not directly related to credit reports, so Choice *C* is incorrect. The Public Credit Information Act is a made-up act, so Choice *D* is incorrect.

27. B: Amortization is the process by which lenders set a fixed payment amount for a mortgage loan. Amortization accounts for a decreasing loan balance and decreasing interest payments throughout the loan repayment term. Choice *A* refers to the accrual rate. Choice *C* is the interest rate, and Choice *D* refers to the down payment.

28. C: If an MLO is retaking the SAFE test to reactivate their license, they need to score at least 75 percent to pass. Both 55 and 60 percent are too low, so Choices *A* and *B* are incorrect, and 90 percent is too high for the minimum passing grade, so Choice *D* is incorrect.

29. B: For construction mortgages, the down payments required typically run between 20 percent and 25 percent. 5–10 percent and 10–15 percent are too low, so Choices *A* and *C* are incorrect. 30–35 percent is too high, even for the risks involved in a construction mortgage, so Choice *D* is incorrect.

30. B: An appraiser must disclose if the property they are being asked to appraise has already been appraised within the last three years. Choices *A*, *C*, and *D* are not the correct time frames for this disclosure.

31. D: A clear title refers to a title without encumbrances or liens against it. A title search does not necessarily turn up a clear title; therefore, a title insurance policy guaranteeing a clear title may not be issued. Choices *A, B*, and *C* are all parts of the title search.

32. D: Financial institutions must disclose, among other things, if the consent to use electronic signatures will apply to only one transaction or to multiple transactions over time. Electronic signatures have the same authority as pen-and-paper signatures under the E-Sign Act, so Choice *A* is incorrect. Choice *B* is incorrect because electronic consent is required to be affirmative consent; assumed consent is not allowed. Choice *C* is incorrect because explaining the full definition of an electronic signature is not required.

33. D: The borrower of an interest-only mortgage can make payments on the principal by simply adding more to their regular monthly interest payment. Whatever is left over after covering the interest payment will go towards the principal of the loan. There is no special procedure necessary, so Choice *A* is incorrect. Borrowers aren't forced to wait until later, so Choice *B* is incorrect. The borrower technically could pay off the principal in a single lump sum, but it is not required and is typically much more difficult for borrowers to make one large payment rather than smaller incremental payments, making Choice *C* less correct than Choice *D*.

34. D: If an MLO has a change of employment, they must report that to the NMLS within five days of the change. If they change employers on Monday, they will need to report this by Saturday of the same week. Wednesday and Friday are both within that five-day time window, but the question is asking for the last possible day, so Choices *A* and *B* are incorrect. Sunday is too late, so Choice *C* is incorrect.

35. D: Final termination of private mortgage insurance (PMI) occurs on the first day of the month following the midpoint of a loan's repayment period, assuming the borrower is current on payments. It does not occur on the seventh day of a month, so Choices *A* and *B* are both incorrect automatically. Choice *C* is incorrect because the PMI Cancellation Act specifies that final termination must be after the midpoint of loan repayment and not after the first year.

36. A: The cushion in the escrow account helps to ensure that there is enough money in the account to pay the annual taxes and insurance premiums. It also helps to cover any unexpected increases in these amounts. Choices *B, C*, and *D* do not accurately describe the purpose of a cushion in an escrow account.

37. A: The Dodd-Frank Act was passed as a result of the Great Recession in 2008. Choice *B* is incorrect because the Great Depression was in 1929. Choice *C* is incorrect because the recession in 1990 was caused by buyout and oil price crises. Choice *D* is incorrect because 2001 was the year of several terrorist attacks on the U.S. that led to the Patriot Act.

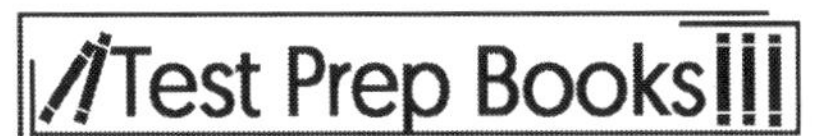

38. A: The Fair Housing Act prohibits discrimination based on factors such as age and race. Choice *B* was passed to prevent future financial crises by regulating industry practices. Choice *C* prohibits practices such as kickbacks and finder's fees. Choice *D* requires financial institutions to disclose their information protection practices.

39. B: While the exact amount may vary depending on the lender, the minimum down payment on conventional loans, which are the most common mortgages, is typically 3 percent. 5 percent, 10 percent, and 8 percent are all too high, making Choices *A*, *C*, and *D* incorrect.

40. C: MLOs must be reasonably certain that a borrower has not maintained property insurance or failed to comply with any other loan obligations before imposing force-placed insurance on the loan. Choices *B* and *D* might be solid reasons to file a suspicious activity report (SAR) or alert authorities, but are unrelated to force-placed insurance, so they are incorrect. Choice *A* is irrelevant to the act of imposing certain property insurance and is also incorrect.

41. A: If a revised Loan Estimate becomes necessary, the new disclosure must be provided to the borrower at least four days prior to the loan closing. The initial Loan Estimate form must be provided to the borrower within three days of the loan application; therefore, Choice *D* is incorrect. Choices *B* and *C* are also incorrect.

42. D: Requiring a co-signer is not one of the actions taken by a lender. The lender can suggest a co-signer in the event that the lender returns with a counteroffer, Choice *B*, in which the lender offers a loan under different terms, or in the event of an adverse action, Choice *C*, in which the lender denies the loan as submitted. An approval, Choice *A*, is also one of the possible actions a lender can take.

43. D: The borrower must give the loan officer the following information before the loan officer can generate a Loan Estimate: the borrower's name, income, and social security number; the address and estimated value of the property involved; and the requested loan amount. The lender must provide the borrower with a Loan Estimate form within three days of receiving all necessary information; therefore, Choice *A* is incorrect because the lender does not have all of the necessary information. The borrower does not need to submit a request in writing, so Choice *B* is incorrect. The form is not dependent upon receipt of an appraisal, so Choice *C* is incorrect.

44. D: Borrowers who pay less than 10 percent down must pay mortgage insurance for the life of the loan. Borrowers who pay at least 10 percent down can stop paying mortgage insurance after eleven years, Choice *C*. Choices *A* and *B* are incorrect.

45. A: Although prospective MLOs do need to provide various pieces of personal information when first registering, they do not need to provide their birth city and country. Employment and civil lawsuit history are both required to be presented, so Choices *B* and *C* are incorrect. Fingerprints are necessary for the Federal Bureau of Investigation to conduct a background check, so Choice *D* is incorrect.

46. B: Reverse occupancy fraud is listing a property as part of someone's assets when in reality it is used as their primary residence. Choice *A* is lying about the total amount of assets someone has. Choice *C* is lying about someone's employment status. Choice *D* is listing a property as owner-occupied when it is actually an investment property where the owner does not live.

47. C: Fines for TRID violations can range from $5,000 per day for first-tier infractions up to $100,000 per day for third-tier deliberate violations. Choices *A*, *B*, and *D* are incorrect.

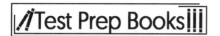

48. D: An escrow account is established to hold monies paid by the borrower towards the taxes and insurance premium, which are usually paid on an annual basis. Choices *A, B,* and *C* are made-up answers.

49. A: GSEs are government-sponsored enterprises. In the mortgage arena, these include Federal National Mortgage Association (Fannie Mae) and Federal Home Loan Mortgage Corporation (Freddie Mac). Choices *B, C,* and *D* are incorrect.

50. D: A state-level financial regulation organization is the most likely of these choices to hire an MLO for mortgage regulations. A benefits distribution organization such as a welfare or government support organization might hire an MLO, but the question is specifically asking for the most likely choice, and financial regulator is a better fit, so Choice *A* is incorrect. State courts and infrastructure planners are very unlikely to hire an MLO, so Choices *B* and *C* are incorrect.

51. B: The deed is the physical document that transfers property ownership. The title, Choice *A*, is not a document; instead, it refers to legal ownership of the property. The Closing Disclosure, Choice *C*, refers to the document that details the loan transaction. Choice *D*, the Purchase Contract, is the agreement between the seller and buyer for the sale of the property.

52. A: Phishing is the act of using a fake email, website, or other bait to try to trick people into voluntarily giving up private information. There is no specific term for violating the National Do Not Call Registry, so Choice *B* is incorrect. Choice *C* is incorrect because phishing usually involves misdirection and false appearances rather than a direct theft. Choice *D* is incorrect because it would be a better description of the crime of identity theft.

53. B: Loan processors are people who assist MLOs by verifying borrower-submitted information and collecting all the paperwork, processing it, and sending it to whoever needs it. Underwriters assist MLOs by making risk assessments, so Choice *A* is incorrect. Mortgage clerk is a false term, so Choice *C* is incorrect. Bank tellers don't have anything to do with processing mortgages, so Choice *D* is incorrect.

54. D: The typical splitting fee for joint advertising is fifty/fifty. Choices *A*, *B*, and *C* are incorrect rates.

55. C: VA loans are guaranteed through the Department of Veterans Affairs and are specifically for members of the military. USDA loans, Choice *A*, are generally for rural properties. FHA loans, Choice *B*, are federally guaranteed loans, but they are not military-specific. Conventional mortgage loans, Choice *D*, are the most common mortgage loans and are not federally guaranteed.

56. B: A licensed MLO is the only person who is legally allowed to determine if the information provided in an application allows an applicant to qualify for a mortgage. Although all of the other tasks may be a part of the application process, they are parts that someone without an MLO license is allowed to assist with or perform, so Choices *A*, *C*, and *D* are all incorrect.

57. C: The three-day right of rescission period for a loan closing on Thursday would end at midnight on Monday. The rescission period begins on the first day after closing, and does not include Sundays, Choice *B*. Because Saturdays do count for the recission period, Choice *D*, Tuesday, is one day too long. Choice *A* is too short. In this example, Saturday would be day two.

58. B: A non-resident co-borrower can help someone secure a loan because they will promise to help pay for the property. Choice *A* is a finder's fee. Choice *C* is one purpose of fraud. Choice *D* is incorrect because listing a non-resident co-borrower can actually lower interest rates.

59. A: PITI refers to a payment that includes principal, interest, taxes, and insurance. Choices *B*, *C*, and *D* are made-up answers.

60. D: Conforming loans are called this because they conform to the strict guidelines set for purchase by Fannie Mae and Freddie Mac. Choice *A*, secondary loans, generally refers to loans that are in subsequent lien positions to first-lien mortgage loans. There are no federal loans, Choice *B*, although FHA and VA loans are sometimes referred to as government loans, Choice *C*.

61. B: The borrower must receive the Closing Disclosure at least three days prior to closing. There must be at least seven days, Choice *C*, between the borrower's receipt of the Loan Estimate form and the closing of the loan, unless the Loan Estimate has been revised, in which case the revised Loan Estimate must be received four days before the closing of the loan, Choice *D*. Choice *A* is a made-up answer.

62. B: Jumbo loans are nonconforming mortgage loans that exceed the maximum loan limits of conforming mortgage loans. Alt-A loans, Choice *A*, are a type of nonconforming mortgage loan, but they are not classified specifically based on the loan amount. Prime and subprime, Choices *C* and *D*, are types of loans made to certain classifications of borrowers based on the strength of their creditworthiness and the amount of risk they pose to the lender.

63. C: There are five rights included in the bundle of rights: the Right of Possession, meaning that the owner has a right to possess the property; the Right of Control and the Right of Enjoyment, meaning that the owner can use and enjoy the property as they see fit; the Right of Disposition, giving the owner the right to rent, sell, or transfer ownership of the property; and the Right of Exclusion, meaning that the owner can control who is permitted to enter the property. Therefore, Choices *A, B*, and *D* are incorrect.

64. C: The mother is straw buying, or purchasing on behalf of someone else, because her son is unable to obtain a loan based on his poor credit history. Choice *A* is refusing service to someone based on factors such as race and ethnicity. Choice *B* attempts to influence a borrower's decisions on purchasing property. Choice *D* is lying about the total amount of assets in a borrower's possession to obtain better terms.

65. C: Subprime borrowers are usually classified as borrowers who have credit scores between 580 and 620. FHA will guarantee loans for borrowers with credit scores of 580, Choice *B*, and even as low as 500, Choice *A*, depending on the borrower's down payment amount. FHA loans, however, are not considered subprime loans. Choice *D* is a credit score for a prime borrower.

66. A: The loan originator is not permitted to ask the borrower about their family plans because it would violate the Fair Housing Act and the Americans with Disabilities Act. Choices *B, C*, and *D* contain information that the originator needs to determine the best loan product for the specific buyer.

67. C: The most popular repayment term for fixed-rate mortgages is 30 years. 15 years is the second most popular, but not the top, so Choice *A* is incorrect. Neither 10- nor 20-year terms are as popular as either 15 or 30, so Choices *B* and *D* are incorrect.

68. C: The borrower must be given an initial escrow statement within forty-five days of the loan closing. Choices *A, B*, and *D* are made-up answers.

69. A: The mortgage loan processor assists with gathering information and preparing the loan package for submission. The underwriter, Choice *B*, receives the loan package and decides whether to approve the loan. The underwriter usually works for the lender, Choice *C*, which is the company that will fund the loan. The loan originator, Choice *D*, accepts the loan application and starts the process on behalf of the borrower.

70. A: In an adjustable-rate mortgage (ARM), the interest rate can change due to changes in the housing market, but it is not necessarily required to. There is no limit on how much the interest rate can change in, specifically, the second half of the mortgage's term, so since the question is looking for the odd rule out, Choice *A* is correct. The first change, all subsequent changes, and the total change to the interest rate are all limited by the federal government, so Choices *B*, *C*, and *D* are incorrect.

71. B: The Department of Housing and Urban Development does not have anything to do with the Home Mortgage Disclosure Act (HMDA); that information can be found on the Consumer Financial Protection Bureau's website. It does contain lists for the process of becoming a homeowner, lists of frequently asked questions, and lists of approved lenders, so Choices *A*, *C*, and *D* are all incorrect.

72. B: The personal relationship between the appraiser and the borrower may compromise the integrity of the financial transaction, resulting in a conflict of interest. Choice *A* allows for someone else to act on behalf of another person if they become incapacitated. Choice *C* is a person who is added to a mortgage loan who does not live at the property but is responsible for paying the loan if the borrower cannot. Choice *D* describes someone illegally buying property for another person.

73. A: A 7/1 ARM means that the interest rate stays fixed for the first seven years of the loan and then adjusts annually for the remainder of the loan term. Choice *B* is incorrect because, while the monthly payment will stay the same for the first seven years, it will adjust annually after that based on the interest rate rather than monthly. Choice *C* is a made-up answer; there is no maximum interest rate change in the 7/1 designation. Choice *D* is incorrect because although the interest rate can change annually, there is no maximum interest rate adjustment indicated in the 7/1 designation.

74. A: A timeline for occupancy is not necessarily relevant to what a lender needs to see to approve a construction mortgage. A lender will need to see the exact details of the construction plans, who is being hired, and what the estimated value of the completed house is compared to comparable housing. Because all these details are needed to make an informed decision, Choices *B*, *C*, and *D* are all incorrect.

75. D: One of the qualities of a loan that must be reported according to the HMDA is the number of months until the interest rate is allowed to change. The amount and interest rate of the loan must always be reported, so Choices *A* and *B* are incorrect. While some borrower information is collected, the name of the borrower is not, so Choice *C* is also incorrect.

76. D: The LTV ratio is calculated using the amount borrowed on a loan and dividing that by the property's appraised value. Loan interest rates are lowest when the ratio is around 80 percent, which can be achieved with a 20 percent down payment on the property. Choices *A*, *B*, and *C* are not the ideal initial down payment to achieve an 80 percent LTV ratio.

77. B: Jobs that depend on tips for their income have fluctuating incomes. Lenders should determine the tip average obtained over the last two years in order to verify the amount of income and its stability, which will affect the offered loan terms. Choices *A*, *C*, and *D* are not the correct actions to take.

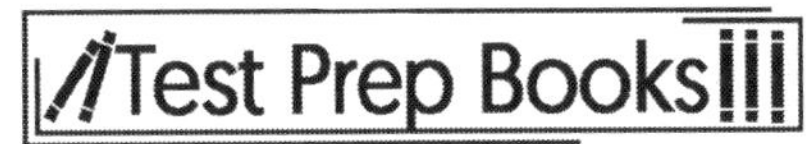

78. D: Regulation P, the Privacy of Consumer Financial Information rule, governs the disclosure requirements regarding borrowers' privacy. Choice *A*, Regulation X, is the Real Estate Settlement Procedures Act. Regulation B, Choice *B*, is the Equal Credit Opportunity Act (ECOA), and Choice *C*, Regulation Z, is the Truth in Lending regulation.

79. C: Before December 2020, a borrower's debt-to-income ratio (DTI), meaning the percentage of monthly debt payments as compared to a borrower's total monthly income, was capped at 43 percent. After December 2020, that calculation was replaced with a maximum APR calculation instead. Choices *A*, *B*, and *D* are incorrect.

80. A: When a borrower applies for a loan against a property they already own, the loan is called a refinance loan. This term applies even if the borrower does not currently have a mortgage on the property. A balloon mortgage, Choice *B*, is a loan in which the borrower has a large balloon payment at the end of the loan term. An adjustable-rate mortgage (ARM), Choice *C*, is one in which the interest rate can vary based on the current market. A subordinate lien, Choice *D*, refers to a second or subsequent mortgage that is positioned behind a first, or primary, mortgage lien.

81. A: The Gramm-Leach-Bliley Act (GLBA) mandated that financial institutions must make efforts to keep personal information safe and secure. Choice *B* is the purpose of the Home Ownership and Equity Protection Act (HOEPA). Choice *C* is the purpose of the Bank Secrecy Act (BSA). Choice *D* is outlined by the Dodd-Frank Act.

82. C: Appraisal fees fall under the 10 percent tolerance category when the appraiser is chosen from a list provided by the lender. If the borrower chooses a service provider on their own, then the fee falls under the no tolerance category. Therefore, Choice *A* is incorrect. Choice *B*, zero tolerance fees, are those that the lender is expected to know ahead of time; these fees cannot change during the course of the loan process. Choice *D* is a made-up answer.

83. D: Lenders make qualified mortgage loans in order to ensure that they can be purchased by Fannie Mae or Freddie Mac on the secondary market. Selling the loans gives capital back to the lender so it can make more loans. FHA and VA loans, Choices *A* and *B*, can be sold on the secondary market, but they are already guaranteed by these agencies. Choice *C* is incorrect.

84. D: Finder's fees are obtained after a successful referral. Choices *A, B,* and *C* are not associated with finder's fees.

85. C: Lenders typically require one month's worth of paystubs to verify a borrower's monthly income. For a borrower who is paid weekly, four paystubs would be required. Choice *A* would be sufficient for a borrower who is paid monthly, and Choice *B* works for a borrower who is paid biweekly. Choice *D* is a made-up answer.

86. A: The CFPB mandates that any advertisements for an MLO's services must have that MLO's NMLS identifier number displayed for consumer verification. The company the MLO works for and the MLO's phone number are certainly important in an advertisement, but not necessarily mandated—the MLO may work as an individual or prefer not to be contacted by phone. Because of this, Choices *B* and *D* are incorrect. The results of their last ten mortgage offers are not required information, so Choice *C* is also incorrect.

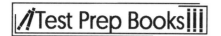

87. C: The Consumer Financial Protection Bureau focuses on providing a large amount of consumer information about the process and nature of mortgages, but also plays a minor enforcement role by monitoring financial institutions and warning them of suspicious or abusive practices. The CFPB does have some rule-making authority on mortgages, but it also plays an active role in informing and policing them, so Choice *A* is incorrect. Other organizations serve larger enforcement roles, so Choice *B* is incorrect. The CFPB does not ignore mortgages at all, so Choice *D* is incorrect.

88. A: Along with finder's fees, RESPA prohibited kickbacks. Choices *B*, *C*, and *D* are not outlined in RESPA.

89. D: Mortgages made between two individuals without the use of a financial institution are called purchase-money mortgages. One-on-one mortgage, private mortgage, and cash mortgage are all false terms, making Choices *A*, *B*, and *C* incorrect.

90. B: Tax returns are used to determine the average monthly income for borrowers who earn irregular income, including tips, commissions, and bonuses. Paystubs, Choice *A*, are used to determine regular, consistent income such as wages and salaries. The employment verification, Choice *C*, is used to verify that the borrower is currently employed and their start date. Questions regarding income are not legally permitted during the verification of employment. Similarly, an income statement from the employer, Choice *D*, would not be sufficient for verifying income.

91. A: When reviewing asset documentation, lenders may question large deposits that are not in line with the borrower's income and that are not readily explained. Deposits of slightly more (or less) than the regular monthly income, Choice *B*, are not usually a concern. Choices *C* and *D* are incorrect because the borrower has clear explanations for the large deposits.

92. B: If a customer seems to be avoiding reporting requirements, then a suspicious activity report (SAR) should be filed. Currency transaction reports are for cash transactions that exceed $10,000 in one day, so Choice *C* is incorrect. Pretexting report and customer investigation report are both made-up terms, so Choices *A* and *D* are incorrect.

93. C: The Dodd-Frank Act was passed to protect large financial institutions from collapse and to protect consumers by regulating risky financial transactions, such as issuing loans to people with poor credit history. Choice *A* requires financial institutions to implement ways to protect borrower information. Choice *B* was passed to outline discrimination and prohibited factors. Choice *D* is a part of the Civil Rights Act.

94. D: If an applicant has been convicted of a felony within seven years prior to their application, their license application will be denied. One, three, and five years are all too short of a time period, so Choices *A*, *B*, and *C* are all incorrect.

95. C: In a reverse mortgage, all monthly interest is added onto the total balance due when the mortgage eventually becomes due in the future. The interest does not have to be repaid on a monthly basis, either in full or in part, so Choices *A* and *B* are incorrect. There is monthly interest, so Choice *D* is also incorrect.

96. D: Appraisals help the lender determine the fair market value of a property in the event the property is surrendered or foreclosed. Although an appraisal can help a borrower know if they are overpaying for a property, Choice *A*, and/or help the borrower negotiate a lower purchase price if the appraisal came in

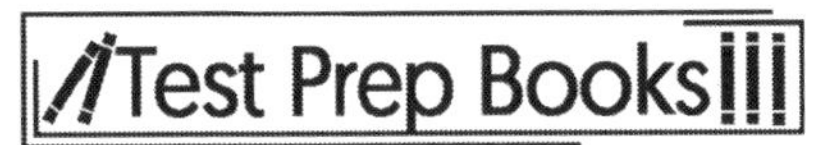

lower than expected, Choice *B*, these are not the primary purposes. The appraisal does not make any determinations about repairs or maintenance, Choice *C*.

97. C: Title III is the part of the Patriot Act that requires financial institutions to cooperate with law enforcement on responding to money laundering crimes. Title IX is about intelligence, Title VII is about information sharing for protecting infrastructure, and Title IV is about border security, so Choices *A*, *B*, and *D* are all incorrect.

98. A: The income approach is used primarily for investment properties because it includes a determination of income potential as part of the property valuation. Choice *B*, the sales comparison approach, uses recently sold properties as comps for the subject property, and the cost approach, Choice *D*, determines the replacement value of the property. Choice *C* is a made-up answer.

99. C: If the automated system triggers a warning on an account in this way, that would be an example of detecting red flags during daily operations, making Choice *C* correct. "Identifying red flags" refers to institutions knowing what red flags to look for in the first place, so Choice *A* is incorrect. The warning itself doesn't do anything to prevent identity theft, making Choice *D* incorrect. The system doesn't have anything to do with ongoing training, so Choice *B* is also incorrect.

100. D: Due diligence is a way for both loan originators and consumers to protect themselves from risky financial transactions. Choice *A* describes making a person choose one community over another or pushing them towards a less advantageous loan. Choice *B* refers to how joint marketing is split between two business partners. Choice *C* allows someone to make decisions for someone else.

101. A: The money a borrower puts towards the purchase of a property is called the down payment. Choice *B* is a made-up answer. Choice *C* refers to the additional costs associated with the transaction, such as taxes and the appraisal fee. Choice *D* is the amount of money borrowed.

102. D: A 2-1 buy-down offer is used to attract business from new homebuyers. The interest rate is low for the first year, increases the second year, and increases to its permanent rate by the third year. The borrower is responsible for interest accumulated during the low interest years. Choice *A* is an account that helps make automatic payments for borrowers. Choice *B* is a loan offered to people with low income or credit scores. Choice *C* is a way for buyers to take over a seller's existing loan.

103. B: It is not a direct violation of 12 CFR Part 1014 Regulation N to misrepresent the number of mortgages the financial institution has approved. It is a violation to misrepresent the existence of fees, variability of interest rates, or the type of mortgage being advertised, making Choices *A*, *C*, and *D* all incorrect.

104. D: This lender is denying service based on perceived financial risk, which is a sign of redlining. Choice *A* describes any action that threatens or intimidates a borrower into making a decision. Choice *B* is attempting to influence a borrower to make purchases in certain communities or to accept unfavorable loan terms. Choice *C* happens when there is a personal relationship between business partners.

105. A: The Real Estate Settlement Procedures Act (RESPA) regulates several aspects of real estate and loans, including kickbacks and finder's fees. Choice *B* requires banks and other financial institutions to monitor suspicious financial transactions. Choice *C* was passed after the 2008 financial crisis to regulate large financial institutions. Choice *D* prohibits discrimination and provides equal opportunities for everyone under the Fair Housing Act.

106. B: Only state-chartered financial institutions that are also subject to a similar state-level reporting law like the HMDA may apply for exemption from the HMDA's reports. Not all institutions are accepted, so Choice *A* is incorrect. State institutions must apply to have their eligibility determined, so Choice *C* is incorrect. Since it is possible to be eligible for exemption, Choice *D* is also incorrect.

107. C: The preliminary title report verifies that there are no liens or claims against a property. The property appraisal, Choice *A*, is used to determine the value of the property. The title commitment, Choice *D*, is the guarantee issued by the title company once the title search and preliminary title report are completed. Choice *B* is a made-up answer.

108. A: No, because the building is being purchased as a business enterprise. Residential mortgage loans are only used to finance a borrower's primary residential dwelling. Choice *B* is incorrect because, while this purchase doesn't qualify for a residential mortgage loan, there are other types of mortgages that can be used to finance the property. Choices *C* and *D* are incorrect because whether the property contains residential units or whether tenants will live there as a primary residence is irrelevant to the qualification (or not) for a residential mortgage loan.

109. C: Straw buying is illegally purchasing property for another person; it is considered fraud. Listing a non-resident co-borrower is a legal practice. Choice *A* prohibits kickbacks and finder's fees; it does not directly address straw buying or listing a non-resident co-borrower. Choice *B* prohibits discrimination when handling real estate and home buying; it does not directly address straw buying or listing a non-resident co-borrower. Choice *D* is incorrect because listing a non-resident co-borrower will result in lower interest rates or help with loan approval.

110. C: Costs that the seller agrees to pay for the buyer at closing are called seller concessions. Settlement costs, Choice *A*, include all fees and charges associated with the closing. Choice *B*, origination fees, are charges that the mortgage broker assesses for their service. Choice *D* is a made-up answer.

111. C: Hazard insurance covers the property in the event of damages from natural disasters, including hurricanes. Homeowner's insurance, Choice *A*, offers additional protection, covering the homeowner's personal property in the event of loss or damage. Flood insurance, Choice *B*, specifically covers damage from flooding. Mortgage insurance, Choice *D*, is not related to physical property coverage but instead protects the lender against default on the loan.

112. A: Regulation B is enforced by the Consumer Financial Protection Bureau. It was originally enforced by the Federal Reserve, Choice *B*, but the CFPB took over in 2011. Choices *C* and *D* are made-up answers. Though these are real government agencies, they do not oversee Regulation B.

113. A: 20 percent is the ideal initial down payment for a property. Borrowers who are unable to offer a 20 percent down payment will need to purchase private mortgage insurance (PMI). This protects the lender in case the borrower stops their mortgage payments. Choice *B* is used to decide loan terms. Choice *C* is an unethical act in which a straw buyer will purchase property on behalf of another person by using fraudulent information. Choice *D* is required at the time of a referral.

114. D: VA loans allow for a 4 percent seller concession towards escrow accounts and funding fees. VA allows an unlimited amount, Choice *A*, towards other closing costs, such as the appraisal and origination

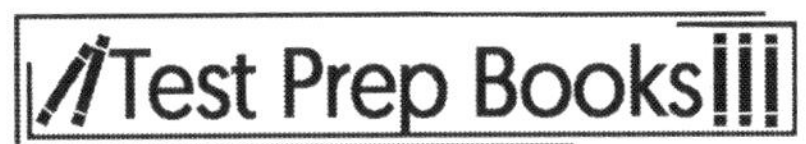

fees. FHA loans and some conventional mortgage loans allow a maximum of 6 percent, Choice *B*. Choice *C* is a made-up answer.

115. A: Third-party providers are any entities that are not the main lender handling a loan. They offer services such as underwriting and appraisals. Conventional mortgages, the most common type of loan, are typically sold to investors or to the secondary market after closing, whether they are originated by a third-party provider or not. Choice *B* refers to government mortgage loans, which are sponsored by entities such as the Federal Housing Administration (FHA) and the Department of Veteran Affairs (VA). While they can sometimes be sold on the secondary market, they are considered non-conforming loans and are much more difficult to sell than conforming loans. They are less common than conventional loans, which makes this answer incorrect. Choice *C* is a way to decrease closing costs for borrowers by increasing the loan interest rate. These transactions happen at closing rather than after closing. Choice *D* is purchased alongside conventional mortgage loans with a down payment of less than 20 percent. Again, this happens at closing rather than after closing.

116. B: The estimated cash to close is listed at the bottom of page one, and a breakdown of the closing costs and total cash to close is also found on the bottom of page two of the form. The top of page one, Choice *A*, includes details about the borrower, the property address, the loan product, and the terms of the loan. Again, the cash to close is shown at the bottom of page two, but page three, which is included in Choices *C* and *D*, includes notes about the appraisal, late payment information, and whether the loan is assumable or not.

117. A: The Closing Disclosure provides the borrower and the seller with the details of the transaction, including the loan terms, the closing costs, and who is paying what. Choice *B* refers to the Notice of Right to Cancel and is only used in a refinance transaction. Choice *C* refers to a borrower's title insurance policy, and Choice *D* refers to the deed.

118. C: Disclosure must be given before or at the time of the referral. Choices *A*, *B*, and *D* do not describe the correct time to disclose a business relationship with a consumer.

119. A: Balloon mortgages typically require a higher credit score to obtain, as well as needing a larger down payment. A smaller debt-to-income ratio (DTI) and a greater percentage of mortgage insurance would be positive things to a lender, but aren't always a different requirement compared to normal mortgages, so Choices *B* and *D* are incorrect. A lower maximum limit would just reduce the total possible amount of a balloon mortgage, so Choice *C* is incorrect.

120. C: The Consumer Financial Protection Bureau (CFPB) handles consumer complaints and also lists this data on its website. RESPA, Choice *A*, is a law, not an organization. Choice *B*, National Association of Realtors (NAR), and Choice *D*, Federal Trade Commission (FTC), regulate various aspects of real estate and mortgage, such as advertising laws.

Practice Test #3

1. What happens when a potential borrower does not have an established credit history with the three main credit bureaus?
   a. The lender can accept a written promise to pay from the borrower in lieu of a credit history.
   b. The lender can review paid utility bills, rent payments, and car insurance payments to determine creditworthiness.
   c. The lender can require a larger down payment in lieu of an established credit history.
   d. The borrower will not be able to qualify for a loan until they have established at least a five-year credit history.

2. Housing advertisements must always include which of the following?
   a. A statement that outlines terms such as predatory lending and steering
   b. Details about fees such as closing costs, transfer fees, and referral fees
   c. The Fair Housing logo and/or the Equal Housing Opportunity slogan
   d. An Affiliated Business Arrangement (AfBA) Disclosure

3. What is the person who oversees the closing transaction called?
   a. Closing coordinator
   b. Mortgage broker
   c. Settlement agent
   d. Underwriter

4. The Federal Housing Finance Agency took control of Freddie Mac in response to the housing crisis of what year?
   a. 1837
   b. 2008
   c. 1873
   d. 2016

5. When a borrower refinances a property, the transaction sometimes includes a right to rescind, meaning the borrower has a set number of days to cancel the transaction. How many days is the right of rescission?
   a. One day
   b. Three days
   c. Seven days
   d. Five days

6. When the Consumer Financial Protection Bureau (CFPB) is investigating an MLO for compliance, what do they NOT have authority to do?
   a. Require a testimony under oath
   b. Temporarily suspend the MLO's license
   c. Examine all books and records
   d. Require the MLO to personally submit all documents related to the investigation

7. What is the purpose of tolerance limits?
    a. They dictate how much a fee can change from the Loan Estimate to the Closing Disclosure.
    b. They specify how much a fee can change from the Closing Disclosure to the loan closing date.
    c. They specify how much a lender can add to the fee quoted by a service provider.
    d. They specify how much a borrower can be off on their income and debts on the loan application.

8. What is the bundle of rights?
    a. The five specific rights that are transferred when a buyer purchases a property
    b. The legal ownership of a property
    c. The physical document that transfers property ownership
    d. The rights that are guaranteed to any borrower in a loan transaction

9. Under what circumstances can certain fees be changed in a Loan Estimate?
    a. When fee splitting occurs
    b. Fees can never be changed on a loan.
    c. When a triggering event occurs
    d. At the time of a referral

10. A Good Faith Estimate (GFE) must include which of the following on the document?
    a. The list of tolerances and fees
    b. Details of new ownership of a property
    c. Changes made to the loan during service transfers
    d. A summary of the total interest and charges that will be paid for the loan duration

11. What organization enforces rules on mortgage advertising?
    a. Federal Trade Commission
    b. Consumer Financial Protection Bureau
    c. Federal Bureau of Investigation
    d. Financial Crimes Enforcement Network

12. How much prison time is involved if an MLO knowingly violates compliance laws?
    a. Six months
    b. Twelve months
    c. Eighteen months
    d. Twenty-four months

13. How many annual tax returns are required to determine income for self-employed borrowers?
    a. One
    b. Two
    c. Three
    d. Four

14. RESPA is alternately known by which regulation in the Code of Federal Regulations?
    a. Regulation B
    b. Regulation X
    c. Regulation Z
    d. Regulation G

15. What does a tri-merge credit report consist of?
    a. Information from three different major credit agencies
    b. The number of properties owned within the last three years
    c. The most recent paystubs from the last three years
    d. The first three complaints made by a borrower to the CFPB

16. Which of the following is NOT one of the four criteria that lenders use to determine the interest rate for subprime loans?
    a. The number of late payments on the borrower's credit report
    b. The types of delinquencies on the borrower's credit report
    c. The amount of the borrower's down payment
    d. The value of the property being financed

17. What is the threshold that requires borrowers to obtain private mortgage insurance (PMI)?
    a. The down payment is between 10 percent and 15 percent of the property value
    b. The down payment is less than 20 percent of the property value
    c. The down payment is less than 20 percent of the loan amount
    d. The down payment is less than 50 percent of the loan amount

18. What is an assumable mortgage?
    a. A mortgage with an assumed market value
    b. A mortgage that the buyer of a home takes over from the seller
    c. A mortgage that a financial institution takes over from the borrower
    d. A mortgage with no specified amortization date, just regular payments

19. Which of the following is NOT one of the discriminatory identifiers specified in ECOA?
    a. Receipt of public assistance
    b. Employment
    c. Use of consumer rights protections
    d. Marital status

20. Why might an ARM loan be appealing to borrowers?
    a. ARM loans require less paperwork than fixed-rate mortgage loans.
    b. Borrowers do not have to provide as much information on an ARM loan application.
    c. Lower credit scores are more acceptable on ARM loans.
    d. ARM loans often have a lower introductory interest rate than fixed-rate mortgage loans.

21. A reverse mortgage is similar to which of the following other types of loans?
    a. Purchase-money mortgage
    b. Interest-only mortgage
    c. Fixed-rate mortgage
    d. Home equity line of credit

22. A bank keeps the lien stated on a loan even after the property has been fully paid off. According to the Dodd-Frank Act, what is this bank committing?
    a. Predatory lending
    b. Money laundering
    c. Unsolicited advice
    d. Unfair, deceptive, or abusive acts and practices

23. Which of the following is the strongest red flag of identity theft for a typical financial institution?
    a. A call from a family member of the account owner informing the institution of the account holder's death
    b. The full upfront purchase of a new car in a different state
    c. A written request for new copies of all terms of service documents
    d. Several small incidental purchases at a popular vacation destination in a different state

24. Which acronym does NOT correspond to a type of report required by the Bank Secrecy Act?
    a. SAR
    b. CTR
    c. FBAR
    d. AML

25. How much is the up-front premium amount required for an FHA loan with an LTV of 93 percent?
    a. 1.75 percent of the loan amount
    b. 2.00 percent of the loan amount
    c. 2.50 percent of the loan amount
    d. 3.00 percent of the loan amount

26. Which of the following is NOT a prohibited act for MLOs?
    a. Using bait-and-switch advertising tactics
    b. Omitting debt from credit reports
    c. Using the identifier number of a supervisor
    d. Purchasing ads for themselves

27. An online advertisement on social media was reported to a regulatory organization because it included false statements. What regulatory organization is involved, and what action can it take in this case?
    a. The CFPB can sue the false advertiser.
    b. HUD can delete false advertisements that appear on social media.
    c. The IRS can file a complaint.
    d. The FTC can issue a warning or initiate a lawsuit.

28. Which subtitle of the Dodd-Frank Act's Title XIV created the Office of Housing Counseling?
    a. Third
    b. Fourth
    c. Sixth
    d. Seventh

29. Susan is taking out a mortgage loan for the purchase of a property. The purchase price of the property is $175,000, and the lender requires that Susan put down 15 percent. How much money must Susan put down on the property?
    a. $17,500
    b. $26,250
    c. $35,000
    d. $43,750

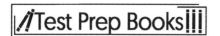

30. What is the typical accrual rate for most mortgage loans?
    a. Daily
    b. Weekly
    c. Monthly
    d. Yearly

31. While working on a mortgage request, a consumer asks a mortgage loan originator (MLO) for his identifier number. What should the MLO do?
    a. Give the consumer his supervisor's identifier number.
    b. Ask what the reason is; if it's sufficient, provide his identifier number.
    c. Provide his identifier number right away.
    d. Tell the consumer that the identifier is private information.

32. What was the goal of the E-Sign Act?
    a. To require all financial institutions to transition to electronic signatures
    b. To set the conditions under which electronic signatures have more or less authority than pen-and-paper signatures
    c. To make electronic signatures as valid as pen-and-paper signatures
    d. To ban the use of electronic signatures

33. Why might a borrower opt to take out a homeowner's title insurance policy?
    a. To protect the lender if the borrower cannot repay the loan and must foreclose on the property
    b. To protect the property from false claims to ownership
    c. To protect the borrower against outstanding liens, lawsuits, or encumbrances on the property
    d. To protect any heirs that the borrower may choose to inherit the property

34. A financial institution generating closed-end mortgage loans is exempt from reporting them if, in the past two calendar years, it originates less than how many of them?
    a. 100
    b. 150
    c. 50
    d. 200

35. When a lender pushes risky loans onto borrowers with poor credit history, this behavior is considered to be which of the following?
    a. Material
    b. Predatory
    c. Fee splitting
    d. Redlining

36. If a borrower is seeking a loan amount of $238,000 for a property with a purchase price of $280,000, what is the loan-to-value (LTV) ratio?
    a. 80 percent
    b. 85 percent
    c. 90 percent
    d. 75 percent

37. The TRID rule was designed to close some loopholes in the mortgage finance laws. It combines elements of which two prior laws?
    a. Truth in Lending Act and Equal Credit Opportunities Act
    b. Equal Credit Opportunities Act and Regulation B
    c. Real Estate Settlement Procedures Act and Regulation X
    d. Truth in Lending Act and Real Estate Settlement Procedures Act

38. What exactly is meant when an MLO is "negotiating loan terms"?
    a. Presenting a loan offer to a consumer
    b. Discussing what loan types a consumer may qualify for
    c. Explaining the steps required to apply for a loan
    d. Receiving a loan application from a consumer

39. If a closing occurs at the end of July, how many months of property taxes will be paid by the seller?
    a. Six
    b. Seven
    c. Eight
    d. Twelve

40. A mortgage broker is defined as what?
    a. Any person who buys or sells real property
    b. Any person who originates a loan
    c. Any person who facilitates a real estate purchase transaction
    d. Any person who makes loans or offers credit to finance a real estate purchase

41. Why would a borrower list a property as owner-occupied when it is not?
    a. To hide the finder's fees they will receive after the property is sold
    b. In order for their straw buyer to maintain ownership of the property
    c. To use the property as their primary residence instead of as an investment property
    d. To get better interest rates for a loan

42. A bank hires a team of programmers to create and implement a digital security system to store the private information of the bank's clients. Which of the following rules does this action best represent?
    a. Financial Privacy Rule
    b. Anti-Money Laundering Rule
    c. Safeguards Rule
    d. Red Flags Rule

43. What is the maximum amount that can be borrowed through a HELOC, based on the home's value and assuming the borrower has no other outstanding obligations?
    a. 85 percent
    b. 65 percent
    c. 70 percent
    d. 90 percent

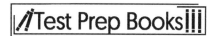

44. Which of the following is the process of verifying the borrower's information and deciding whether to approve the loan?
    a. Applying
    b. Processing
    c. Underwriting
    d. Closing

45. What happens if an MLO fails to renew their license before December 31?
    a. It becomes inactive, and they must renew before continuing MLO work.
    b. They are fined $500 for being late on their license renewal.
    c. Their license is suspended and they have to retake the Secure and Fair Enforcement (SAFE) test to regain it.
    d. Their license will automatically renew and they will be charged $100.

46. What is the difference between a loan's interest rate and the annual percentage rate (APR)?
    a. The APR is the money the lender charges for the loan; the interest rate includes the total of all fees and costs for the loan.
    b. The interest rate is shown as a percentage; the APR is a specific dollar figure.
    c. The APR is shown as a percentage; the interest rate is a specific dollar figure.
    d. The interest rate is the money the lender charges for the loan; the APR includes the interest rate and any other fees or costs.

47. What type of loans are best for borrowers who agree to pay brokers yield spread premiums?
    a. Loans with a rate lock agreement
    b. FHA mortgage loans
    c. Loans provided by third-party providers
    d. Short-term loans

48. A third-party bank asks a borrower to view their credit history for verification purposes. The borrower refuses. What law permits the borrower to prevent third parties from viewing their information?
    a. Home Ownership Protection Equity Act
    b. Civil Rights Act
    c. Fair Credit Reporting Act
    d. Home Mortgage Disclosure Act

49. Since its inception, how many instances of mortgage-related warnings has the Consumer Financial Protection Bureau publicly issued?
    a. Three
    b. Four
    c. Seven
    d. Twelve

50. What does the acronym PITI mean?
    a. Payment, interest, taxes, insurance
    b. Principal, interest rate, taxes, insurance
    c. Principal, interest, taxes, insurance
    d. Prepaids, interest rate, taxes, insurance

51. Qualified mortgage loans must meet specific guidelines with regards to what aspect of mortgage lending?
    a. The value of the property being financed
    b. That the title is free and clear of liens
    c. That the seller is the legal owner and able to sell the property
    d. The borrower's ability to repay the loan

52. Which of the following is NOT a prepaid cost at closing?
    a. Interest
    b. Property taxes
    c. Homeowner's insurance
    d. Origination fees

53. Which of the following statements best describes the payment structure of a balloon mortgage?
    a. Total term of 7 years, monthly payments based on a 10-year term
    b. Total term of 10 years, monthly payments based on a 10-year term
    c. Total term of 7 years, monthly payments based on a 7-year term
    d. Total term of 10 years, monthly payments based on a 7-year term

54. Which of the following is NOT one of the basic requirements to qualify for an MLO license?
    a. Demonstrating financial responsibility
    b. Sponsorship from a licensed institution
    c. Background check from the Financial Crimes Enforcement Network
    d. Passing a written test

55. Which of the following is NOT one of the seven items that must be included on the annual escrow statement?
    a. The current monthly mortgage payment
    b. The total amount paid into the escrow account during the previous year
    c. The balance of the escrow account at the end of the period
    d. The amounts paid for taxes and insurance since the opening of the account

56. What is the maximum percentage of seller concessions allowed on an FHA loan?
    a. 9 percent
    b. 6 percent
    c. 4 percent
    d. 3 percent

57. According to the CFPB, when do companies usually respond to complaints?
    a. Five days
    b. Ten days
    c. Fifteen days
    d. Twenty days

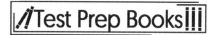

58. On which page in the Closing Disclosure can the buyer find contact information for the lender and the settlement agent?
    a. Page one
    b. Page three
    c. Page four
    d. Page five

59. At what threshold does a financial institution in the U.S. enter the Consumer Financial Protection Bureau's jurisdiction?
    a. $1 billion in assets and at least 300,000 employees
    b. $10 billion in assets
    c. $500 million in assets and at least 1,000 employees
    d. $10 million in assets

60. Which of the following is required as part of an annual MLO license renewal?
    a. Retaking the SAFE test with a score of at least 75 percent
    b. Submitting a copy of all loans originated in the past year for verification
    c. Eight hours of continuing education
    d. A $25 licensing fee

61. What can an underwriter do to verify if information regarding employment is correct?
    a. Appoint a POA to verify employment history.
    b. Request pay stubs and W-2 forms from the borrower.
    c. Request assistance from the Mortgage Bankers Association.
    d. Ask the borrower's bank to share their credit history.

62. Which of the following is the best reason for a purchase-money mortgage to be recorded in a public security document?
    a. To allow a financial institution to purchase and oversee the mortgage.
    b. Federal law requires public disclosure of the agreement.
    c. To protect both parties from disputes over terms.
    d. To protect the borrower from sudden changes in the mortgage terms.

63. Which of the following might be required to verify a borrower's employment income?
    a. Pay stubs and W2s
    b. A letter from the borrower's employer
    c. Bank statements
    d. Retirement account statements

64. What is an escrow account used for?
    a. To pay the mortgage payments for the first few months of a loan
    b. To disburse the closing costs after the loan transaction has closed
    c. To distribute payments to third-party service providers
    d. To collect and hold money to pay annual property taxes and homeowner's insurance premiums

65. What is dual compensation?
   a. When an MLO gets paid for both the amount of credit in the mortgage and the mortgage terms
   b. When an MLO gets paid once up front and once at the end of negotiations
   c. When an MLO gets paid by both the borrower and lender
   d. When an MLO gets paid for working for two different financial institutions

66. The USDA guarantees loans made by participating lenders; however, the USDA does make one type of loan to borrowers itself. Which loan is made by the USDA?
   a. USDA Rural Loan Program loans
   b. USDA Home Improvement loans
   c. USDA Loans
   d. USDA Direct loans

67. What should the loan originator do if the borrower does not complete the ethnicity questions on the loan application?
   a. Ask the borrower to complete that section.
   b. Make a visual assessment of the borrower's ethnicity.
   c. Leave that section blank.
   d. Refuse to accept the application if the borrower does not provide the information.

68. Which of the following refers to the loss mitigation option known as forbearance?
   a. The borrower pays an extra amount each month to catch up on missed payments.
   b. The terms of the loan are restructured.
   c. The borrower brings the loan current and resumes making regular payments.
   d. The borrower temporarily stops making payments.

69. A lender recommends a service to a consumer, but the consumer refuses to use the suggested service and goes elsewhere. What law permits the consumer to choose a different service?
   a. Gramm-Leach-Bliley Act
   b. Bank Secrecy Act
   c. Fair Housing Act
   d. Real Estate Settlement Procedures Act

70. Money that the borrower has left over after the down payment and loan closing costs are paid is called what?
   a. Reserve funds
   b. Remaining capital
   c. Additional monies
   d. Finance dividends

71. What is one disadvantage to using third-party providers for a loan?
   a. A variable APR will be placed on the loan.
   b. They operate in the primary market.
   c. They do not have a long-term responsibility for the mortgage.
   d. They charge simple daily interest for their services.

72. Who is responsible for verifying that all information submitted on the final loan application is correct?
   a. Loan officer
   b. Borrower's bank
   c. IRS
   d. The person designated as power of attorney (POA)

73. Second-tier TRID violations, those resulting from recklessness, carry fines of up to how much per day?
   a. $5,000
   b. $10,000
   c. $20,000
   d. $25,000

74. The Department of Housing and Urban Development was created in what year?
   a. 2010
   b. 1947
   c. 1970
   d. 1965

75. Alex is applying for a new MLO license. He used to work as an MLO ten years ago, but his license was previously revoked due to being involved with a bank committing money laundering. What is the most likely outcome of his application?
   a. His application will be accepted without issue.
   b. His application will be accepted, but he'll be on probation and closely monitored.
   c. His application will be denied because he was convicted of a felony.
   d. His application will be denied because his previous license was revoked.

76. What type of loan is typically for borrowers whose credit score falls somewhere between 620 and 660?
   a. Alt-A loans
   b. Prime loans
   c. Subprime loans
   d. Jumbo loans

77. A consumer sees a newspaper advertisement explaining a new, low-interest loan but does not see any information about associated fees or costs. This advertisement can be reported to which of the following organizations?
   a. IRS
   b. Mortgage Bankers Association
   c. A third-party bank
   d. FTC

78. Which government agency is responsible for designating flood-prone areas?
   a. Red Cross
   b. Federal Emergency Management Agency
   c. Federal Housing Administration
   d. Flood Zone Authority

79. What can happen if an institution has a bad track record of dealing with money laundering?
    a. Investigators could be brought in to oversee daily operations.
    b. Assets and operations could be seized by the Federal Trade Commission.
    c. The institution could be shut down by the Federal Trade Commission.
    d. Mergers could be blocked by the Department of the Treasury.

80. A borrower announces that he has lost his job recently and will need to discuss the terms on the Loan Estimate with the lender. Losing a job is an example of which of the following?
    a. Tri-merge credit report
    b. Unreported income
    c. Triggering event
    d. Employment fraud

81. How long is the draw period of a typical HELOC?
    a. Ten years
    b. Fifteen years
    c. Seven years
    d. Fourteen years

82. What are the allowable debt-to-income (DTI) ratios for Federal Housing Administration (FHA) loans?
    a. 25 percent and 50 percent
    b. 28 percent and 36 percent
    c. 31 percent and 43 percent
    d. There are no DTI ratios for FHA loans.

83. Information that is false, omitted, or misrepresented is considered to be which of the following?
    a. Fraud
    b. Permitted
    c. Predatory
    d. Due diligence

84. What credit score would be considered below average but would not prevent a borrower from applying for a mortgage loan?
    a. 400
    b. 600
    c. 680
    d. 750

85. Which of the following statements does NOT describe adjustable-rate mortgages (ARMs)?
    a. Adjustable-rate mortgages are carefully regulated by the federal government.
    b. Adjustable-rate mortgages are a type of qualified mortgage.
    c. There are several limits to how much the interest rate of an adjustable-rate mortgage can change.
    d. The adjustments made to the interest rate are based on annual stock market trends.

86. What organization states that advertisements need to be fair, truthful, and evidence based?
   a. FTC
   b. IRS
   c. CFPB
   d. Mortgage Bankers Association

87. What is the minimum credit score required to obtain an interest-only mortgage?
   a. 550
   b. 600
   c. 650
   d. 700

88. What is a borrower's monthly income if the October 15 paystub shows a year-to-date amount of $27,550 and the borrower has been employed for the full year?
   a. $2900
   b. $3061
   c. $2295
   d. $2755

89. Which method of holding title to a property is used by married couples to give each spouse an equal share of the property with separate rights of survivorship?
   a. Sole ownership
   b. Joint tenancy
   c. Tenancy in common
   d. Tenancy by the entirety

90. A lender may take adverse action on a loan application in which of the following circumstances?
   a. The borrower is married but does not include their spouse on the loan application.
   b. The borrower does not disclose their race and national origin on the loan application.
   c. The borrower's application shows that they receive welfare income.
   d. The borrower is unable to demonstrate sufficient income to qualify for the loan.

91. A borrower contacted Tom, a loan originator, about refinancing their current home mortgage loan. What information does Tom need to find a suitable loan product for the borrower?
   a. The purchase price of the home
   b. The borrower's income at the time of their original loan application
   c. The interest rate and terms of the current mortgage loan
   d. How much money the borrower put as a down payment

92. A person is hired by a financial institution to assist their MLO in analyzing the risk of lending to mortgage applicants. What is this job position called?
   a. Loan analyst
   b. Loan processor
   c. Private investigator
   d. Underwriter

93. How is a construction loan allocated to the borrower?
    a. Half at the start, half when construction is halfway completed
    b. All at once at the start of construction
    c. Incrementally during the construction phase
    d. Incrementally at preset dates

94. Certain situations, called changed circumstances, require a lender or loan originator to provide the borrower with a new Loan Estimate disclosure. Which of the following is an example of a changed circumstance?
    a. The borrower financed the purchase of new appliances after applying for the mortgage loan.
    b. The lender increased their origination fee after the borrower received the initial Loan Estimate disclosure.
    c. The homeowner's association where the property is located increased their fees and reported a past-due amount to the lender.
    d. The home inspector was unavailable, and the new inspector charges $50 less than the previous one.

95. What needs to accompany a gift made to a borrower?
    a. Verification of Employment, pay stubs, and W-2 forms
    b. Affiliated Business Arrangement (AfBA) Disclosure
    c. A letter that lists the donor's name, contact information, and the specific amount of the gift
    d. Closing costs

96. A lender who refuses to do business with a client because of their religion is in violation of which law?
    a. Fair Credit Reporting Act
    b. Fair Housing Act
    c. Dodd-Frank Act
    d. Bank Secrecy Act

97. What does the term loan consummation mean?
    a. The closing date
    b. The end of the right of rescission period
    c. The date the borrower becomes legally obligated to repay the loan
    d. The date of the loan application

98. Conventional mortgage loans usually requirement mortgage insurance when the down payment is less than what percentage?
    a. 25 percent
    b. 20 percent
    c. 15 percent
    d. 10 percent

99. What should an MLO do if they discover falsified information on a loan application?
    a. Demand payment from the borrower to correct the change.
    b. Send a complaint to the Consumer Financial Protection Bureau (CFPB).
    c. Change the information to help the borrower.
    d. Contact the loan compliance officer.

100. Which percentage increment is usually used when advertising fixed-rate mortgages?
    a. 0.5 percent
    b. 0.125 percent
    c. 1 percent
    d. 0.333 percent

101. Which of the following is NOT information found on the borrower's credit report?
    a. Financial legal actions
    b. Payment history on all accounts
    c. How long each account has been open
    d. Current employer information

102. What does the CFPB do with the information it obtains from complaints?
    a. Compiles the information into a database for its own use only
    b. Posts the information on its own website to help people learn from the complaints
    c. Shares the information with banks to determine loan terms for borrowers
    d. Discards the information

103. Which rule establishes allowed tolerances?
    a. ECOA
    b. TRID
    c. CFPB
    d. HUD

104. At least how old do you have to be in order to be eligible for a reverse mortgage?
    a. 57 years old
    b. 62 years old
    c. 67 years old
    d. 72 years old

105. Which of the following is NOT a stated goal of the Home Mortgage Disclosure Act (HMDA)?
    a. Assisting with distributing public-sector investments
    b. Determining if financial institutions are serving the needs of their communities
    c. Encouraging financial institutions into specific lending practices
    d. Assisting with identifying possible discrimination in lending

106. What is the role of GSEs in the mortgage industry?
    a. Purchase loans on the secondary market
    b. Oversee that mortgage regulations are being maintained
    c. Verify that mortgages meet qualifying loan standards
    d. Verify that properties meet the appropriate value for the mortgage amount

107. What year was the Civil Rights Act passed?
    a. 1968
    b. 1970
    c. 1974
    d. 2008

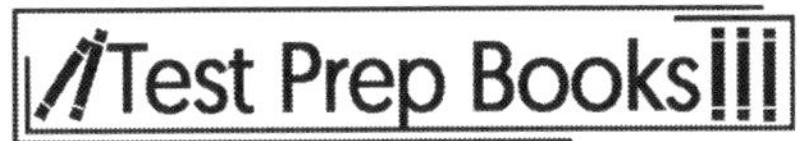

108. Loans that do not meet the underwriting standards and requirements of the CFPB for sale on the secondary market, especially with regards to the ability to repay rule, are called what?
    a. Subprime mortgages
    b. Alt-A mortgages
    c. Non-qualified mortgages
    d. Negative amortization mortgages

109. The Homeownership Counseling Disclosure, required by the Home Ownership and Equity Protection Act (HOEPA), must include which of the following?
    a. A list of at least ten HUD-approved counseling services in the borrower's area
    b. A list of all counseling services in the borrower's area
    c. A list of all counseling services approved by HUD in the last year
    d. A list of at least ten HUD-approved counseling services in the U.S.

110. If a borrower has unreported tip income, who should they report this to?
    a. Consumer Financial Protection Bureau (CFPB)
    b. Federal Trade Commission (FTC)
    c. National Association of Realtors (NAR)
    d. Internal Revenue Service (IRS)

111. What is a mortgage called when it exceeds the maximum amounts set by the Federal Housing Finance Agency?
    a. Jumbo loan
    b. High-cost loan
    c. Higher-priced loan
    d. Balloon mortgage

112. How often does a federally insured financial institution need to maintain its registration with the National Mortgage Licensing System and Registry (NMLS)?
    a. Every six months
    b. Every year
    c. Every two years
    d. Every five years

113. What does USPAP stand for?
    a. Universal Standards of Professional Appraisal Practice
    b. United States Professional Appraisal Practice
    c. Universal Standards of Property Appraisal Practice
    d. United States Property Appraisal Practice

114. For qualified mortgage loans, the loan's annual percentage rate (APR) cannot exceed what percentage range above the average prime offer rate?
    a. 2.5 to 4.5 percent
    b. 3.5 to 6.5 percent
    c. 2.5 to 6.5 percent
    d. 3.5 to 8.5 percent

115. What is one advantage to purchasing an assumable mortgage loan?
   a. The loan would be sponsored by Fannie Mae or Freddie Mac.
   b. Appraisals are not required for the property.
   c. The loan will have a fixed APR.
   d. Private mortgage insurance is included in the loan.

116. What is the person who completes the title research and report called?
   a. Abstractor
   b. Processor
   c. Underwriter
   d. Loan officer

117. The mortgage broker or lender must provide the borrower with a Truth in Lending (TIL) Disclosure within how many days of receipt of the borrower's loan application?
   a. The same day
   b. Three days
   c. Seven days
   d. Ten days

118. The privacy disclosure provided to borrowers must include the types of information collected, what information may be shared with third parties, an explanation of the borrower's rights, and what else?
   a. The circumstances under which the information could be shared
   b. Information on how the borrower can opt out of sharing their information
   c. The purpose behind sharing the information
   d. Which specific loan the information will be collected from

119. What is the maximum loan amount for FHA loans in high-cost areas like metropolitan cities?
   a. $420,680
   b. $647,200
   c. $970,800
   d. $1,001,270

120. Which federal agency is in charge of enforcing RESPA?
   a. Housing and Urban Development
   b. Consumer Financial Protection Bureau
   c. Federal Reserve
   d. Department of Justice

Answer Explanations #3

1. B: Lenders can accept alternate credit sources and information in lieu of an established credit bureau history. However, not all lenders allow such alternate credit information. Choices *A, C,* and *D* are made-up answers.

2. C: Advertisements need to include the Fair Housing logo and/or the Equal Housing Opportunity slogan. Choices *A*, *B*, and *D* are not required for advertisements.

3. C: The settlement agent oversees the closing transaction and ensures that all necessary information and documentation have been completed and provided to and from the appropriate parties to the transaction. A closing coordinator, Choice *A*, is sometimes employed by a real estate office to coordinate and oversee the sale of a property, but they are not involved specifically in the closing. The mortgage broker, Choice *B*, assists the borrower in choosing and applying for a loan program, and the underwriter, Choice *D*, ensures that all of the borrower's documentation is complete and that the borrower is financially able and responsible enough to repay the loan.

4. B: The mortgage crisis of 2008 prompted the FHFA to take over control of Freddie Mac and make it the second GSE in the secondary market. Choices *A, C,* and *D* are all years of volatility in the housing and mortgage markets, but these were not when Freddie Mac became a GSE.

5. B: The borrower has three days after closing to rescind the loan agreement and cancel the transaction. Choices *A, C,* and *D* are made-up answers. However, the right of rescission does not apply to refinances that are for less than the current mortgage or for consolidation of loans with the same lender.

6. B: The CFPB does not have the authority to temporarily suspend an MLO's license while an investigation is ongoing. They do have the authority to examine all books and records as well as require in-person testimony and document delivery, so Choices *A*, *C*, and *D* are all incorrect.

7. A: Tolerance limits specify how much any particular fee can change from the initial Loan Estimate to the final Closing Disclosure. They are designed to prevent lenders from increasing the fees outside of reasonable expectations. Fees cannot change between the date of the Closing Disclosure and the loan closing date, Choice *B*. Lenders cannot pad the fees charged by the service providers, Choice *C*. Borrowers are expected to provide accurate information on their loan application, but there are no specific tolerance limits for errors, making Choice *D* incorrect.

8. A: The bundle of rights includes the five specific rights that are transferred when a buyer purchases a property. These include the Right of Possession, the Right of Control, the Right of Enjoyment, the Right of Disposition, and the Right of Exclusion. Choice *B* refers to the title, Choice *C* refers to the deed, and Choice *D* is a made-up answer.

9. C: Triggering events can change the Loan Estimate but do not affect fees such as referral and borrowing fees. Choice *A* refers to the distribution of funds after joint marketing, which is usually a fifty/fifty split. Choice *B* does not recognize that some aspects of the loan can be affected by job loss and require a revised Loan Estimate. Choice *D* refers to disclosing the affiliation between two service providers.

10. A: A Good Faith Estimate (GFE) lists the fees for closing a loan under different tolerance levels, which detail which fees may or may not change. Choice *B* refers to a deed of conveyance. Choice *C* is required when a borrower's loan is transferred to another company. Choice *D* is the finance charges, a list of all interest and charges made on a loan.

11. A: The Federal Trade Commission is responsible for enforcing rules regarding mortgage advertising. The Consumer Financial Protection Bureau has rulemaking authority, but not enforcement authority, so Choice *B* is incorrect. Neither the Federal Bureau of Investigation nor the Financial Crimes Enforcement Network (FinCEN) is responsible for enforcing mortgage advertising violations, so Choices *C* and *D* are also incorrect.

12. B: A willful violation of MLO compliance law carries a fine and an additional penalty of up to one year in prison. Six months is too short, so Choice *A* is incorrect. Eighteen and twenty-four months are too long, so Choices *C* and *D* are incorrect.

13. B: Self-employed borrowers need to provide two years of tax returns to verify their average monthly income. Choices *A, C*, and *D* are made-up answers.

14. B: RESPA is Chapter 10 of Title 12 of the CFR, commonly referred to as Regulation X or Reg X. Regulation B, Choice *A*, is the Equal Credit Opportunity Act (ECOA). Regulation Z, Choice *C,* is the Truth in Lending Act (TILA), and Choice *D* refers to the SAFE Mortgage Licensing Act.

15. A: The tri-merge credit report consists of information from Experian, Equifax, and TransUnion. Choices *B*, *C*, and *D* are not components of a tri-merge credit report.

16. D: The interest rate on subprime loans is calculated based on the borrower's credit report, not the value of the property being financed. Choices *A, B*, and *C* are some of the factors that are considered when determining the interest rate for a subprime borrower.

17. B: Most loans require private mortgage insurance (PMI) if the down payment of the loan is less than 20 percent of the property value in question. It isn't as specific as between 10 percent and 15 percent, so Choice *A* is incorrect. It also specifically has to do with the property value, not the amount of the loan, so Choices *C* and *D* are incorrect.

18. B: An assumable mortgage is a mortgage that the buyer of a property takes over from the property's seller. It isn't a mortgage with an assumed market value, so Choice *A* is incorrect. It isn't a mortgage that the lending institution takes responsibility for, so Choice *C* is incorrect. It isn't a mortgage with no specified amortization date, so Choice *D* is incorrect.

19. B: Employment is not one of the protected identifiers under ECOA. ECOA prohibits discrimination based on race, color, religion, national origin, sex, and age. It also prohibits discrimination based on participation in public assistance programs, Choice *A*; whether or not a consumer has exercised any consumer rights protections, Choice *C*; and marital status, Choice *D*.

20. D: ARM loans often have a lower introductory interest rate than fixed-rate mortgage loans, which can be appealing to borrowers who intend to move or refinance the property within the initial fixed-rate period of the loan. Choices *A, B*, and *C* are incorrect answers.

21. D: Reverse mortgages use a homeowner's equity in their home to get a loan in a similar manner to a home equity line of credit (HELOC), as they both advance a loan using the home's equity as collateral.

The difference is that a HELOC is more like a credit card with a limit and repayment plan, whereas a reverse mortgage advances all of the money upfront and has conditions upon which the whole amount becomes due instead of having a set payment plan. Purchase-money, interest-only, and fixed-rate mortgages are not as similar to a reverse mortgage as a HELOC is, so Choices *A*, *B*, and *C* are all incorrect.

22. D: The Dodd-Frank Act defines unfair, deceptive, or abusive acts and practices (UDAAP) and prohibits them under penalty of law. Keeping a lien despite having a loan paid off is an example of a UDAAP. Choice *A* describes approving risky loans for people who would struggle to pay them off. Choice *B* is a crime that bank institutions monitor. Choice *C* is advice that the loan originator gives without being asked.

23. B: Depending on the situation or warnings from other organizations, all of these could be under consideration for being an identity theft red flag. However, the strongest option here is Choice *B*—a distant and full purchase of an expensive item is the most suspicious. Smaller incidental or daily item purchases such as in Choice *D* are not as suspicious, so it's incorrect compared to Choice *B*. Requesting new copies of terms of service documents is not outwardly suspicious, so Choice *C* is incorrect. Relatives calling to tie up the loose ends of a departed family member and close financial accounts could be suspicious depending on other warnings, but isn't necessarily suspicious behavior by itself, so Choice *A* is also incorrect.

24. D: AML refers to anti-money laundering, an alternate name for the type of law the Bank Secrecy Act represents. SAR, CTR, and FBAR respectively correspond to suspicious activity report (SAR), currency transaction report (CTR), and foreign bank account report (FBAR), all of which are required by the BSA. Therefore, Choices *A*, *B*, and *C* are incorrect.

25. A: All FHA loans more than 90 percent LTV require an up-front MIP premium payment of 1.75 percent of the loan amount in addition to annual premiums of between 0.45 percent and 1.05 percent of the loan balance. Choices *B, C*, and *D* are made-up answers.

26. D: MLOs are allowed to purchase advertisements for themselves to solicit borrowers, provided they openly display their NMLS identifier number. Bait-and-switch tactics, omitting debt from credit reports, and using another's identifier number are all prohibited, so Choices *A*, *B*, and *C* are all incorrect.

27. D: The FTC regulates advertisements and can issue lawsuits if necessary. Choices *A*, *B*, and *C* are not involved in regulating advertisements.

28. B: The fourth subtitle of the Dodd-Frank Act's Title XIV created the Office of Housing Counseling to coordinate regulations related to housing and mortgage counseling. The third subtitle was one of several that set many standards for mortgage loan originators (MLOs), so Choice *A* is incorrect. The sixth subtitle set more MLO requirements regarding insurance and property appraisal, so Choice *C* is incorrect. The seventh subtitle featured miscellaneous provisions such as extending the Protecting Tenants at Foreclosure Act, so Choice *D* is incorrect.

29. B: To determine the down payment amount, convert the percentage to a decimal and multiply the decimal by the purchase price. In this case, $\$175{,}000 \times 0.15 = \$26{,}250$. Choices *A, C*, and *D* represent down payments of 10, 20, and 25 percent, respectively.

30. C: Most mortgage loans include a monthly accrual rate. Some loans use a daily rate, Choice *A*, but that is not standard. Though some loan types allow lenders to calculate the accrual rate as they see fit, making weekly or yearly rates possible, this again is not typical. Therefore, Choices *B* and *D* are also incorrect.

31. C: Regardless of a consumer's reason, if an MLO is asked to provide their identifier number, they must provide it without question or delay. Giving a supervisor's number instead is lying and prohibited, so Choice *A* is incorrect. The reason a consumer is asking is irrelevant, so Choice *B* is incorrect. MLO identifiers are not private information and should be publicly available, so Choice *D* is incorrect.

32. C: The goal of the E-Sign act was to give equal authenticity to electronic signatures and pen-and-paper signatures. It did not require a transition to electronic signatures entirely or ban them, so Choices *A* and *D* are incorrect. Choice *B* is incorrect because the goal was to give equal authority to both types of signatures, not set rules for when one has more authority than another.

33. C: A homeowner's title policy protects the borrower from undiscovered liens, lawsuits, or encumbrances against the property. Choice *A* is the reason that lenders require title insurance policies. This protects the lender but not the borrower. Choice *B* is incorrect because title insurance guarantees that there are no existing claims or liens against the property, but it does not protect against future or false claims. While Choice *D* may be a side benefit, any heirs or new owners to the property would still want to have their own title report conducted to ensure that the property remains free and clear for the new owner.

34. A: This exemption requirement states that financial institutions are exempt from reporting closed-end mortgage loans if they originated less than one hundred of them in the past two calendar years. The other three choices are all the wrong number, so Choices *B*, *C*, and *D* are incorrect.

35. B: Predatory lending takes advantage of consumers by offering financially risky loans to people who would not qualify for other loans. Choice *A* is any information that could influence the value of a property. Choice *C* happens at the end of joint advertising, when fees are split between two partnering services. Choice *D* involves not doing business with others based on a discriminating factor.

36. B: Loan-to-value (LTV) is determined by dividing the loan amount by the purchase price of the property. The LTV for this purchase is 85 percent ($238,000 divided by $280,000). Choices *A*, *C*, and *D* are made-up answers.

37. D: TRID is also known as the TILA-RESPA Integrated Disclosure Rule, combining elements of the Truth in Lending Act (TILA) and the Real Estate Settlement Procedures Act. It does not involve ECOA, Choice *A*. In Choice *B*, ECOA is the same thing as Regulation B; it is not one of the acts combined to make TRID. RESPA and Regulation X, Choice *C*, are the same thing; while RESPA/Regulation X is one of the acts combined to make TRID, the question asks for two acts that are combined.

38. A: "Negotiating loan terms" as it applies to MLOs refers to the exact act of offering a loan to a consumer. Discussing what loans a consumer may qualify for does not count if it doesn't lead to a specific offer, so Choice *B* is incorrect. Explaining the steps required to apply is not the act of negotiating loan terms, so Choice *C* is incorrect. Receiving a loan application refers to directly receiving the information from a consumer to make a decision about loan qualification, so Choice *D* is incorrect.

39. B: The seller would have owned the property for seven months of the year, so they would pay for seven months of property taxes. The borrower would pay for the five remaining months that they will own the property in that year. Therefore, Choices *A*, *C*, and *D* are incorrect.

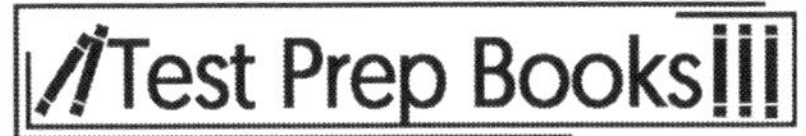

40. B: A mortgage broker is defined as any person who originates loans and/or serves as an intermediary between a borrower and a mortgage lender or finance company. Choice *A* is a made-up answer. Choice *C* loosely refers to a real estate agent, and Choice *D* loosely refers to a lender or finance company.

41. D: Fraud is usually committed to obtain better terms on the loan. Choice *A* refers to the finder's fees that a service or company receives after a referral; the borrower does not receive those fees and therefore does not need to hide them. Choice *B* is incorrect because straw buyers usually buy property for someone else and receive payment for relinquishing the property to them; this does not change as a result of listing the property as owner-occupied. Choice *C* is reverse occupancy fraud, in which a borrower says that a property is an investment property when it is actually their primary residence. It is the opposite type of fraud referenced in this scenario.

42. C: Creating a digital security system to protect client information would be best described as a result of the Safeguards Rule, which requires all financial institutions to have a written security plan explaining how they protect their clients' private information. The Financial Privacy Rule sounds similar but refers to rules regarding the exact private information financial institutions may collect and how they inform consumers of the data collection, so Choice *A* is incorrect. The Red Flags Rule has to do with identity theft, so Choice *D* is incorrect. Anti-Money Laundering Rule is a made-up name, so Choice *B* is also incorrect.

43. A: 85 percent of a home's value is the maximum amount that can be borrowed through a home equity line of credit (HELOC), minus any extra that may still be owed in an existing mortgage. 65 percent and 70 percent are too low, making Choices *B* and *C* incorrect. 90 percent is a bit too high, making Choice *D* also incorrect.

44. C: Underwriting is the process of verifying the borrower's information and determining if the borrower is creditworthy and qualified for loan approval. Choices *A, B*, and *D* are all different parts of the loan process. Choice *A*, applying, is when the loan originator collects the borrower's information at the beginning of the process. Choice *B*, processing, involves gathering information and preparing it for submission to underwriting. Choice *D*, closing, is when the loan is completed and funded.

45. A: If an MLO's license isn't renewed in time, it becomes inactive. There is no penalty for this, but the MLO must renew their license, which they can do at any time, in order to continue working as an MLO. They won't be fined for being late, so Choice *B* is incorrect. Their license isn't suspended and a test retake isn't required, so Choice *C* is incorrect. There is no automatic renewal system, so Choice *D* is incorrect.

46. D: The interest rate is the amount of money the lender charges for the loan. The annual percentage rate (APR) is the total cost of the loan, including the interest and any fees or additional finance charges. Choice *A* is the opposite of the correct answer; APR and interest rate are reversed. Choices *B* and *C* are both incorrect because the APR and the interest rate are both shown as percentages.

47. D: Short-term loans are best for borrowers who agree to pay their broker yield spread premiums because borrowers will save money by paying reduced upfront fees in exchange for a higher interest rate. If borrowers can pay off the loan quickly, they will save money despite the higher interest rate. Choices *A, B*, and *C* do not involve yield spread premiums. Choice *A* is an agreement to lock an interest rate until a borrower secures a loan. Choice *B* are loans offered by the government to help people with low income or credit scores. Choice *C* are loans that third-party providers help to fund and sell after closing a loan.

48. C: The Fair Credit Reporting Act (FCRA) protects consumers by regulating who can view their personal information. Choice *A* protects against paying too much for mortgage insurance. Choice *B* was a landmark decision that prohibited discrimination. Choice *D* mandates that credit unions must retain all details about loans.

49. A: The Consumer Financial Protection Bureau has publicly issued three warning letters about mortgages: two similar warnings in 2012 and a third warning in 2016. Four, seven, and twelve are all too high, so Choices *B*, *C*, and *D* are incorrect.

50. C: PITI refers to the principal, interest, taxes, and insurance that comprise the total monthly mortgage payment. Choice *A* has payment instead of principal. Choice *B* has interest rate instead of interest. Choice *D* has prepaids instead of principal and interest rate instead of interest.

51. D: Qualified mortgages have met compliance guidelines with regards to verifying a borrower's ability to repay the loan. While Choices *A, B*, and *C* are important aspects of mortgage financing, they are not specifically addressed with regards to qualified mortgage standards.

52. D: Origination fees are the costs that the mortgage broker charges for assisting the borrower with the mortgage. They are not considered prepaid costs. Prepaid costs include Choices *A, B*, and *C* as well as any monies used to establish the initial escrow account.

53. A: Balloon mortgages calculate their monthly payments as if the total loan term is longer than it actually is, so a 7-year loan with the monthly payments of a 10-year term is correct. Choices *B* and *C* describe the payment structure of a standard loan, so they are incorrect. Choice *D* would result in the loan being fully paid off three years before the end of the total loan term, so it is incorrect.

54. C: MLOs do need to undergo a background check, but it is not performed by the Financial Crimes Enforcement Network (FinCEN). It is performed by the Federal Bureau of Investigation. Demonstrating financial responsibility, sponsorship from a licensed financial institution, and passing a written test are all required to qualify, so Choices *A*, *B*, and *D* are all incorrect.

55. D: The annual escrow statement must include the amounts paid for taxes, insurance, and any other payments for the year, but it does not have to show all payments made since the opening of the account. Choices *A, B*, and *C* are all required information, as are the total amount paid into the escrow account during the year and explanations for any surplus or shortage in the account.

56. B: The maximum allowable seller contribution on an FHA loan is 6 percent. Choice *A* represents seller contributions on a conventional mortgage loan with 25 percent or more down, and Choice *D* represents seller contributions on a conventional mortgage loan with less than 10 percent down. Choice *C* represents the maximum seller concession towards escrow accounts and funding fees on a VA loan.

57. C: Most companies respond to complaints within fifteen days of receiving them. Choices *A*, *B*, and *D* are not the correct time frame.

58. D: Contact information for the lender and the settlement agent, as well as for the mortgage broker and the real estate agents, can be found at the bottom of page five of the Closing Disclosure. Page one, Choice *A*, includes the names of the borrower(s) and seller(s), the property address, and the loan terms.

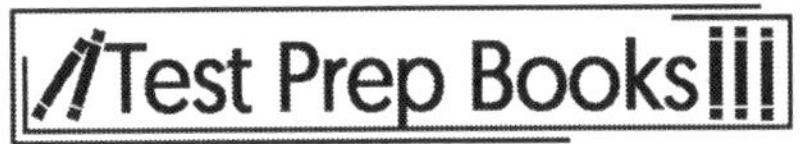

Page three, Choice *B*, shows the breakdown of costs assigned to the borrower and the seller as well as the cash to close calculations. Choice *C*, page four, includes the loan disclosures and escrow information.

59. B: Once a financial institution has obtained $10 billion in assets, it enters the CFPB's jurisdiction. There are no employee requirements, so Choices *A* and *C* are incorrect automatically. $10 million in assets is much too low, so Choice *D* is incorrect.

60. C: Continuing education is important to make sure all MLOs are up to date with current events and laws, so at least seven to eight hours of continuing education classes are required every year to renew a license. Test retakes aren't required for regular license renewal, so Choice *A* is incorrect. There is no need to submit copies of every loan originated, so Choice *B* is incorrect. No fee is required to keep an MLO license, so Choice *D* is incorrect.

61. B: Underwriters can request Verification of Employment, pay stubs, and W-2 forms to verify employment status. Choice *A* is requested in case a person is unable to make decisions for themselves; it is not involved with income verification. Choice *C* is not involved in employment verification. Choice *D* is violating the Fair Credit Reporting Act (FCRA).

62. C: Purchase-money mortgages are kept in public security documents in order to protect both the lender and the borrower from future arguments about the terms. Financial institutions don't need to take over the supervising the mortgage, so Choice *A* is incorrect. Purchase-money mortgages don't have a federal law requiring public disclosure, so Choice *B* is incorrect. Choice *D* is relatively accurate, but only describes protections for the borrower when the intent of public disclosure is to protect both the borrower and the seller, so it is less correct than Choice *C*.

63. A: Generally, a borrower must provide pay stubs, W2s, and/or tax returns that the lender can use to verify their income. Choice *B*, a letter from the employer, can verify that the borrower is currently employed, but it is not sufficient to determine income. Bank and retirement account statements, Choices *C* and *D*, can verify assets (including income from investments) but are not generally acceptable for determining employment income.

64. D: The escrow account is used to collect and hold the monthly tax and insurance payments until the annual amounts are due. Choices *A*, *B*, and *C* are incorrect.

65. A: Dual compensation specifically refers to the act of an MLO being paid for both the amount of credit involved with a mortgage as well as the terms and conditions of the mortgage. This is prohibited, and only the amount of credit involved should affect an MLO's pay. It doesn't have to do with an MLO getting paid twice, so Choice *B* is incorrect. Being paid by both the borrower and lender could cause this situation, but it is not what defines the act, so Choice *C* is incorrect. It doesn't have to do with an MLO working for multiple financial institutions, so Choice *D* is incorrect.

66. D: The USDA makes USDA Direct loans directly to borrowers, without the need to go through participating lenders. The other two USDA programs are the USDA Loans, Choice *C*, and the USDA Home Improvement loans, Choice *B*, which are made through participating lenders. Choice *A* is incorrect.

67. B: The loan originator should make a visual assessment of the borrower's race for the application, as per HUD regulations. Choices *A*, *C*, and *D* are in violation of the Equal Credit Opportunity Act (ECOA).

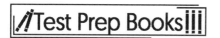

68. D: A forbearance is when the borrower is allowed to stop making payments, or to make smaller payments, for a set period of time. Choice *A* refers to a repayment plan. Choice *B* refers to a loan modification, and Choice *C* is a reinstatement.

69. D: In addition to prohibiting kickbacks and finder's fees, RESPA allows consumers to choose services that are not recommended to them. Choice *A* requires companies to explain their process of keeping information safe. Choice *B* requires financial institutions to work together with the government to identify suspicious activity such as money laundering. Choice *C* is a part of the Civil Rights Act of 1968.

70. A: Once the borrower has paid their down payment and loan closing costs, any money left over is called reserve funds. Choices *B, C,* and *D* are made-up answers.

71. C: Third-party providers do not have a long-term responsibility to the loan because they are not the main lender. They typically sell the mortgage shortly after closing the mortgage. Choice *A* is an interest rate that has changing rates throughout the year. Choice *B* refers to most loans that borrowers are offered when they are first looking for a loan. Choice *D* is interest that is accrued daily on a loan, but this is not applied to third-party providers for their service.

72. A: The loan officer is ultimately responsible for their client and must verify that all information is correct before final submission. Choices *B, C,* and *D* do not verify the information on a loan application.

73. D: Second-tier TRID violations carry fines of up to $25,000 per day that the violation goes uncorrected. Second-tier violations involve errors of recklessness, such as incorrect closing cost calculations. First-tier TRID violations carry a fine of up to $5,000 per day; therefore, Choice *A* is incorrect. First-tier violations involve civil penalties and are generally errors of omission. Choices *B* and *C* are also incorrect.

74. D: The Department of Housing and Urban Development was formed in 1965 as part of President Lyndon Johnson's Great Society plan. 2010 is when the Consumer Financial Protection Bureau was formed, so Choice *A* is incorrect. 1947 is when the Housing and Home Financing Agency was formed. That is an origin point for the HUD but isn't when the department itself formed, so Choice *B* is incorrect. 1970 is when the Bank Secrecy Act was passed, but that act didn't create the HUD, so Choice *C* is incorrect.

75. D: Alex's application will be denied specifically because his previous MLO license was revoked. His application will not be accepted, so Choices *A* and *B* are incorrect. Choice *C* is incorrect because the incident occurred ten years ago, and the threshold for a felony conviction causing an application to be denied is seven years prior to application.

76. A: Alt-A loans are a type of nonconforming mortgage loan that is meant for borrowers who do not qualify as prime borrowers, Choice *B*, who typically have a credit score of 660 or up. Alt-A borrowers also are not considered subprime borrowers, Choice *C*, who typically have a credit score lower than 620. Choice *D*, jumbo loans, are classified based on the high loan amount rather than on the quality of the borrower.

77. D: The FTC regulates advertisements and explains the statements allowed on an advertisement. Choices *A, B,* and *C* do not regulate advertising.

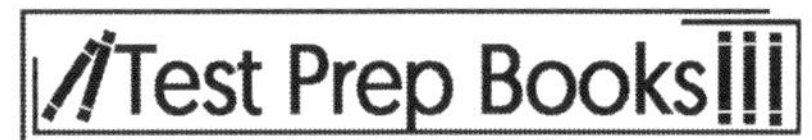

78. B: Flood- prone areas are determined by the Federal Emergency Management Agency (FEMA). Choice *A* is not a government agency. Choice *C*, although it is a government agency, does not make that determination. Choice *D* is a made-up answer.

79. D: Institutions that don't correctly handle issues with money laundering can have mergers and acquisitions blocked by the Department of the Treasury. They won't have investigators overseeing their operations or be shut down, so Choices *A* and *C* are incorrect. Assets may be seized when money laundering crimes are first discovered, but operations will not be taken over and a single incident may not establish a bad track record, so Choice *B* is incorrect here.

80. C: A triggering event, such as job loss or incapacitation, can change the Loan Estimate. Choice *A* is a credit report that consists of information from three credit agencies. Choice *B* is handled by the Internal Revenue Service (IRS). Choice *D* is lying about employment status to get better loan terms.

81. A: The most common length of the draw period in a home equity line of credit (HELOC) is ten years. Fifteen and fourteen years are too long, making Choices *B* and *D* incorrect. Seven years is too short, so Choice *C* is incorrect.

82. C: FHA loans allow a housing DTI of up to 31 percent and a total DTI of up to 43 percent. Choice *B* is the standard, "ideal" DTI ratios. Choice *D* refers to Veterans Affairs (VA) loans, not FHA loans. Choice *A* is a made-up answer.

83. A: Fraud is the act of providing false and misleading information. Choices *B*, *C*, and *D* are not terms used to describe false and misleading information.

84. B: Borrowers with credit scores between 580 and 620 are typically considered subprime borrowers, so a score of 600 is the best choice here. It is low, but not so low that the borrower will not be able to apply for a subprime loan. 400 is too low, so Choice *A* is incorrect. 680 is considered a good credit score and 750 is a great score, so Choices *C* and *D* are also incorrect.

85. D: Adjustments made to the interest rate of an adjustable-rate mortgage (ARM) are not based on stock market trends, but by referring to federal government-published indexes of information used to calculate the cost of lending money. Choice *A* is incorrect because adjustable-rate mortgages undergo careful regulation from the federal government to prevent rising interest rates from causing too much financial damage to borrowers. Choice *B* is incorrect because many adjustable-rate mortgages meet the federal qualifications to be classified as qualified mortgages. Choice *C* is incorrect because there are three specific limits on how much the interest rate of an adjustable-rate mortgage is allowed to change.

86. A: The FTC regulates real estate and mortgage advertisements no matter where they appear and states that all advertisements must be fair, truthful, and evidence based. Choice *B* handles taxes. Choice *C* handles borrower complaints. Choice *D* represents the real estate finance industry.

87. D: Interest-only mortgage loans require a much higher credit score than any other typical mortgages—a minimum of 700. 550 and 600 are too low for even most standard mortgages, so Choices *A* and *B* are incorrect. 650 would qualify for typical mortgages, but not an interest-only mortgage, so Choice *C* is also incorrect.

88. A: The borrower has worked nine- and one-half months by October 15. Dividing the total income by 9.5 equals $2900 per month. Choice *B* is the total income divided by nine months rather than nine and one half. Choice *C* is the total income divided by twelve months, although it is actually only nine and one half months' worth of income. Choice *D* is the full income divided by ten months, but the borrower has not yet worked (shown income for) the full month of October.

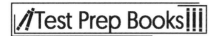

89. B: Joint tenancy is often used by married couples because it gives each spouse equal ownership shares in the property and because it includes separate rights of survivorship (each spouse can designate an heir for their portion of the property ownership). Sole ownership, Choice *A*, can be used by married couples, but it does not give each spouse a separate right of survivorship. Choice *C*, tenancy in common, is like joint tenancy, except each owner may not hold an equal share in the property. With Choice *D*, tenancy by the entirety, the married couple is viewed as a single entity.

90. D: Lenders are permitted to require that borrowers demonstrate an acceptable ability to repay the loan, including showing sufficient income. Choices *A, B*, and *C* are examples of violations of ECOA.

91. C: The loan originator needs to know the interest rate, payment amount, and terms of the current mortgage loan. He can then compare that information with the available loan programs to determine if a better option is available for the borrower. Choices *A* and *D* are usually only relevant if the borrower is purchasing a home as opposed to refinancing their current home. Choice *B* is not relevant for a refinance loan.

92. D: Underwriters assist MLOs by performing risk assessments on mortgage applicants, making sure they are safe to lend to. Loan analyst is a false term, so Choice *A* is incorrect. Loan processors do paperwork and pass it along to the relevant parties rather than performing any kind of risk assessment, so Choice *B* is incorrect. Private investigators don't have anything to do with mortgage risk assessment, so Choice *C* is incorrect.

93. C: Construction mortgages are given out in increments as the construction on the house progresses. It isn't split in half or handed out all at once, so Choices *A* and *B* are incorrect. The dates on these increments are not fixed, so Choice *D* is incorrect.

94. A: The most common changed circumstances involve changes to the borrower's creditworthiness and/or their ability to repay the loan. Taking on a new debt affects the borrower's debt-to-income ratio (DTI), which could impact their ability to repay the loan and could trigger a revised Loan Estimate disclosure. An increase in lender fees, Choice *B*, is not permitted; the lender is not allowed to increase their fees once the Loan Estimate disclosure has been provided (except under changed circumstances). Changes in the homeowner's association fees, Choice *C*, fall under the "no tolerance" category and would not require a new Loan Estimate disclosure. Similarly, a new disclosure is not generally required when costs or fees are reduced, as in Choice *D*.

95. C: Monetary gifts made to borrowers must include a letter that lists the gift giver's name, contact information, bank and account information, and relationship to the borrower; the address of the property the borrower wishes to buy; the date of the gift; the specific amount of the gift; and a statement that the gift is not a loan and does not need to be repaid. Choice *A* can be requested by an underwriter to verify employment status. Choice *B* is given at the time of a referral or before a referral. Choice *D* are the fees required to complete a real estate transaction.

96. B: Discrimination is prohibited under the Fair Housing Act, which was written into law as a part of the Civil Rights Act. Choice *A* guarantees that financial institutions will protect consumer data. Choice *C* regulated risky financial transactions that contributed to the 2008 financial crisis. Choice *D* mandates

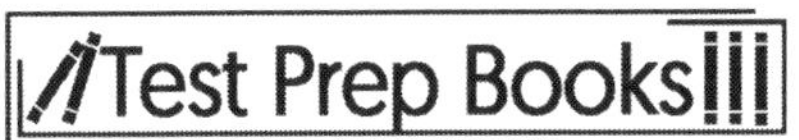

that financial institutions need to monitor for suspicious activity, such as identity theft and money laundering.

97. C: Loan consummation is a legal term that refers to the date when the borrower becomes legally obligated to repay the loan. This is often the closing date, Choice *A*, but not always. Loan consummation is not affected by the rescission period, Choice *B*, and it comes well after the loan application date, Choice *D*.

98. B: In order to avoid having to pay mortgage insurance, borrowers must usually pay a down payment of at least 20 percent of the purchase price. Choices *A, C,* and *D* are incorrect.

99. D: The loan originator can work together with the loan compliance officer to handle falsified information on an application. Choice *A* is coercion. Choice *B* is incorrect because the Consumer Financial Protection Bureau (CFPB) will handle borrower complaints, not falsified loan information. Choice *C* is a prohibited act and can result in punishment for the MLO.

100. B: Fixed-rate mortgages are often advertised with interest rates in increments of 0.125 percent or sometimes 0.25 percent. While 0.5 percent is itself a multiple of 0.125 percent, interest rates are calculated at a more fine-tuned rate than that, so Choice *A* is incorrect. 1 percent is too high since interest rates often change in even smaller amounts than that, so Choice *C* is incorrect. The interest rates don't change in increments of thirds since they can be awkward to divide by, so Choice *D* is incorrect.

101. D: The credit report does not show employment information. It does include the information shown in Choices *A, B*, and *C*.

102. B: After resolving borrower complaints about companies, the CFPB compiles the information into a database and posts it on their website. Choice *A* is incorrect because the database is public knowledge. Choices *C* and *D* are not actions that the CFPB takes with the information.

103. B: The TILA-RESPA Integrated Disclosure Rule (TRID) categorizes loan fees into three tolerance classifications: zero tolerance, 10 percent tolerance, and no tolerance. ECOA, Choice *A*, is the Equal Credit Opportunity Act. CFPB, Choice *C*, is the Consumer Financial Protection Bureau. Choice *D*, HUD, is the U.S. Department of Housing and Urban Development.

104. B: In order to qualify for a reverse mortgage, borrowers must be at least 62 years old, among other requirements. 57 is too young, so Choice *A* is incorrect. Choices *C* and *D* are incorrect because while 67 and 72 are both eligible ages, they are not the minimum required age.

105. C: The three stated goals of the Home Mortgage Disclosure Act (HMDA) are to assist public officials with distributing public sector investments; to help determine whether or not financial institutions are serving the housing needs of their communities; and to assist in identifying possible discriminatory lending patterns. These correspond to Choices *A*, *B*, and *D* respectively, making Choice *C* the odd one out and therefore the correct answer.

106. A: GSEs like Fannie Mae and Freddie Mac purchase home loans on the secondary market, which frees up funds so that lenders can make more loans. The Consumer Financial Protection Bureau is responsible for overseeing qualified mortgage regulations, Choice *B*. Each lender is responsible for verifying that their mortgages meet the required qualifying mortgage standards, Choice *C*. This is usually handled by the lender's loan underwriters. Choice *D* is also usually handled by underwriters.

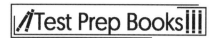

107. A: The Civil Rights Act was passed in 1968 and prohibited discrimination due to characteristics such as race and religion. Choice *B* is the passing of the Bank Secrecy Act (BSA). Choice *C* is the passing of the Real Estate Settlement Procedures Act (RESPA). Choice *D* is the financial crisis that eventually led to the Dodd-Frank Act being passed in 2010.

108. C: Non-qualified mortgages are loans that do not meet the strict requirements for sale to Fannie Mae or Freddie Mac on the secondary market. Choices *A, B,* and *D* are all different types of non-qualified mortgages.

109. A: The Homeownership Counseling Disclosure must include a list of at least ten counseling agencies in the borrower's area that are approved by HUD. The list cannot be more than thirty days old. Choices *B, C,* and *D* are incorrect.

110. D: The IRS handles unreported tip income. Failure to report the income to the IRS could result in more taxes being owed and punishment for withholding taxes. Choice *A* compiles borrower complaints about companies into a database and posts it on their website. Choice *B* handles advertising and regulation of numerous service industries, including real estate and mortgage. Choice *C* works together with the Federal Trade Commission (FTC) to regulate advertisements and monitors the real estate industry for compliance with its rules.

111. A: A jumbo mortgage is one that exceeds the amounts set by the FHFA. High-cost loans and higher-priced loans, Choices *B* and *C* respectively, are both determined based on the APR as compared to the average prime offer rate and the total fees charged for the transaction. A balloon mortgage, Choice *D*, includes a large lump-sum payment due at the end of the loan.

112. B: Federally insured or chartered financial institutions follow the same rules as MLOs and perform annual license maintenance as well. Every six months is too short, so Choice *A* is incorrect. Two and five years are too long, so Choices *C* and *D* are incorrect.

113. A: The USPAP is the Universal Standards of Professional Appraisal Practice. It is the standards and guidelines that licensed appraisers must follow in their work. Choices *B, C,* and *D* are made-up answers.

114. C: Depending on the type of loan, the APR on qualified mortgage loans cannot exceed 2.5 to 6.5 percent above the average prime offer rate. First-lien mortgage loans over $110,260 cannot have an APR of more than 2.5 percent above, while subordinate mortgage loans under $66,156 are capped at 6.5 percent above. Other types of loans have other caps within this range, as well. Choices *A, B,* and *D* are incorrect.

115. B: Appraisals are not required for assumable mortgage loans because the process has already been done for the previous owner. Choice *A* is incorrect because these two companies purchase mortgages on the secondary market; they do not sponsor assumable loans. Choice *C* is an annual interest rate that accumulates at a fixed, unchanging rate and is not necessarily part of an assumable loan. Choice *D* is insurance that must be purchased when a borrower puts less than 20 percent down on a conventional loan; it is not an advantage of assuming a mortgage loan.

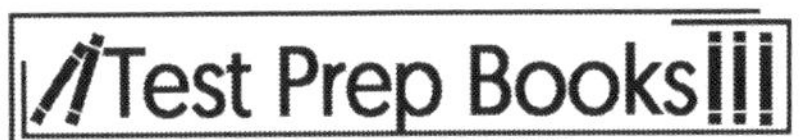

116. A: The title research and report are done by an abstractor. A processor, Choice *B*, and the underwriter, Choice *C*, work on gathering and reviewing the loan documentation and approving the loan. Title research is also not the responsibility of the loan officer, Choice *D*.

117. B: The TIL must be provided to the borrower within three days of receipt of the loan application. Choices *A, C*, and *D* are made-up answers.

118. B: The privacy disclosure must give the borrower information on how they can opt out of having their information shared. Choices *A, C*, and *D* are incorrect.

119. C: The maximum FHA loan in high-cost areas is $970,800. Choice *A* is the maximum FHA loan amount outside of high-cost areas. Choice *B* is the maximum loan amount for conventional mortgage loans, and Choice *D* is also incorrect.

120. B: RESPA is enforced by the Consumer Financial Protection Bureau, though it was originally under the Department of Housing and Urban Development, Choice *A*, when it was enacted in 1975. The Federal Reserve and the Department of Justice, Choices *C* and *D* respectively, will aid in prosecuting violations, but they are not actively involved in oversight.

Index

Dear NMLS Test Taker,

Thank you again for purchasing this study guide for your NMLS exam. We hope that we exceeded your expectations.

Our goal in creating this study guide was to cover all of the topics that you will see on the test. We also strove to make our practice questions as similar as possible to what you will encounter on test day. With that being said, if you found something that you feel was not up to your standards, please send us an email and let us know.

We have study guides in a wide variety of fields. If you're interested in one, try searching for it on Amazon or send us an email.

Thanks Again and Happy Testing!
Product Development Team
info@studyguideteam.com

FREE Test Taking Tips Video/DVD Offer

To better serve you, we created videos covering test taking tips that we want to give you for FREE. **These videos cover world-class tips that will help you succeed on your test.**

We just ask that you send us feedback about this product. Please let us know what you thought about it—whether good, bad, or indifferent.

To get your **FREE videos**, you can use the QR code below or email freevideos@studyguideteam.com with "Free Videos" in the subject line and the following information in the body of the email:

a. The title of your product

b. Your product rating on a scale of 1-5, with 5 being the highest

c. Your feedback about the product

If you have any questions or concerns, please don't hesitate to contact us at info@studyguideteam.com.

Thank you!

Made in the USA
Las Vegas, NV
04 October 2023